Test Item File

SECOND EDITION
FUNDAMENTALS of
MANAGEMENT

Test Item File
Morgan Bridge

SECOND EDITION
FUNDAMENTALS of MANAGEMENT

ESSENTIAL CONCEPTS AND APPLICATIONS

Stephen P. Robbins
David A. De Cenzo

Prentice Hall, Upper Saddle River, NJ 07458

Acquisitions editor: *Stephanie Johnson*
Associate editor: *Lisamarie Brassini*
Project editor: *Richard Bretan*
Manufacturing buyer: *Ken Clinton*

 © 1998 by Prentice Hall, Inc.
A Simon & Schuster Company
Upper Saddle River, New Jersey 07458

All rights reserved. No part of this book may be reproduced, in any form or by any means, without permission in writing from the publisher.

Printed in the United States of America

10 9 8 7 6 5 4 3 2

ISBN 0-13-725426-1

Prentice-Hall International (UK) Limited, *London*
Prentice-Hall of Australia Pty. Limited, *Sydney*
Prentice-Hall Canada Inc., *Toronto*
Prentice-Hall Hispanoamericana, S.A., *Mexico*
Prentice-Hall of India Private Limited, *New Delhi*
Prentice-Hall of Japan, Inc., *Tokyo*
Simon & Schuster Asia Pte. Ltd., *Singapore*
Editora Prentice-Hall do Brasil, Ltda., *Rio de Janeiro*

TABLE OF CONTENTS

Chapter 1:	Managers and Management	1
Chapter 2:	The Changing Face of Management	20
Chapter 3:	Foundations of Planning	41
Chapter 4:	Planning Tools and Techniques	59
Chapter 5:	Foundations of Decision Making	77
Chapter 6:	Technology and the Design of Work Processes	97
Chapter 7:	Basic Organization Designs	119
Chapter 8:	Staffing and Human Resource Management	140
Chapter 9:	Managing Change and Innovation	163
Chapter 10:	Foundations of Individual and Group Behavior	182
Chapter 11:	Understanding Work Teams	205
Chapter 12:	Motivating and Rewarding Employees	221
Chapter 13:	Leadership and Supervision	239
Chapter 14:	Communication and Interpersonal Skills	259
Chapter 15:	Foundations of Control	278
Chapter 16:	Control Tools and Techniques	293

Chapter 1: Managers and Management

True/False

1. There is a universally accepted model of a successful manager.

   Answer: F Difficulty: 1 Page: 3

2. The primary distinction between operatives and managers is that operatives have employees that report directly to them.

   Answer: F Difficulty: 2 Page: 4

3. Middle managers may have titles such as department head, project leader, unit chief, or district manager.

   Answer: T Difficulty: 2 Page: 5

4. An organization can be efficient and yet not effective.

   Answer: T Difficulty: 2 Page: 6

5. The four functions of management are completely independent and should be treated as separate activities.

   Answer: F Difficulty: 1 Page: 7

6. Fayol derived his original functions of management from his observations of an Irish potato processing plant.

   Answer: F Difficulty: 3 Page: 8

7. Evidence supports the idea that managers - regardless of the type of organization or the level in the organization - perform similar roles.

   Answer: T Difficulty: 1 Page: 11

8. According to Luthans, mangers who are the most effective in their jobs are also the ones who are promoted the fastest.

   Answer: F Difficulty: 2 Page: 11

9. With today's dynamic world, managing chaos has become the rule - not the exception.

   Answer: T Difficulty: 2 Page: 15

10. A manager's job differs in profit and not-for-profit organizations.

    Answer: F Difficulty: 1 Page: 15

Chapter 1: Managers and Management

11. Profit acts as an unambiguous measure of the effectiveness of a business organization.

    Answer: T Difficulty: 2 Page: 15

12. The growth in small businesses is a phenomenon that has been confined in large part to the United States.

    Answer: F Difficulty: 3 Page: 16

13. While there may be differences in degree and emphasis of functions, the same management functions apply to owners of small businesses as well as to the CEO of major corporations.

    Answer: T Difficulty: 3 Page: 17

14. Studies that have compared managerial practices between countries have generally supported the universality of management concepts.

    Answer: F Difficulty: 3 Page: 17

15. Organizational survival often depends on successful interactions with the external environment.

    Answer: T Difficulty: 2 Page: 21

16. Employees, customers, suppliers, labor unions and government agencies are examples of stockholders.

    Answer: F Difficulty: 2 Page: 21

Multiple Choice

17. Referring to the scenario at the beginning of the chapter, which of the following managers made a difference at Autodesk, Inc.?
    A. Carol Hardy
    B. Carol Bartz
    C. Becky Hardy
    D. Becky Bartz

    Answer: B Difficulty: 1 Page: 2

18. An organization must contain all but which of the following characteristics?
    A. A purpose
    B. People
    C. A structure
    D. A product

    Answer: D Difficulty: 2 Page: 4

19. The person who sells you the new pair of jeans is known as
    A. A middle manager
    B. A first-line manager
    C. An operative
    D. A top manager

    Answer: C Difficulty: 3 Page: 4

20. Managers primarily perform which of the following tasks?
    A. Selling
    B. Stocking merchandise
    C. Directing the activities of other people
    D. Ordering merchandise

    Answer: C Difficulty: 3 Page: 4

21. The managers who work most closely with the operatives are known as
    A. Top management
    B. Middle management
    C. First-line managers
    D. Operative managers

    Answer: C Difficulty: 1 Page: 5

22. The level of management that translate the goals of the organization into specific plans that can then be implemented is known as
    A. Top management
    B. Middle management
    C. First-line managers
    D. Operative managers

    Answer: B Difficulty: 2 Page: 5

23. Operatives can best be described as
    A. Those who actually perform the service or produce the product
    B. Those who work anonymously behind the scenes
    C. Those who set the goals of the organization
    D. Those who supervise others

    Answer: A Difficulty: 2 Page: 5

24. Performing the task right and considering the relationship between inputs and outputs is known as
    A. Effectiveness
    B. Goal attainment
    C. Efficiency
    D. Management characteristics

    Answer: C Difficulty: 2 Page: 6

Chapter 1: Managers and Management

25. Actually doing the right thing is known in management as which of the following?
    A. Effectiveness
    B. Goal attainment
    C. Efficiency
    D. Management characteristics

    Answer: A Difficulty: 2 Page: 6

26. Tim's Tire Shop is concerned only with using the least amount of labor possible as it repairs/replaces the tires of its customers. Their primary goal is
    A. Effectiveness
    B. Goal attainment
    C. Efficiency
    D. Management characteristics

    Answer: C Difficulty: 3 Page: 6

27. Defining goals, establishing an overall strategy and developing a comprehensive hierarchy of plans is known as which of the following functions of management?
    A. Planning
    B. Leading
    C. Organizing
    D. Controlling

    Answer: A Difficulty: 2 Page: 7

28. Determining the tasks to be accomplished, how the tasks are to be grouped and who is responsible for the various tasks is known as which of the following functions of management?
    A. Planning
    B. Organizing
    C. Leading
    D. Controlling

    Answer: B Difficulty: 2 Page: 7

29. When managers motivate employees, direct the activities of others, select the most effective communication channel and resolve conflicts they are performing which of the following functions of management?
    A. Controlling
    B. Organizing
    C. Leading
    D. Planning

    Answer: C Difficulty: 2 Page: 7

30. The process of monitoring performance, comparing it with goals and correcting any significant deviations is known as which of the following functions of management?
    A. Planning
    B. Organizing
    C. Leading
    D. Controlling

    Answer: D Difficulty: 2 Page: 8

31. Ann is the CEO of a large manufacturing plant. She has spent her day trying to ensure that the light bulbs coming off the assembly line light 99.4 percent of the time. She has spent her day performing which function of management?
    A. Planning
    B. Organizing
    C. Leading
    D. Controlling

    Answer: D Difficulty: 3 Page: 8

32. John is the CEO of a major hospital. He has spent his day planning the schedules of employees for the next month. He had to ensure that there was a Registered Nurse on every shift. He spent his day performing which function of management?
    A. Planning
    B. Organizing
    C. Leading
    D. Controlling

    Answer: B Difficulty: 3 Page: 8

33. Linda has spent the day in a session where the future of her company was discussed. The people involved were trying to determine what the role of their company was as the 21st century approaches. Goals were then developed based upon their vision of the company's mission. Linda spent her day performing which of the functions of management?
    A. Planning
    B. Organizing
    C. Leading
    D. Controlling

    Answer: A Difficulty: 3 Page: 8

34. Mintzberg found that managers' activities were constantly interrupted approximately every
    A. Three minutes
    B. Six minutes
    C. Nine minutes
    D. Eleven minutes

    Answer: C Difficulty: 2 Page: 9

Chapter 1: Managers and Management

35. According to Mintzberg, which management role includes figurehead, leader and liaison activities?
    A. Interpersonal roles
    B. Informational roles
    C. Decisional roles
    D. Planning roles

    Answer: A Difficulty: 1 Page: 9

36. According to Mintzberg, which management role includes monitor, disseminator and spokesperson activities?
    A. Interpersonal roles
    B. Informational roles
    C. Decisional roles
    D. Planning roles

    Answer: B Difficulty: 1 Page: 9

37. According to Mintzberg, which management role includes entrepreneur, disturbance handler, resource allocator, and negotiator?
    A. Interpersonal roles
    B. Informational roles
    C. Decisional roles
    D. Planning roles

    Answer: C Difficulty: 1 Page: 9

38. George is representing his company at the local Chamber of Commerce Annual Business Recognition Luncheon. He is performing which managerial role?
    A. Negotiation
    B. Monitor
    C. Figurehead
    D. Liaison

    Answer: C Difficulty: 3 Page: 9

39. Susan spends 1/2 hour every morning reading the current periodicals concerned with her business. She is performing which managerial role?
    A. Negotiation
    B. Monitor
    C. Figurehead
    D. Liaison

    Answer: B Difficulty: 3 Page: 9

40. Jose is involved with discussions between employees, management and the Union to which his employees belong. They are discussing wage issues. Management is interested in keeping the wages at minimum wage. The employees/Union want $.50 plus minimum wage. Jose is performing which managerial role?
    A. Monitor
    B. Entrepreneur
    C. Negotiator
    D. Organizer

    Answer: C Difficulty: 3 Page: 9

41. Which of the following is not one of the four managerial activities that Luthans found all managers engage in?
    A. Communication
    B. Human resource management
    C. Networking
    D. Controlling

    Answer: D Difficulty: 2 Page: 12

42. Which managerial activity according to Luthans, made the biggest relative contribution to the success of a manager?
    A. Networking
    B. Communication
    C. Human resource management
    D. Traditional management

    Answer: A Difficulty: 2 Page: 12

43. Which managerial activity according to Luthans, made the largest relative contribution to the effectiveness of a manager?
    A. Networking
    B. Communication
    C. Human resource management
    D. Traditional management

    Answer: B Difficulty: 2 Page: 12

44. Katz developed four critical competencies that managers must possess. Which of the following is not one of those four competencies?
    A. Conceptual competencies
    B. Human competencies
    C. Technical competencies
    D. Connection competencies

    Answer: D Difficulty: 1 Page: 13

Chapter 1:   Managers and Management

45. The competency that centers on a manager's mental ability to coordinate all of the organization's interests and activities is known as which competency?
    A. Conceptual competency
    B. Human competency
    C. Technical competency
    D. Networking competency

    Answer: A Difficulty: 2 Page: 13

46. The competency that centers on a manager's ability to work with, understand, and motivate other people is known as which competency?
    A. Conceptual competency
    B. Human competency
    C. Technical competency
    D. Networking competency

    Answer: B Difficulty: 2 Page: 13

47. The competency that centers on a manager's ability to use the tools, procedures, and techniques of a specialized field is known as which competency?
    A. Conceptual competency
    B. Human competency
    C. Technical competency
    D. Networking competency

    Answer: C Difficulty: 2 Page: 13

48. The competency that centers on a manager's ability to build a power base and establish the "right" connections is known as which competency?
    A. Conceptual competency
    B. Human competency
    C. Technical competency
    D. Networking competency

    Answer: D Difficulty: 2 Page: 13

49. Becky has joined an organization which promotes the discussion of current management topics. The majority of the managers in the State belong to the organization. Which managerial competency is Becky addressing?
    A. Conceptual competency
    B. Human competency
    C. Technical competency
    D. Networking competency

    Answer: D Difficulty: 3 Page: 13

50. Angelo is well-known for his skills in using the advanced programming software of the engineering field. In fact it was his specialized knowledge that led to his promotion as manager. Which managerial competency is Angelo demonstrating?
    A. Conceptual competency
    B. Human competency
    C. Technical competency
    D. Networking competency

    Answer: C Difficulty: 3 Page: 13

51. Destiny's strength as a manager lies in her ability to work with people. She is able to work with, motivate and lead others easily. Destiny is demonstrating which managerial competency?
    A. Conceptual competency
    B. Human competency
    C. Technical competency
    D. Networking competency

    Answer: B Difficulty: 3 Page: 13

52. Which of the following acts as an unambiguous measure of the effectiveness of a business organization?
    A. Efficiency
    B. Employee satisfaction
    C. Increased revenues
    D. Profits

    Answer: D Difficulty: 2 Page: 15

53. A business is classified as small if it has fewer than which of the following amount of employees?
    A. 50
    B. 100
    C. 250
    D. 500

    Answer: D Difficulty: 2 Page: 16

54. All but which of the following are criteria used in determining a definition for a small business?
    A. Profits
    B. Sales
    C. Total assets
    D. Number of employees

    Answer: A Difficulty: 3 Page: 16

Chapter 1:   Managers and Management

55. According to the author, small businesses will account for which amount of new job growth in the next decade?
    A. 25%
    B. 33%
    C. 50%
    D. 75%

    Answer: C Difficulty: 3 Page: 16

56. Small businesses account for which percentage of all nonfarm businesses in the United States?
    A. 27%
    B. 38%
    C. 79%
    D. 97%

    Answer: D Difficulty: 1 Page: 16

57. The small business owner's most important managerial role is which of the following?
    A. Monitor
    B. Spokesperson
    C. Leader
    D. Negotiator

    Answer: B Difficulty: 2 Page: 16

58. Compared to the manager of a large organization, a small business manager is more likely to be a
    A. Specialist
    B. Figurehead
    C. Generalist
    D. Information monitor

    Answer: C Difficulty: 3 Page: 16

59. The universality of management concept typically applies to all but which of the following countries?
    A. United States
    B. Chile
    C. Canada
    D. Australia

    Answer: B Difficulty: 3 Page: 17

60. The annual income of senior managers at large toy manufacturing firms ranges between
    A. $100,000-$200,000
    B. $200,000-$600,000
    C. $225,000-$750,000
    D. $300,000-$1,000,000

    Answer: C Difficulty: 1 Page: 18

61. The average cash compensation for chief executives at 317 publicly held U.S. corporations was which amount?
    A. $100,000
    B. $1,000,000
    C. $2,000,000
    D. $2,800,000

    Answer: D Difficulty: 2 Page: 19

62. Milton Kim of Ssangyong Investment and Securities Company resides in Seoul, Korea. All but which of the following are a part of Seoul's culture?
    A. Consensus-building
    B. Compromise
    C. Merit-based career promotions
    D. Egalitarianism

    Answer: C Difficulty: 3 Page: 18

63. The management theory jungle was developed by which of the following people?
    A. Maslow
    B. Herzberg
    C. Ouchi
    D. Koontz

    Answer: D Difficulty: 2 Page: 20

64. All but which of the following are components of the process approach to management?
    A. Planning
    B. Organizing
    C. Controlling
    D. Negotiating

    Answer: D Difficulty: 1 Page: 20

Chapter 1: Managers and Management

65. All but which of the following are the integrative frameworks that have evolved to help organize the subject matter of management?
    A. Process Approach
    B. Function Approach
    C. Systems Approach
    D. Contingency Approach

    Answer: B Difficulty: 2 Page: 20

66. Which of the following approaches is used the most in organizing management subject matter?
    A. Process Approach
    B. Function Approach
    C. Systems Approach
    D. Contingency Approach

    Answer: A Difficulty: 3 Page: 20

67. Which approach focuses on a set of interrelated and interdependent parts arranged in a manner that produces a unified whole?
    A. Process Approach
    B. Function Approach
    C. Systems Approach
    D. Contingency Approach

    Answer: C Difficulty: 2 Page: 20

68. Systems that are not influenced by and do not interact with their environment are known as which type of system?
    A. Closed system
    B. Open system
    C. Structured system
    D. Non-structured system

    Answer: A Difficulty: 1 Page: 20

69. The author states that today it is assumed organizations will be which of the following types of system?
    A. Closed system
    B. Open system
    C. Structured system
    D. Non-structured system

    Answer: B Difficulty: 2 Page: 20

70. Labor unions, employees, suppliers, customers, clients, and public interest groups are all examples of which of the following?
    A. Management constituencies
    B. Stockholders
    C. Stakeholders
    D. Business owners

    Answer: C Difficulty: 2 Page: 21

71. Any group that is affected by organizational decisions and policies is known as which of the following?
    A. Management constituencies
    B. Stockholders
    C. Stakeholders
    D. Business owners

    Answer: C Difficulty: 1 Page: 21

72. Which of the following approaches recognizes differences among organizations and categorizes variables that affect an organization's performance?
    A. Process Approach
    B. Function Approach
    C. Systems Approach
    D. Contingency Approach

    Answer: D Difficulty: 1 Page: 22

73. All but which of the following are variables that are considered when using the contingency approach to management?
    A. Organization size
    B. Individual differences
    C. Environmental uncertainty
    D. Management experience

    Answer: D Difficulty: 2 Page: 22

74. Focusing on the degree of uncertainty caused by politics, technology, and the economy would fall under which of the following contingency variables?
    A. Organization size
    B. Individual differences
    C. Environmental uncertainty
    D. Management experience

    Answer: C Difficulty: 2 Page: 22

Chapter 1: Managers and Management
Scenario

Table 1-1
Suzanne was amazed. She had just spent the day with the CEO of a major manufacturing firm through a "Visit with a Manager Program" developed by the College where she attended. She was exhausted and wondered how the CEO managed the hectic pace. Suzanne was also amazed by the number of "hats" that the CEO had worn throughout the day. The day had started with a general manager's meeting where the latest news concerning the competition had been announced by the CEO. Then Suzanne and the CEO had spent an hour completing a report to be given the following day to the Board of Directors. Lunch, where Suzanne had hoped to have time to ask questions, was an informal meeting with a group of suppliers who were concerned about their increasing costs. As soon as they had returned to the office, they received a message of a fire in one of the major warehouses. They were immediately off to the location to assess the damage. Then that evening, there was a formal dinner sponsored by the local Chamber of Commerce which the CEO had invited Suzanne to attend. Suzanne had declined. She was exhausted.

75. Referring to Table 1-1, the numerous roles played by the CEO is a demonstration of which of the following?
    A. Maslow's Hierarchy
    B. Fayol's Management Functions
    C. Herzberg's Maintenance Factors
    D. Mintzberg's Management Roles

    Answer: D Difficulty: 2

76. Referring to Table 1-1, when the CEO was speaking at the manager's meeting, which of the following roles was being performed?
    A. Figurehead
    B. Entrepreneur
    C. Resource allocator
    D. Disseminator

    Answer: D Difficulty: 2

77. Referring to Table 1-1, lunch was an example of which of the following roles?
    A. Monitor
    B. Negotiator
    C. Resource allocator
    D. Disseminator

    Answer: B Difficulty: 3

78. Referring to Table 1-1, preparing the report for the Board of Directors is an example of which of the following roles?
    A. Monitor
    B. Negotiator
    C. Resource allocator
    D. Spokesperson

    Answer: D Difficulty: 3

79. Referring to Table 1-1, attending the supper held by the Chamber of Commerce is an example of which of the following roles?
    A. Monitor
    B. Negotiator
    C. Figurehead
    D. Spokesperson

    Answer: C Difficulty: 3

Table 1-2
Shawna had spent the day "tagging" her uncle. He was the CEO of a large firm that manufactures cereal and related products. Shawna was a management major at a local college and one of her class assignments was to interview a business manager. When she approached her uncle about the assignment, he had told her that he felt she would get a better feel for management if she would "shadow" him for a day. So over Fall Break she had spent the day with him. He had spent his day dealing with a variety of issues. The first agenda item for the day had been a meeting with the division manager who was having difficulties meeting his target amount due to his inability to motivate his employees. Then it had been off to the assembly line floor to inspect a new procedure for filling cereal boxes. Lunch had been with a group of local CEOs where everything from the new hiring laws to the latest economic reports had been discussed. After lunch, Shawna had sat in on a meeting where the five-year strategic plan for the company was being evaluated. All in all it had been a day full of information Shawna could use for her class assignment.

80. Referring to Table 1-2, all but which of the following are the managerial competencies successful managers must possess?
    A. Political competencies
    B. Human competencies
    C. Technical competencies
    D. Organizational competencies

    Answer: D Difficulty: 1

Chapter 1: Managers and Management

81. Referring to Table 1-2, the meeting with the division manager concerning his inability to motivate his employees is a demonstration of which of the following competencies?
    A. Political competencies
    B. Human competencies
    C. Technical competencies
    D. Organizational competencies

    Answer: B Difficulty: 2

82. Referring to Table 1-2, lunch was an example of which of the following managerial competencies?
    A. Political competencies
    B. Human competencies
    C. Technical competencies
    D. Conceptual competencies

    Answer: A Difficulty: 2

83. Referring to Table 1-2, inspecting the new procedure for filling cereal boxes is an example of which of the following competencies?
    A. Political competencies
    B. Human competencies
    C. Technical competencies
    D. Organizational competencies

    Answer: C Difficulty: 2

84. Referring to Table 1-2, evaluating the strategic plan for the next five years would be an example of which of the following competencies?
    A. Political competencies
    B. Human competencies
    C. Technical competencies
    D. Conceptual competencies

    Answer: D Difficulty: 2

Table 1-3
John is the CEO of a large manufacturing firm which produces construction equipment. George is the owner and operator of a small business that produces one of the key engine components for John's manufacturing firm. Both are managers, however, George has noticed some differences between his activities and the activities John performs. George spends much of his time in outwardly directed activities like meeting with customers and potential investors. John seems to spend more of his time on activities that are directed internally, like allocating resources to appropriate departments. George wonders what accounts for this difference and he goes to a management consultant for input.

85. Referring to Table 1-3, the consultant informs George that the most important role of a small business manager is which of the following?
    A. Monitor
    B. Disseminator
    C. Spokesperson
    D. Negotiator

    Answer: C Difficulty: 3

86. Referring to Table 1-3, the least important role of the manager of a large organization is which of the following?
    A. Monitor
    B. Entrepreneur
    C. Spokesperson
    D. Negotiator

    Answer: B Difficulty: 3

87. Referring to Table 1-3, how many employees must work for John's firm?
    A. 250
    B. 400
    C. 450
    D. 600+

    Answer: D Difficulty: 2

88. Referring to Table 1-3, the most important role played by John will be which of the following?
    A. Resource allocator
    B. Entrepreneur
    C. Spokesperson
    D. Negotiator

    Answer: A Difficulty: 3

Chapter 1: Managers and Management

89. Referring to Table 1-3, the consultant tells George that the major difference between managers of large organizations versus small business owners is which of the following?
    A. The roles that are played by the managers
    B. The manager of a large organization is more likely to be a generalist
    C. The proportion of time spent on each function
    D. There is no difference between manager roles

    Answer: C Difficulty: 3

Essay

90. Compare and contrast the three levels of management.

    Answer:
    First-line managers - usually called supervisors, responsible for day-to-day activities, work with the operatives
    Middle managers - usually called department or agency head, or project leader, manage other managers, responsible for translating the goals set by top management into specific details that lower managers can perform
    Top managers - usually called president, CEO, or managing director, responsible for making decisions about the direction of the organization and establish policies that affect all organizational members

91. Briefly describe the four management functions.

    Answer:
    Planning - defining goals, establishing strategy, and developing plans to coordinate activities
    Organizing - includes determining what tasks are to be done, who is to do them, how the tasks are to be grouped and who reports to whom
    Leading - includes motivating employees, directing the activities of others, selecting the most effective communication channels and resolving conflicts
    Controlling - the process of monitoring performance, comparing it with goals, and correcting any significant deviations

92. Compare and contrast Mintzberg's managerial roles.

    Answer:
    Interpersonal - roles consists of being the figurehead for the organization, assuming the leadership role and acting as a liaison for the organization
    Informational - roles consist of being a monitor of current information which is then dispersed to employees needing that information, also involves being the spokesperson for the organization
    Decisional - roles consist of being an entrepreneur for the organization, handling disturbances, allocating resources, and negotiating

93. Briefly describe the four competencies that successful managers must possess.

    Answer:
    Conceptual competencies - the ability to coordinate all of the organization's interests and activities
    Human competencies - the ability to work with, understand and motivate people
    Technical competencies - the ability to use the tools, procedures, and techniques of a specialized field
    Political competencies - the ability to enhance one's own power, build a power base, and establish the right connections

94. Compare and contrast the three integrative frameworks that organize the subject matter of management.

    Answer:
    Process approach - based upon the four functions of management, planning, organizing, leading, and controlling
    Systems approach - views an organization as a set of interrelated and interdependent parts arranged in a manner that produces a unified whole
    Contingency approach - recognizes differences among organizations and categorizes variables that affect an organization's performance

Chapter 2: The Changing Face of Management

True/False

1. The key to success for Zane's Cycles is that it has no competition.

    Answer: F Difficulty: 1 Page: 31

2. The key for the corporate stars of the 1990s is their ability to predict what will be happening in their business and then utilize economies of scale.

    Answer: F Difficulty: 2 Page: 32

3. One of the biggest problems in managing organizations today is that they try to hold onto the past.

    Answer: T Difficulty: 1 Page: 33

4. Part of the rapidly changing environment that managers face today is the globalization of business.

    Answer: T Difficulty: 1 Page: 34

5. In order to be effective in a boundaryless world, managers need to focus on their own cultures, systems, and techniques.

    Answer: F Difficulty: 2 Page: 34

6. There is a growing independence between countries of the world.

    Answer: F Difficulty: 2 Page: 36

7. Flexibility and adaptability are key components for managers who cross national borders.

    Answer: T Difficulty: 1 Page: 38

8. Technological advances make organizations less productive and thus able to maintain their competitive advantage.

    Answer: F Difficulty: 2 Page: 39

9. Moral responsibility refers to a business firm's obligation to pursue long-term goals that are good for society.

    Answer: F Difficulty: 2 Page: 42

10. Social responsiveness has occurred when a business has met only its economic and legal responsibilities.

    Answer: F Difficulty: 3 Page: 42

11. Fran Sussner Rogers believes that helping employees will demonstrate not only social responsibility but will also enhance worker performance and profitability.

    Answer: T Difficulty: 2 Page: 43

12. Almost two-thirds of all new entrants into the work force will be Latinos.

    Answer: F Difficulty: 2 Page: 48

13. TQM focuses on irregular improvements where major changes are implemented.

    Answer: F Difficulty: 2 Page: 50

14. The redesigning of jobs in order to increase the decision-making discretion of workers is known as reengineering.

    Answer: F Difficulty: 2 Page: 55

15. The diversity that exists in the work force requires managers to be less sensitive to the differences each group brings to the work setting.

    Answer: F Difficulty: 1 Page: 56

Multiple Choice

16. Who sells the most bikes in the New Haven, Connecticut, area?
    A. Sears
    B. WalMart
    C. K-Mart
    D. Zane's Cycles

    Answer: D Difficulty: 1 Page: 31

17. At what age did Chris Zane begin his own bicycle shop?
    A. 12
    B. 18
    C. 22
    D. 36

    Answer: A Difficulty: 2 Page: 31

18. What is the key to the success of Zane's Cycles?
    A. Low prices
    B. High quality
    C. Focus on customer satisfaction
    D. Little competition

    Answer: C Difficulty: 3 Page: 31

Chapter 2:   The Changing Face of Management

19. All but which of the following are characteristics of the corporate stars of the 1990s?
    A. Quality
    B. Team work
    C. Entrepreneurial skills
    D. Stability

    Answer: D Difficulty: 2 Page: 31

20. According to Toffler, the first wave of modern civilization was which of the following?
    A. Agriculture
    B. Industrialization
    C. Manufacturing
    D. Information

    Answer: A Difficulty: 1 Page: 33

21. According to Toffler, which wave of modern civilization focused on the individual who was his/her own boss performing a variety of tasks?
    A. Agriculture
    B. Industrialization
    C. Manufacturing
    D. Information

    Answer: A Difficulty: 2 Page: 33

22. According to Toffler, which wave of modern civilization focused on mass production, specialized jobs, and authority relationships?
    A. Agriculture
    B. Industrialization
    C. Manufacturing
    D. Information

    Answer: B Difficulty: 2 Page: 34

23. According to Toffler, which wave of modern civilization changed the lives of skilled craftsmen so that no longer did they see a product to completion?
    A. Agriculture
    B. Industrialization
    C. Manufacturing
    D. Information

    Answer: B Difficulty: 3 Page: 34

24. Which wave of modern civilization, according to Toffler, eliminated many low-skilled, blue-collar workers?
    A. Agriculture
    B. Industrialization
    C. Manufacturing
    D. Information

    Answer: D Difficulty: 3 Page: 34

25. Which wave of modern civilization transformed society from a manufacturing focus to a focus on service?
    A. Agriculture
    B. Industrialization
    C. Manufacturing
    D. Information

    Answer: D Difficulty: 2 Page: 34

26. The concept of a boundaryless world where goods and services are produced and marketed worldwide is known as which of the following?
    A. The global village
    B. The global community
    C. MNCs
    D. International businesses

    Answer: A Difficulty: 1 Page: 34

27. Which of the following corporations initiated the rapid growth in international trade?
    A. Transnational Corporations
    B. Uninational Corporations
    C. Multinational Corporations
    D. Blue-chip Corporations

    Answer: C Difficulty: 2 Page: 34

28. Multinational Corporations maintain significant operations in _____ or more countries but are based in _____ home country/countries.
    A. Four, one
    B. Two, one
    C. One, two
    D. One, four

    Answer: B Difficulty: 1 Page: 34

Chapter 2:   The Changing Face of Management

29. Decision making in Transnational Corporations occurs at which of the following?
   A. Local level
   B. Home office level
   C. Continental level
   D. Regional level

   Answer: A Difficulty: 2 Page: 35

30. Who runs operations in each country for a Transnational Corporation?
   A. Management teams sent from the Home Office
   B. Management teams sent from the Regional Office
   C. Nationals
   D. Management teams sent from the United States

   Answer: C Difficulty: 2 Page: 35

31. All but which of the following are options if a business decides to go global?
   A. Export its product
   B. Contract with foreign manufacturers
   C. Franchising
   D. Importing its product

   Answer: D Difficulty: 2 Page: 35

32. A narrow focus where managers see things solely through their own eyes and within their own perspective is known as which of the following?
   A. Ethnocentric view
   B. World view
   C. Parochialism
   D. Global view

   Answer: C Difficulty: 2 Page: 36

33. John is a manager from the United States. He firmly believes the only way to do things is the "American Way", since it is the best way. He is holding which point of view?
   A. Ethnocentric view
   B. World view
   C. Parochialism
   D. Global view

   Answer: A Difficulty: 3 Page: 36

34. In France, status is often the result of all but which of the following factors?
    A. Seniority
    B. Education
    C. Personal accomplishment
    D. Organizational factors

    Answer: C Difficulty: 2 Page: 36

35. Which of the following reflects the attitudes and perspectives shared by individuals from a specific culture or country that shapes individual behavior and the way the world is perceived?
    A. World view
    B. Focused view
    C. Cultural environments
    D. Behavior environments

    Answer: C Difficulty: 2 Page: 37

36. Which of the following has a major impact on employees' work-related values and attitudes, according to Hofstede?
    A. National culture
    B. Company culture
    C. International culture
    D. Regional culture

    Answer: A Difficulty: 2 Page: 37

37. All but which of the following are the four specific dimensions of national culture, according to Hofstede?
    A. Power distance
    B. Uncertainty avoidance
    C. Space acceptance
    D. Individualism versus collectivism

    Answer: C Difficulty: 2 Page: 37

38. The fact that Jenny feels responsible for herself and her family but not necessarily the neighbor down the street is an example of which of the following dimensions of national culture?
    A. Power distance
    B. Uncertainty avoidance
    C. Space acceptance
    D. Individualism versus collectivism

    Answer: D Difficulty: 3 Page: 37

Chapter 2: The Changing Face of Management

39. The fact that in the United States employees are generally not in fear or awe of their managers is an example of which of the following dimensions of national culture?
    A. Power distance
    B. Uncertainty avoidance
    C. Space acceptance
    D. Individualism versus collectivism

    Answer: A Difficulty: 3 Page: 37

40. A society where there is relatively little job mobility and life-time employment is widely practiced would be an example of which of the following dimensions of national culture?
    A. Power distance
    B. Quality of life
    C. Uncertainty avoidance
    D. Individualism versus collectivism

    Answer: C Difficulty: 3 Page: 37

41. All but which of the following countries are strongly individualistic but low on power distance?
    A. United States
    B. England
    C. New Zealand
    D. Singapore

    Answer: D Difficulty: 3 Page: 38

42. Which of the following are key components for managers who cross national borders?
    A. Efficiency and flexibility
    B. Flexibility and adaptability
    C. Adaptability and effectiveness
    D. Effectiveness and an ethnocentric viewpoint

    Answer: B Difficulty: 2 Page: 38

43. Technology includes all but which of the following?
    A. Equipment
    B. Operating methods
    C. Knowledge
    D. Tools

    Answer: C Difficulty: 1 Page: 39

44. Technology has made it possible to enhance production processes by replacing
    A. Human labor with electronic/computer equipment
    B. Electronic/computer equipment with human labor
    C. Human labor with assembly lines/manufacturing firms
    D. Assembly lines/manufacturing firms with electronic/computer equipment

    Answer: A Difficulty: 3 Page: 39

45. Technology has provided the capability where a worker's computer and modem can be linked to those of coworkers and managers in offices basically anywhere in the global village, thus allowing workers for the same organization to be located around the world. This is known as which of the following?
    A. Video conferencing
    B. Down-loading
    C. Telecommuting
    D. Internet surfing

    Answer: C Difficulty: 2 Page: 40

46. Jane does not go into the office every day. Instead she works at home and through the use of her computer and modem links to the home office. Jane is
    A. Video conferencing
    B. Down-loading
    C. Telecommuting
    D. Internet surfing

    Answer: C Difficulty: 2 Page: 40

47. The classical viewpoint states that management's only social responsibility is to
    A. Maximize sales
    B. Maximize profits
    C. Maximize philanthropy
    D. Maximize ethical decision making

    Answer: B Difficulty: 1 Page: 42

48. All but which of the following are arguments for the assumption of social responsibility by business?
    A. Long-run profits
    B. Stockholder interests
    C. Ethical obligations
    D. Costs

    Answer: D Difficulty: 2 Page: 41

Chapter 2: The Changing Face of Management

49. All but which of the following are arguments for the assumption of social responsibility by business?
    A. Possession of resources
    B. Balance of responsibility and power
    C. Public image
    D. Dilution of purpose

    Answer: D Difficulty: 2 Page: 41

50. All but which of the following are arguments against the assumption of social responsibility by business?
    A. Dilution of purpose
    B. Costs
    C. Too much power
    D. Public expectations

    Answer: D Difficulty: 2 Page: 41

51. All but which of the following are arguments against the assumption of social responsibility by business?
    A. Lack of skills
    B. Lack of accountability
    C. Lack of broad public support
    D. Possession of resources

    Answer: D Difficulty: 2 Page: 41

52. A firm's obligation, beyond that required by law and economics, to pursue long-term goals that are good for society is known as which of the following?
    A. Social responsiveness
    B. Ethical responsibility
    C. Social responsibility
    D. Social obligation

    Answer: C Difficulty: 3 Page: 42

53. Which of the following deals with the need of a business to meet only basic economic and legal standards?
    A. Social responsibility
    B. Social obligation
    C. Moral obligation
    D. Social responsiveness

    Answer: B Difficulty: 3 Page: 42

54. Which of the following deals with the ability of a firm to adapt to changing societal conditions?
    A. Social responsibility
    B. Social obligation
    C. Moral obligation
    D. Social responsiveness

    Answer: D Difficulty: 3 Page: 42

55. A large chemical company not only disposes of all toxic waste properly as outlined by law but it also spends $1 million dollars each year on research to determine better processes for all businesses to use in disposing of toxic wastes. This company is exhibiting which of the following?
    A. Social responsibility
    B. Social obligation
    C. Moral obligation
    D. Social responsiveness

    Answer: A Difficulty: 2 Page: 42

56. A large pulp and paper company meets all federal guidelines and obeys all laws rigorously as it cuts down timber. The primary concern of this company is compliance and profit maximization for its stockholders. This company is exhibiting which of the following?
    A. Social responsibility
    B. Social obligation
    C. Moral obligation
    D. Social responsiveness

    Answer: B Difficulty: 2 Page: 42

57. A large manufacturer of home appliances offers on-site daycare for its employees. This company is exhibiting which of the following?
    A. Social responsibility
    B. Social obligation
    C. Moral obligation
    D. Social responsiveness

    Answer: D Difficulty: 3 Page: 43

58. Those people who are independent workers that initiate a business venture, who take calculated risks, and who accept the fact that mistakes occur are known as which of the following?
    A. Intrapreneurs
    B. Managers
    C. Entrepreneurs
    D. Venture capitalists

    Answer: C Difficulty: 1 Page: 44

Chapter 2:   The Changing Face of Management

59. In general, entrepreneurs are better able to do which of the following than are managers in a traditional hierarchical organization?
    A. Lead
    B. Organize
    C. Respond to a changing environment
    D. Respond to a static environment

    Answer: C Difficulty: 2 Page: 44

60. Persons within an organization who seize opportunities for change and then capitalize on those changes but who never bear the financial risk are known as which of the following?
    A. Intrapreneurs
    B. Managers
    C. Entrepreneurs
    D. Venture capitalists

    Answer: A Difficulty: 1 Page: 44

61. The majority of the pre-1980s work force in North America consisted of primarily
    A. Male Caucasians
    B. Female Caucasians
    C. Male African Americans
    D. Female Latinos

    Answer: A Difficulty: 1 Page: 45

62. All but which of the following groups of people are additions to the work force since the 1980s?
    A. Female Caucasians
    B. African Americans
    C. Male Caucasians
    D. Latinos

    Answer: C Difficulty: 2 Page: 45

63. Growth in the U.S. work force from 1990-2000 will occur most rapidly among which of the following groups?
    A. Latinos
    B. Women
    C. Physically disabled
    D. African Americans

    Answer: B Difficulty: 2 Page: 48

Testbank

64. A wide range of benefits including on-site day care, flexible working hours, job sharing and parental leave are all examples of which of the following?
   A. Cafeteria benefits
   B. Productivity benefits
   C. Family-friendly benefits
   D. Performance Plus benefits

   Answer: C Difficulty: 2 Page: 48

65. A philosophy stated by W. Edwards Deming which emphasizes customer needs and expectations and a commitment to continuous improvement is known as which of the following?
   A. Kaizen
   B. Downsizing
   C. Reengineering
   D. Total quality management

   Answer: D Difficulty: 2 Page: 49

66. A company that is committed to continuous improvement would be exhibiting which of the following?
   A. Kaizen
   B. Downsizing
   C. Reengineering
   D. Total quality management

   Answer: A Difficulty: 1 Page: 49

67. The Japanese demonstrated that it was possible for manufacturers of the highest-quality products to also have which of the following?
   A. High costs
   B. Low costs
   C. Larger profits
   D. Lower profits

   Answer: B Difficulty: 3 Page: 50

68. All but which of the following are components of total quality management?
   A. Concern for continuous improvement
   B. Accurate measurement
   C. Employee empowerment
   D. Focus on the stockholders of the company

   Answer: D Difficulty: 2 Page: 49

Chapter 2: The Changing Face of Management

69. Radical, quantum change within an organization is known as which of the following?
    A. Kaizen
    B. Downsizing
    C. Reengineering
    D. Total quality management

    Answer: C Difficulty: 2 Page: 50

70. After looking at the competition, your company decides that major changes need to take place. Your product needs to be changed completely. Your company is involved with which of the following?
    A. Kaizen
    B. Downsizing
    C. Reengineering
    D. Total quality management

    Answer: C Difficulty: 2 Page: 50

71. Your company decides that adding a crunch factor to the hot cereal that you produce will benefit the product by increasing the protein level. It is a minor change but one of many that your company makes as it strives to continuously improve its product. Your company is demonstrating which of the following?
    A. Kaizen
    B. Downsizing
    C. Reengineering
    D. Total quality management

    Answer: D Difficulty: 2 Page: 50

72. An activity in an organization designed to create a more-efficient operation through extensive layoffs is known as which of the following?
    A. Outsourcing
    B. Downsizing
    C. Reengineering
    D. Rightsizing

    Answer: B Difficulty: 1 Page: 51

73. Kay's company is using more and more outside firms to provide necessary products and services. This is known as which of the following?
    A. Outsourcing
    B. Downsizing
    C. Reengineering
    D. Rightsizing

    Answer: A Difficulty: 2 Page: 51

Testbank

74. Linking staffing levels to organizational goals is known as which of the following?
    A. Outsourcing
    B. Downsizing
    C. Reengineering
    D. Rightsizing

    Answer: D Difficulty: 1 Page: 51

75. Part-time, temporary and contract works who are available for hire on an as-needed basis are known as which of the following?
    A. Outsourcing
    B. Contingent work force
    C. Reengineering
    D. Rightsizing

    Answer: B Difficulty: 1 Page: 52

76. An employee who comes in only during the restaurant's peak hours of 11:00-1:30 and receives no benefits is known as which of the following?
    A. Part-time employee
    B. Temporary employee
    C. Contract worker
    D. Full-time employee

    Answer: A Difficulty: 3 Page: 53

77. Dejobbing is creating two primary work groups. These two groups are which of the following?
    A. Core employees and contract workers
    B. Core employees and the contingent work force
    C. Core employees and part-time workers
    D. Contract works and temporary workers

    Answer: B Difficulty: 2 Page: 54

78. The redesigning of jobs in order to increase the decision-making discretion of workers is known as which of the following?
    A. Reengineering
    B. Downsizing
    C. Empowering
    D. Rightsizing

    Answer: C Difficulty: 2 Page: 55

Chapter 2:   The Changing Face of Management

79. Ken finds himself spending much less time supervising and more time motivating, empowering and encouraging his employees. Which term best describes Ken?
    A. Empowering
    B. Coach
    C. Downsizing
    D. Supervising

    Answer: B Difficulty: 2 Page: 55

80. The rules or principles that define right and wrong conduct are known as which of the following?
    A. Social responsibility
    B. Moral obligation
    C. Social obligation
    D. Ethics

    Answer: D Difficulty: 1 Page: 57

81. Focusing on the greatest good for the greatest number of people is an example of which of the following views of ethics?
    A. Utilitarian view
    B. Theory justice view
    C. Rights view
    D. Ethical view

    Answer: A Difficulty: 2 Page: 57

82. A formal document that states an organization's primary values and the ethical rules it expects employees to follow is known as which of the following?
    A. Code of conduct
    B. Code of responsibility
    C. Corporate code
    D. Code of ethics

    Answer: D Difficulty: 2 Page: 58

83. The key to success for today's manager can best be stated in which of the following statements?
    A. Be prepared for stability
    B. Be prepared to make adjustments
    C. Be prepared for a static environment
    D. Be prepared for less use of technology

    Answer: B Difficulty: 2 Page: 59

Scenario

Table 2-1
Kerri was confused. Her management class was focusing on social responsibility and her assignment was to find business cases demonstrating social responsibility. She had several examples but now she was not sure which case was an example of which concept. Her first business dealt with the tuna industry, which in response to pressure from environmentalists, had stated dolphins would no longer be caught with the tuna. Her second business dealt with a company whose primary focus was on profit maximization for its stockholders. The primary focus of this company was legal compliance and profit maximization. Her third business was the tobacco industry which each year gives thousands of dollars to the Arts. Her fourth business dealt also with the tobacco companies and the fact they were no longer advertising near local schools. Legislation had been enacted in order to prevent cigarettes from being promoted in locations where children under the age of 18 would be likely to see the advertisements.

84. Referring to Table 2-1, a firm's obligation to pursue long-term goals that are good for society is known as which of the following?
    A. Social responsibility
    B. Social obligation
    C. Social responsiveness
    D. Moral obligation

    Answer: A Difficulty: 2

85. Referring to Table 2-1, the first business is an example of which of the following?
    A. Social responsibility
    B. Social obligation
    C. Social responsiveness
    D. Moral obligation

    Answer: C Difficulty: 2

86. Referring to Table 2-1, the second business is an example of which of the following?
    A. Social responsibility
    B. Social obligation
    C. Social responsiveness
    D. Moral obligation

    Answer: B Difficulty: 2

Chapter 2: The Changing Face of Management

87. Referring to Table 2-1, the third business is an example of which of the following?
    A. Social responsibility
    B. Social obligation
    C. Social responsiveness
    D. Moral obligation

    Answer: A Difficulty: 2

88. Referring to Table 2-1, the fourth business is an example of which of the following?
    A. Social responsibility
    B. Social obligation
    C. Social responsiveness
    D. Moral obligation

    Answer: C Difficulty: 2

Table 2-2
Kevin knew that it was likely his corporation was going to ask him to go abroad and manage the new chemical factory they were building. He was excited about the prospects but also apprehensive. He had never traveled before and as far as he was concerned, there was only one way to do anything, his way which was also the "American Way". He decided some research was in order to at least get an idea about other countries. In his reading he learned that some cultures place a high priority on a loose social framework where they feel primarily responsible for themselves and their immediate family. He also learned that in some societies, employees show a great deal of respect for those in authority and titles and rank carry much weight. Some countries have little job mobility and practice life-time employment. He also learned that some countries are characterized by assertiveness and materialism. Now he wondered if there was any framework to help organize his thoughts.

89. Referring to Table 2-2, who developed a framework describing specific dimensions of national culture that John could use in order to organize his information?
    A. Maslow
    B. Herzberg
    C. Hofstede
    D. Zane

    Answer: C Difficulty: 2

90. Referring to Table 2-2, Kevin could be said to have which of the following points of view?
    A. Ethnocentric view
    B. World view
    C. Parochialism
    D. Focused view

    Answer: A Difficulty: 2

91. Referring to Table 2-2, a culture where employees show a great deal of respect for authority and titles and rank are important would be an example of which dimension of national culture?
    A. Individualism versus collectivism
    B. Power distance
    C. Uncertainty avoidance
    D. Quantity versus quality of life

    Answer: B Difficulty: 2

92. Referring to Table 2-2, a culture that is characterized by assertiveness and materialism would be demonstrating which dimension of national culture?
    A. Individualism versus collectivism
    B. Power distance
    C. Uncertainty avoidance
    D. Quantity versus quality of life

    Answer: D Difficulty: 2

93. Referring to Table 2-2, a culture that practices life-time employment would be demonstrating which dimension of national culture?
    A. Individualism versus collectivism
    B. Power distance
    C. Uncertainty avoidance
    D. Quantity versus quality of life

    Answer: C Difficulty: 2

Chapter 2:   The Changing Face of Management

Table 2-3
Jenny had been reading several management periodicals for her class assignment. She was confused by all the terms she had come across in her search for changes that were reshaping contemporary organizations. The first article had described a new business owner who had taken a large calculated risk to initiate his new business venture where he had become quite successful at the age of 26. The next article dealt with a process that managers were using for quality control at a local cheese producing plant. The company was constantly monitoring the cheese-making process and little by little improving the quality of their cheese. The next article was in direct contrast. This roller blading company had decided that their product needed to be completely remade in order to keep up with the competition. So they had basically started from scratch and developed a new revised product. Several of the articles Jenny had read talked about companies laying off numerous employees. And the practice was not limited to the United States. It was occurring world wide. Finally several articles had also mentioned that businesses were hiring less core employees and using more contingent workers. Many larger businesses were hiring people to fill in for those employees off for an extended time period, like a new dad off for twelve weeks after the birth of a child.

94. Referring to Table 2-3, the new business owner could best be described by which of the following?
    A. Reengineering
    B. Downsizing
    C. Entrepreneur
    D. Intrapreneur

    Answer: C   Difficulty: 2

95. Referring to Table 2-3, the cheese factory was using which of the following techniques.
    A. Reengineering
    B. Downsizing
    C. Total quality management
    D. Rightsizing

    Answer: C   Difficulty: 3

96. Referring to Table 2-3, the roller blading company was using which of the following techniques?
    A. Reengineering
    B. Downsizing
    C. Total quality management
    D. Rightsizing

    Answer: A   Difficulty: 3

97. Referring to Table 2-3, the practice of laying off employees is known as which of the following?
   A. Reengineering
   B. Downsizing
   C. Total quality management
   D. Rightsizing

   Answer: B   Difficulty: 2

98. Referring to Table 2-3, which type of worker is replacing the new father who is staying home with his baby?
   A. Part-time employee
   B. Temporary employee
   C. Contract employee
   D. Project employee

   Answer: B   Difficulty: 3

Essay

99. Compare and contrast the following: global village, multinational corporations, and transnational corporations.

   Answer:
   Global village - a boundaryless world where the production and marketing of goods and services is worldwide
   Multinational corporations - companies that maintain significant operations in two or more countries simultaneously but are based in one home country
   Transnational corporations - a company that maintains significant operations in more than one country simultaneously and decentralizes decision making in each operation to the local country

100. Briefly describe two of Hofstede's four cultural variables.

   Answer:
   Individualism versus collectivism - a loosely knit social framework as opposed to a more tightly knit social framework - the individual versus the group
   Power distance - the amount of acceptance for the unequal distribution of power in institutions and organizations
   Uncertainty avoidance - a culture with high uncertainty avoidance has a high level of anxiety among its people so formal rules are developed with strict compliance expected
   Quantity versus quality of life - quantity of life refers to values that are characterized by assertiveness and materialism where quality of life focuses on relationships and concern for others

Chapter 2: The Changing Face of Management

101. Discuss two arguments for social responsibility and two arguments against social responsibility.

    Answer:
    Arguments for:
    Public expectations
    Long-run profits
    Ethical obligations
    Public image
    Possession of resources

    Arguments against:
    Violation of profit maximization
    Dilution of purpose
    Costs
    Too much power
    Lack of skills

102. Compare and contrast social responsibility, social obligation, and social responsiveness.

    Answer:
    Social responsibility - a firm's obligation to pursue long-term goals that are good for society
    Social obligation - the obligation to meet economic and legal responsibilities
    Social responsiveness - the ability of a firm to adopt changing societal conditions

103. Describe the work force in the year 2000.

    Answer:
    Growth will occur primarily among women and Hispanics
    Almost 2/3 of the new work force entrants will be women
    More emphasis on employee training
    Modification of employee benefit programs
    Family-friendly benefit packages

Chapter 3: Foundations of Planning

True/False

1. If managers performed their jobs in organizations that never faced changes in the environment, there would be a great need for planning.

   Answer: F Difficulty: 2 Page: 71

2. Planning increases uncertainty.

   Answer: F Difficulty: 1 Page: 71

3. Planning is exactly what is needed in order to more effectively manage a chaotic environment.

   Answer: T Difficulty: 2 Page: 72

4. Without planning, there can be no effective control.

   Answer: T Difficulty: 3 Page: 72

5. Once a plan is established, it should never be changed.

   Answer: F Difficulty: 2 Page: 72

6. Plans cannot be developed in a dynamic environment.

   Answer: F Difficulty: 2 Page: 73

7. The evidence suggests organizations should have formal plans.

   Answer: T Difficulty: 1 Page: 73

8. Organizations with formal plans will always outperform those organizations without formal plans.

   Answer: F Difficulty: 3 Page: 75

9. Tactical plans form a basis for strategic plans.

   Answer: F Difficulty: 3 Page: 76

10. Feedback favorably affects performance.

    Answer: T Difficulty: 2 Page: 79

11. MBO is most effective if the goals set are difficult enough to require the person to stretch.

    Answer: T Difficulty: 3 Page: 79

Chapter 3: Foundations of Planning

12. Before the early 1970s, plans for the future were mere extensions of where the organization had been in the past.

    Answer: T Difficulty: 2 Page: 81

13. As long as businesses are in the same industry, an opportunity for one business will also be an opportunity for another business.

    Answer: F Difficulty: 3 Page: 83

14. A strong culture may act as a significant barrier to acceptance of change.

    Answer: T Difficulty: 2 Page: 84

15. In order to fulfill the grand strategy, managers will seek to position their units so that they can gain a relative advantage over their competition.

    Answer: T Difficulty: 3 Page: 86

16. Product innovations offer little opportunity for sustained competitive advantage.

    Answer: T Difficulty: 3 Page: 89

17. Entrepreneurs are willing to take huge risks.

    Answer: F Difficulty: 3 Page: 92

Multiple Choice

18. Watson Pharmaceutical centers around
    A. Name brand drugs
    B. Drugs used only in hospitals
    C. Discovery of new drugs
    D. Generic drugs

    Answer: D Difficulty: 2 Page: 70

19. Allen Chao turned to his family and friends in Taiwan for _____ for his new business.
    A. Chemicals
    B. Start-up capital
    C. Expertise
    D. Governmental resources

    Answer: B Difficulty: 2 Page: 70

20. When objectives are not written down or rarely verbalized, and the planning is general and lacks continuity, which of the following types of planning was used?
    A. Environmental planning
    B. Economic planning
    C. Informal planning
    D. Formal planning

    Answer: C Difficulty: 2 Page: 71

21. When planning involves specific objectives that cover a period of years which are then written down and made available to organization members with specific action programs for achieving the goal, which of the following types of planning was used?
    A. Environmental planning
    B. Economic planning
    C. Informal planning
    D. Formal planning

    Answer: D Difficulty: 2 Page: 71

22. All but which of the following are reasons for planning?
    A. Provides direction
    B. Reduces the impact of change
    C. Maximizes waste and redundancy
    D. Sets standards to facilitate control

    Answer: C Difficulty: 1 Page: 71

23. In a chaotic environment, what clarifies the consequences of actions managers might take in response to the continual change?
    A. Controlling
    B. Organizing
    C. Leading
    D. Planning

    Answer: D Difficulty: 2 Page: 72

24. Once a plan is established, it should always be
    A. Followed
    B. Changed
    C. Flexible
    D. Long-term

    Answer: C Difficulty: 2 Page: 72

Chapter 3:   Foundations of Planning

25. The organizational formality of Apple Computer, ultimately led to
    A. A successful organization
    B. Hampered creativity
    C. Increased creativity
    D. Increased market share

    Answer: B Difficulty: 3 Page: 73

26. Successful plans may provide
    A. A false sense of security
    B. Only success
    C. Increased awareness of the environment
    D. Increased awareness of change

    Answer: A Difficulty: 3 Page: 73

27. Where formal planning occurs, all but which of the following generally occur?
    A. Higher profits
    B. Higher return on assets
    C. Negative profits
    D. Positive financial results

    Answer: C Difficulty: 1 Page: 75

28. In those organizations where formal planning did not lead to higher performance, the culprit was which of the following?
    A. The competition
    B. The marketing plan
    C. Management
    D. The environment

    Answer: D Difficulty: 2 Page: 75

29. Body Shop International, based in England, sells
    A. Weight equipment
    B. Health-conscious foods
    C. Natural soaps and lotions
    D. Exercise equipment

    Answer: C Difficulty: 2 Page: 74

30. What was the major downfall in the success of Body Shop International in the United States?
    A. Competition
    B. High prices
    C. Lack of demand
    D. Inability to react to the environment quickly

    Answer: D Difficulty: 3 Page: 74

31. All but which of the following are popular ways to describe plans?
    A. Breadth
    B. Time frame
    C. Specificity
    D. Environmental focus

    Answer: D Difficulty: 2 Page: 75

32. Plans that apply to the entire organization, establish the organization's overall objectives and seek to position the organization in terms of its environment are called
    A. Operational plans
    B. Tactical plans
    C. Strategic plans
    D. Single-use plans

    Answer: C Difficulty: 2 Page: 75

33. How the overall objectives are to be achieved is specified in which of the following?
    A. Operational plans
    B. Tactical plans
    C. Strategic plans
    D. Single-use plans

    Answer: B Difficulty: 2 Page: 76

34. All but which of the following are ways in which tactical and strategic plans differ?
    A. Time frame
    B. Scope
    C. Known set of organizational objectives
    D. Environmental effects

    Answer: D Difficulty: 2 Page: 76

35. Tactical plans tend to cover
    A. Longer time frames
    B. Shorter time frames
    C. Intermediate time frames
    D. The time frame is irrelevant

    Answer: B Difficulty: 1 Page: 76

36. The greater the uncertainty, the more plans should be
    A. Long-term
    B. Short-term
    C. Intermediate in length
    D. The time frame is irrelevant

    Answer: B Difficulty: 3 Page: 76

Chapter 3:   Foundations of Planning

37. When uncertainty is high and management must maintain flexibility, which of the following types of plans are preferable?
   A. Long-term plans
   B. No plans
   C. Directional plans
   D. Specific plans

   Answer: C Difficulty: 2 Page: 76

38. Which types of plans provide general guidelines?
   A. Specific plans
   B. Directional plans
   C. Tactical plans
   D. Operational plans

   Answer: B Difficulty: 1 Page: 76

39. Which of the following types of plans is used to meet a particular or unique situation?
   A. Tactical plan
   B. Operational plan
   C. Single-use plan
   D. Standing plan

   Answer: C Difficulty: 1 Page: 77

40. A system whereby performance objectives are jointly determined by subordinates and their superiors, progress is reviewed, and rewards are then allocated is known as which of the following?
   A. Standing plan
   B. Strategic plan
   C. MBO
   D. MBWA

   Answer: C Difficulty: 1 Page: 77

41. MBO links goals at one level to which of the following?
   A. Top management
   B. Middle management
   C. First-line management
   D. All levels of management

   Answer: D Difficulty: 3 Page: 77

42. All but which of the following are ingredients common to MBO?
   A. Goal specificity
   B. Participative decision making
   C. Performance feedback
   D. General time period

   Answer: D Difficulty: 2 Page: 78

43. Which of the following would be an appropriate statement for a MBO objective?
    A. Improve productivity
    B. Increase sales
    C. Improve training
    D. Decrease waste by 6% over the next six months

    Answer: D Difficulty: 3 Page: 78

44. Who determines employee goals in MBO?
    A. Employees
    B. Managers
    C. Managers and employees
    D. Managers and the CEO

    Answer: C Difficulty: 3 Page: 78

45. Which level of management must have a high level of commitment to MBO in order for MBO to reach its potential?
    A. First-line management
    B. Middle management
    C. Top management
    D. Operative management

    Answer: C Difficulty: 2 Page: 79

46. Deming argued that specific goals may
    A. Increase productivity
    B. Increase performance
    C. Do more harm than good
    D. Be used as floors by employees

    Answer: C Difficulty: 3 Page: 80

47. All but which of the following are steps in goal setting?
    A. Specify deadlines
    B. Allow the employee to actively participate
    C. Link rewards to effort
    D. Prioritize goals

    Answer: C Difficulty: 3 Page: 80

48. All but which of the following undermined the long-range planning of the 1970s where planning for the future was merely an extension of past plans?
    A. Energy crisis
    B. Deregulation
    C. Increasing global competition
    D. Decreasing global competition

    Answer: D Difficulty: 2 Page: 81

Chapter 3: Foundations of Planning

49. Which of the following is a nine-step process that involves strategic planning, implementation and evaluation?
    A. Decision-making process
    B. Strategic management process
    C. Tactical management process
    D. Long-range planning process

    Answer: B Difficulty: 2 Page: 81

50. The purpose of Kerry's Klowns is to "provide healthy entertainment that makes school-age children laugh". The quote could be described as which of the following?
    A. Strategic plan
    B. Mission
    C. Strategic purpose
    D. Tactical objective

    Answer: B Difficulty: 3 Page: 82

51. The statement that answers the question, "what business are we in", is best described by which of the following?
    A. Strategic plan
    B. Mission
    C. Strategic purpose
    D. Tactical objective

    Answer: B Difficulty: 2 Page: 82

52. The second step in the strategic management process is which of the following?
    A. Analyze the environment
    B. Identify strengths and weaknesses
    C. Identify the organization's current mission, objectives and strategies
    D. Formulate strategies

    Answer: A Difficulty: 2 Page: 82

53. A company that is assessing its capital, worker skills, marketing, accounting and patents is analyzing which of the following?
    A. Strength
    B. Weakness
    C. Opportunity
    D. Threat

    Answer: A Difficulty: 1 Page: 83

54. Tim's Company is analyzing the technology that allows them to produce wireless communication equipment for less money. This technological breakthrough for Tim's Company is which of the following?
    A. Strength
    B. Weakness
    C. Opportunity
    D. Threat

    Answer: C Difficulty: 2 Page: 83

55. Kent's Kar Kare has just determined that a competitor is locating in a prime location with the newest in car washing equipment. Kent is bound to his location. The new competitor is an example of which of the following for Kent?
    A. Strength
    B. Weakness
    C. Opportunity
    D. Threat

    Answer: D Difficulty: 2 Page: 83

56. Pat's Pets has developed a reputation for the best in quality pet care. They are known for their humane and loving treatment of animals. Their motto is "We love them like they are our own". This reputation could be classified as which of the following?
    A. Opportunity
    B. Distinctive competence
    C. Strategic competence
    D. Strengths

    Answer: B Difficulty: 3 Page: 83

57. An analysis of an organization's strength, weaknesses, opportunities and threats is known as which of the following?
    A. MBO
    B. MBWA
    C. SWOT Analysis
    D. SWAT Analysis

    Answer: C Difficulty: 2 Page: 84

58. If no changes are necessary in light of the SWOT analysis, management is ready to begin which of the following?
    A. Strategy formation
    B. Tactical formulation
    C. Short-term planning
    D. Controlling

    Answer: A Difficulty: 2 Page: 85

Chapter 3:   Foundations of Planning

59. All but which of the following are types of strategies that would fall under grand strategies?
    A. Growth
    B. Stability
    C. Retrenchment
    D. Cost-leadership

    Answer: D Difficulty: 2 Page: 85

60. Sam's Company is focusing on increasing the size of the company and hiring more employees. Which of the following strategies is Sam's pursuing?
    A. Growth
    B. Stability
    C. Retrenchment
    D. Combination

    Answer: A Difficulty: 2 Page: 85

61. When Northwest Airlines began serving its own in-flight meals, which of the following strategies was it pursuing?
    A. Growth
    B. Stability
    C. Retrenchment
    D. Combination

    Answer: A Difficulty: 1 Page: 85

62. Larry's Company is in the process of buying a smaller competitor and incorporating that company's resources into his business. This is an example of which of the following types of strategies?
    A. Merger
    B. Stability
    C. Retrenchment
    D. Acquisition

    Answer: D Difficulty: 2 Page: 85

63. Stacy's Company continues to offer the same quality beauty products it has for the last 10 years. The company is successful and has no current plans for change. Which of the following types of strategies is it employing?
    A. Growth
    B. Stability
    C. Retrenchment
    D. Combination

    Answer: B Difficulty: 2 Page: 86

64. Harry's Company apparently has overgrown its market. They can no longer compete successfully due to their size and formalization. Thus they are reducing their size in order to once again become competitive. This is known as which of the following strategies?
   A. Growth
   B. Stability
   C. Retrenchment
   D. Combination

   Answer: C Difficulty: 2 Page: 86

65. Susan's Ceramics is expanding the size of its unfinished products while decreasing the amount of firing and finishing of products it does. This is known as which of the following strategies?
   A. Growth
   B. Stability
   C. Retrenchment
   D. Combination

   Answer: D Difficulty: 2 Page: 86

66. All but which of the following are competitive strategies that a business may use in order to gain a distinct advantage, according to Michael Porter?
   A. Retrenchment
   B. Cost-leadership
   C. Focus
   D. Differentiation

   Answer: A Difficulty: 1 Page: 87

67. The strategy that positions a company so that it will have a distinct advantage over its competition is known as which of the following?
   A. Growth advantage
   B. Stability
   C. Retrenchment
   D. Competitive advantage

   Answer: D Difficulty: 2 Page: 87

68. A large discount store, like WalMart, whose primary goal is to have the lowest prices in the industry is using which of the following strategies to maintain a competitive advantage?
   A. Cost-leadership strategy
   B. Differentiation strategy
   C. Focus strategy
   D. Retrenchment strategy

   Answer: A Difficulty: 3 Page: 87

Chapter 3: Foundations of Planning

69. A company who states that their product is reliable, even to the extent of never needing a service call, like Maytag, is practicing which of the following competitive advantage strategies?
    A. Cost-leadership strategy
    B. Differentiation strategy
    C. Focus strategy
    D. Retrenchment strategy

    Answer: B Difficulty: 3 Page: 88

70. A candy store who places their expensive chocolates in only fine hotels and restaurants frequented by the very rich is using which of the following competitive advantage strategies?
    A. Cost-leadership strategy
    B. Differentiation strategy
    C. Focus strategy
    D. Retrenchment strategy

    Answer: C Difficulty: 3 Page: 88

71. Long-term success of any competitive strategy requires that the advantage be which of the following?
    A. Profitable
    B. Similar to the strategy used by the competition
    C. Sustainable
    D. Dissimilar to the strategy used by the competition

    Answer: C Difficulty: 3 Page: 88

72. Which concept of quality and continuous improvement can assist an organization in maintaining its competitive advantage?
    A. SWOT analysis
    B. MBO
    C. MBWA
    D. TQM

    Answer: D Difficulty: 2 Page: 89

73. All but which of the following differentiates Packard Bell from its competitors?
    A. High-quality hardware
    B. Comprehensive service and technical support
    C. Few competitors
    D. Low prices

    Answer: C Difficulty: 3 Page: 90

74. All but which of the following are characteristics that profile a entrepreneurial personality?
   A. High need for achievement
   B. Believe they can control their own destinies
   C. High need for profits
   D. Take only moderate risks

   Answer: C Difficulty: 3 Page: 92

Scenario

Table 3-1
Stacie sighed. Her general manager had just left after giving her the latest assignment - readdress the competitive advantage of their company. By Friday's meeting, Stacie was to have developed three differing strategies the business could use in order to maintain their competitive advantage. Their computer business was slowly losing market share to their competitors and everyone realized something needed to be done. Stacie glanced through the article by Michael Porter her manager had left with her. According to Porter there were three differing types of strategies they could choose from. Stacie began wondering if there was a way they could make their computers cheaper which would allow them to then sell at a lower price. If they could reduce price by $100 a machine, they would be the industry leaders in price. Stacie wondered if they could find any lower-priced suppliers for the more expensive parts of their computers. She knew that their computers appealed particularly to small business owners due in part to price. They were able to offer the lower price because their computers were not as powerful or as fast as some machines but did contain the necessary word processing, database and spreadsheet capabilities necessary for a typical small business owner. The lack of frills with the solid three program capabilities plus their known reputation for quality had worked for them in the past. Stacie wondered if perhaps they needed to look at a smaller segment of the market, maybe small businesses with a large accounts receivable that would fully utilize their specific database. She knew that would cut their market by 1/8 but maybe achieving a definite market niche would help. Stacie began compiling her report for Friday's meeting.

75. Referring to Table 3-1, the long-term success of any competitive strategy Stacie develops requires that the advantage be which of the following?
   A. Profitable
   B. Similar to the strategy used by the competition
   C. Sustainable
   D. Dissimilar to the strategy used by the competition

   Answer: C Difficulty: 3

Chapter 3: Foundations of Planning

76. Referring to Table 3-1, the competitive advantage focusing on a lower price would be which of the following?
    A. Cost-leadership strategy
    B. Differentiation strategy
    C. Focus strategy
    D. Retrenchment strategy

    Answer: A Difficulty: 2

77. Referring to Table 3-1, the competitive advantage based upon their known reputation among small business owners for a computer with few frills but the capabilities of performing word processing, databases and spreadsheets would be known as which of the following?
    A. Cost-leadership strategy
    B. Differentiation strategy
    C. Focus strategy
    D. Retrenchment strategy

    Answer: B Difficulty: 3

78. Referring to Table 3-1, the competitive advantage based upon developing the market of small businesses that had a specific need for a database with the capability for a large accounts receivable billing, would be which of the following?
    A. Cost-leadership strategy
    B. Differentiation strategy
    C. Focus strategy
    D. Retrenchment strategy

    Answer: C Difficulty: 3

79. Referring to Table 3-1, Stacie knew that in order to keep their competitive advantage, her company would have to do which of the following?
    A. Remain profitable
    B. Lower price
    C. Take constant action
    D. Hire new management

    Answer: C Difficulty: 3

Table 3-2
Kay was excited. She had just returned from a manager's retreat where MBO had been discussed. This had never been used in their organization before and she was enthusiastic about implementing the program in her department. She received the OK from her manager, the Division Head who vaguely remembered having heard of the program several years earlier. Kay looked over the handout she had received. She was still somewhat confused on who was to choose the goals for the employees. However, she knew that the goals once chosen needed to be specific and have explicit time periods attached. Even though there was a lot of work to do in order to implement the program, Kay was excited. She knew this would prove to be beneficial to the organization.

80. Referring to Table 3-2, in order for MBO to work most effectively in Kay's department, which level of support did she not receive?
    A. First-line managers
    B. Middle managers
    C. Top managers
    D. She does not need the support of management

    Answer: C Difficulty: 2

81. Referring to Table 3-2, who should develop the employee goals for the MBO program?
    A. Kay
    B. Kay's manager
    C. Employees
    D. Kay and the employees

    Answer: D Difficulty: 2

82. Referring to Table 3-2, which of the following is a well-written objective to be used in MBO?
    A. Increase productivity
    B. Increase sales
    C. Decrease waste by 12% over the next six months
    D. Decrease personnel costs

    Answer: C Difficulty: 2

83. Referring to Table 3-2, Kay knew she wanted her employees to view the objectives as which of the following?
    A. Floors
    B. Ceilings
    C. Unobtainable in order to encourage stretching
    D. Challenging and yet unrealistic

    Answer: A Difficulty: 3

Chapter 3: Foundations of Planning

84. Referring to Table 3-2, Kay knew that the research showed that MBO allows which of the following?
    A. Increased employee performance
    B. Decreased employee performance
    C. Increased profits
    D. Increased sales

    Answer: A Difficulty: 2

Table 3-3
Terry had been told to reexamine the strategic niche their company held in the cosmetic industry. Top management did not want the company caught unaware of any changes occurring. Terry began reviewing a list of factors in his mind. There had been some negative publicity lately due to cosmetic testing on animals. The animals were well-treated but they were used to test new products. Positively, sales industry wide were up 10%. Women were buying more cosmetics in general, which was nothing but good for them. Another positive factor was their personnel. They had good people working in the company, particularly in research and development. The only other negative Terry could find was that the advertising campaign that was begun last year had not shown the results they had hoped for. Something needed to be done in that department. Terry began to compile his report.

85. Referring to Table 3-3, which analysis would assist Terry to identify a strategic niche that the company could exploit?
    A. SWOT analysis
    B. MBO
    C. MBWA
    D. SWAT analysis

    Answer: A Difficulty: 1

86. Referring to Table 3-3, the negative publicity due to the testing of cosmetics on animals would be classified as which of the following?
    A. Weakness
    B. Strength
    C. Threat
    D. Opportunity

    Answer: C Difficulty: 2

87. Referring to Table 3-3, the fact that sales are up 10% industry wide due to the fact women were buying more cosmetics would be which of the following?
    A. Weakness
    B. Strength
    C. Threat
    D. Opportunity

    Answer: D Difficulty: 2

Testbank

88. Referring to Table 3-3, the quality of the company's personnel would be classified as which of the following?
    A. Weakness
    B. Strength
    C. Threat
    D. Opportunity

    Answer: B Difficulty: 2

89. Referring to Table 3-3, the failure of the advertising campaign would be classified as which of the following?
    A. Weakness
    B. Strength
    C. Threat
    D. Opportunity

    Answer: A Difficulty: 3

Essay

90. Discuss two benefits of planning and two arguments against formal planning in an organization.

    Answer:
    Benefits - provides direction, reduces the impact of change, minimizes waste and redundancy
    Arguments against - may create rigidity, cannot be used in a dynamic environment, cannot replace creativity and intuition

91. Compare and contrast the following: strategic plans, tactical plans, specific plans and directional plans.

    Answer:
    Strategic plans - cover an extensive time period, cover broad issues and include the formulation of objectives
    Tactical plans - cover shorter time periods, focus on specifics, and assume objectives are known
    Specific plans - more specific and focused
    Directional plans - provide a general direction of where the company is headed not the specifics of how to get there

92. Explain in detail who is to determine the objectives in MBO and why.

    Answer:
    Objectives are jointly determined by employees and their bosses so that the goals established are participatively set which will lead frequently to higher employee performance
    Goals should cascade down throughout the organization using this approach

Chapter 3: Foundations of Planning

93. Describe SWOT analysis and how it is used in today's business.

    Answer:
    Analyzing a business in relationship to its internal strengths and weaknesses as well as looking at external opportunities and threats in order to find a competitive niche to exploit

94. Choose two grand strategies and describe those strategies giving an example of each.

    Answer:
    Growth - increasing the level of operations
    Stability - making no significant change
    Retrenchment - reducing the size or variety of operations
    Combination - using two or more grand strategies at the same time

Chapter 4: Planning Tools and Techniques

True/False

1. Evaluating changing social and demographic patterns would be factors involved in environmental scanning.

    Answer: T Difficulty: 2 Page: 102

2. Competitive intelligence is simply organized espionage.

    Answer: F Difficulty: 1 Page: 103

3. Environmental scanning creates the foundation for forecasts.

    Answer: T Difficulty: 2 Page: 104

4. Developing a set of scenarios can better prepare a company to initiate changes in strategy and to maintain their competitive advantage.

    Answer: T Difficulty: 2 Page: 104

5. Few organizations are exempt from the possibility that technological innovation will dramatically change the demand for their current products and services.

    Answer: T Difficulty: 3 Page: 105

6. We live in a world where almost everything is expressed in monetary terms.

    Answer: T Difficulty: 1 Page: 108

7. Budgets are one planning device that only top management formulates.

    Answer: F Difficulty: 2 Page: 108

8. The politics of large organizations tend to undermine any potential gain of using zero-based budgeting.

    Answer: T Difficulty: 3 Page: 109

9. A Gantt chart actually becomes a managerial control device as the manager determines deviations from the plan.

    Answer: T Difficulty: 2 Page: 112

10. A Gantt chart can be used to plan a project that requires the coordination of several activities, some of which must be done simultaneously.

    Answer: F Difficulty: 2 Page: 113

Chapter 4: Planning Tools and Techniques

11. Break-even analysis is a widely used technique for helping managers make profit projections.

    Answer: T Difficulty: 1 Page: 116

12. Fixed costs are fixed only in the short run.

    Answer: T Difficulty: 3 Page: 116

13. The point at which total costs equal total revenue is known as the profit point.

    Answer: F Difficulty: 2 Page: 116

14. Regression analysis requires that a change in one variable will be accompanied by an exactly proportional change in another variable.

    Answer: F Difficulty: 3 Page: 118

15. Using queuing theory, a manager can determine how many check-out lines at the grocery store need to be open at any point in time.

    Answer: T Difficulty: 1 Page: 119

16. There are two hard and fast rules for managing time that will work in every case.

    Answer: F Difficulty: 2 Page: 120

17. Time management comes easily to good managers.

    Answer: F Difficulty: 2 Page: 121

18. Efficiently run meetings are time effective.

    Answer: T Difficulty: 2 Page: 124

Multiple Choice

19. Which of the following does the Diesel Apparel Company produce?
    A. Engines that run on diesel
    B. Party dresses
    C. Jeans, sweatshirts and tee shirts
    D. Clothing for heavy construction workers

    Answer: C Difficulty: 2 Page: 101

20. All but which of the following are techniques used by Renzo Rosso to succeed in managing his shops?
    A. Correct timing of inventory replacement
    B. Correct timing of hiring extra personnel
    C. Development of budgets and controls at the store level
    D. Development of budgets and controls at the top management level

    Answer: D Difficulty: 3 Page: 101

21. The screening of large amounts of information to detect emerging trends and create a set of scenarios is called which of the following?
    A. Competitive intelligence
    B. Strategic planning
    C. Environmental scanning
    D. Revenue forecasting

    Answer: C Difficulty: 1 Page: 102

22. An example of a company that neglected to recognize a trend in customer preferences from slender writing instruments to fatter sturdier instruments is which of the following?
    A. Gillette Company's Waterman S.A. fountain pens
    B. Cross pens
    C. Germany's Montblanc pen
    D. England's Sharp fountain pens

    Answer: C Difficulty: 2 Page: 102

23. An activity that seeks to identify who competitors are, what they are doing, and how their actions will affect the focus organization is called which of the following?
    A. Competitive intelligence
    B. Strategic planning
    C. Environmental scanning
    D. Revenue forecasting

    Answer: A Difficulty: 1 Page: 102

24. Which of the following would have assisted the life insurance industry in recognizing the changing social conditions that were affecting the life insurance industry?
    A. Competitive intelligence
    B. Strategic planning
    C. Environmental scanning
    D. Revenue forecasting

    Answer: C Difficulty: 2 Page: 102

Chapter 4:   Planning Tools and Techniques

25. Which of the following are easily available sources of information when evaluating competitive intelligence?
    A. Internet
    B. Advertisements
    C. Annual reports
    D. Minutes of top management meetings

    Answer: D Difficulty: 2 Page: 103

26. The founder of Detroit Diesel, Roger Penske, has increased the market share of his company to which of the following?
    A. 20%
    B. 25%
    C. 35%
    D. 40%

    Answer: B Difficulty: 2 Page: 103

27. The purpose of developing scenarios is to
    A. Predict the future
    B. Reduce uncertainty and plan for changes
    C. Affect the future
    D. Increase uncertainty and determine the changes needed

    Answer: B Difficulty: 3 Page: 104

28. Predictions of future outcomes are known as which of the following?
    A. Competitive intelligence
    B. Strategic planning
    C. Environmental scanning
    D. Forecasting

    Answer: D Difficulty: 3 Page: 104

29. All but which of the following are examples of sources of information used in developing revenue forecasts?
    A. Historical revenue figures
    B. Future revenue figures
    C. Trends
    D. Evolving social and economic conditions

    Answer: B Difficulty: 2 Page: 104

30. The effect on the music industry of the almost total disappearance of vinyl long-playing records and their replacement by compact disks is an example of which of the following?
    A. Revenue forecasting
    B. Technological forecasting
    C. Quantitative forecasting
    D. Qualitative forecasting

    Answer: B Difficulty: 2 Page: 105

Testbank

31. Applying a set of mathematical rules to a series of past data to predict future outcomes is a technique known as which of the following?
    A. Revenue forecasting
    B. Technological forecasting
    C. Quantitative forecasting
    D. Qualitative forecasting

    Answer: C Difficulty: 1 Page: 105

32. The forecasting technique that is most appropriate to use when precise data are scarce or difficult to obtain is known as which of the following?
    A. Revenue forecasting
    B. Technological forecasting
    C. Quantitative forecasting
    D. Qualitative forecasting

    Answer: D Difficulty: 2 Page: 105

33. The basic idea that management can improve quality by analyzing and then copying the methods of leaders in their respective fields is known as which of the following?
    A. Revenue forecasting
    B. Benchmarking
    C. Quantitative forecasting
    D. Qualitative forecasting

    Answer: B Difficulty: 1 Page: 105

34. All but which of the following are examples of qualitative forecasting techniques?
    A. Jury of opinion
    B. Sales-force composition
    C. Substitution-effect
    D. Customer evaluation

    Answer: C Difficulty: 3 Page: 106

35. All but which of the following are examples of quantitative forecasting techniques?
    A. Time-series analysis
    B. Regression model
    C. Econometric models
    D. Sales-force composition

    Answer: D Difficulty: 3 Page: 106

Chapter 4:   Planning Tools and Techniques

36. When Ford compared differing car features with the best of their competitors and then used this information to improve their Taurus, they were using which of the following?
    A. Revenue forecasting
    B. Benchmarking
    C. Quantitative forecasting
    D. Qualitative forecasting

    Answer: B Difficulty: 2 Page: 106

37. A company that obtains this can boast that it has met stringent international quality standards and is one of a select group of companies worldwide to achieve this designation.
    A. ISO 5000
    B. ISO 9000
    C. Worldwide quality certification
    D. Quality standards certification

    Answer: B Difficulty: 3 Page: 107

38. A company that has obtained this has demonstrated that they are environmentally responsible.
    A. ISO 5000
    B. ISO 9000
    C. ISO 14000
    D. Quality environmental certification

    Answer: C Difficulty: 3 Page: 107

39. A standard that assures customers that a company uses specific steps to test products, continuously trains employees, maintains satisfactory records, and corrects problems as they occur has attained which of the following?
    A. ISO 5000
    B. ISO 9000
    C. ISO 14000
    D. Quality standards certification

    Answer: B Difficulty: 2 Page: 107

40. A numerical plan for allocating resources to specific activities is known as which of the following?
    A. Revenue forecasting
    B. Profit and loss statement
    C. Budget
    D. Income statement

    Answer: C Difficulty: 1 Page: 108

41. A budget that is developed based upon the prior time period's budget is known as which of the following?
    A. Incremental budget
    B. Zero-based budget
    C. Revenue budget
    D. Variable budget

    Answer: A Difficulty: 2 Page: 108

42. A budget that is developed starting from scratch, regardless of prior appropriations, is known as which of the following?
    A. Incremental budget
    B. Zero-based budget
    C. Revenue budget
    D. Variable budget

    Answer: B Difficulty: 2 Page: 109

43. Which of the following types of budget lacks sufficient focus specifically due to the fact that money is allocated to units not activities within the units?
    A. Incremental budget
    B. Zero-based budget
    C. Revenue budget
    D. Variable budget

    Answer: A Difficulty: 3 Page: 109

44. Which of the following types of budgets reexamines all organizational activities to see which should be eliminated, funded at a reduced level, funded at the current level of increased?
    A. Incremental budget
    B. Zero-based budget
    C. Revenue budget
    D. Variable budget

    Answer: B Difficulty: 3 Page: 109

45. Which of the following is a document that identifies and describes a specific activity and includes a statement of purpose, costs, personnel requirements, alternative courses of actions and an evaluation of the benefits?
    A. Revenue budget
    B. Decision package
    C. Zero-based budgeting
    D. Expense package

    Answer: B Difficulty: 3 Page: 110

Chapter 4: Planning Tools and Techniques

46. A listing of what activities have to be done, the order in which they are to be done, who is to do each, and when they are completed is known as which of the following?
    A. Scheduling
    B. Forecasting
    C. Strategic planning
    D. Zero-based budgeting

    Answer: A Difficulty: 1 Page: 111

47. A manager at Wendy's who is determining who works which shift, who does what activities and what needs to be accomplished during each shift is performing which of the following?
    A. Scheduling
    B. Forecasting
    C. Strategic planning
    D. Zero-based budgeting

    Answer: A Difficulty: 2 Page: 111

48. Which two variables are used in the Gantt chart?
    A. Time and activities to be scheduled
    B. Time and expenses incurred
    C. Expenses incurred and activities to be scheduled
    D. Efficiency of activities to be scheduled and expenses

    Answer: A Difficulty: 3 Page: 111

49. Which planning technique allows managers to easily determine if they are ahead, behind or on schedule?
    A. Gantt chart
    B. Forecasting
    C. Strategic planning
    D. Zero-based budgeting chart

    Answer: A Difficulty: 2 Page: 112

50. Which types of charts schedule capacity by work stations?
    A. Gantt chart
    B. Forecasting chart
    C. Load chart
    D. Zero-based budgeting chart

    Answer: C Difficulty: 2 Page: 112

51. If a project requires coordinating hundreds of activities, some which must be done simultaneously and some which cannot begin until earlier activities have been completed, which of the following would be used?
    A. Gantt chart
    B. PERT
    C. Load chart
    D. Break-even analysis

    Answer: B Difficulty: 1 Page: 113

52. Which of the following allows managers to monitor the interdependent activities of a project's progress, identify possible bottlenecks and shift resources as necessary in order to keep the project on schedule?
    A. Gantt chart
    B. PERT
    C. Load chart
    D. Break-even analysis

    Answer: B Difficulty: 2 Page: 113

53. All but which of the following are key components of PERT?
    A. Events
    B. Activities
    C. Times
    D. Critical path

    Answer: C Difficulty: 2 Page: 113

54. The longest or most time-consuming sequence of events/activities that is required to complete the project in the shortest amount of time is known as which of the following?
    A. Events
    B. Activities
    C. Times
    D. Critical path

    Answer: D Difficulty: 1 Page: 113

55. Which of the following are the end points that represent the completion of major activities?
    A. Events
    B. Activities
    C. Times
    D. Critical path

    Answer: A Difficulty: 1 Page: 113

Chapter 4: Planning Tools and Techniques

56. Since a delay on this course will delay the whole project, where should management attention be primarily focused?
    A. Events
    B. Activities
    C. Times
    D. Critical path

    Answer: D Difficulty: 2 Page: 116

57. The point at which total revenue equals total costs is known as which of the following?
    A. Gantt chart
    B. PERT
    C. Load chart
    D. Break-even analysis

    Answer: D Difficulty: 1 Page: 116

58. A widely used technique for helping managers make profit projections is known as which of the following?
    A. Gantt chart
    B. PERT
    C. Load chart
    D. Break-even analysis

    Answer: D Difficulty: 1 Page: 116

59. All but which of the following are costs a manager must have in order to figure break-even analysis?
    A. Total fixed costs
    B. Labor costs
    C. Variable costs
    D. Price of the product

    Answer: B Difficulty: 2 Page: 116

60. Insurance, rent, mortgage payments, and property taxes are examples of which of the following?
    A. Fixed costs
    B. Labor costs
    C. Variable costs
    D. Management costs

    Answer: A Difficulty: 2 Page: 116

61. Raw materials, labor costs, and energy costs are examples of which of the following?
   A. Fixed costs
   B. Operating costs
   C. Variable costs
   D. Management costs

   Answer: C Difficulty: 2 Page: 116

62. Sally's Sweets Shop is selling cinnamon rolls for $2.50 a roll. Fixed costs are $30,000 a year and variable costs are $1.75 per roll. How many rolls must Sally sell in order to break-even?
   A. 40,000
   B. 52,500
   C. 75,000
   D. 12,000

   Answer: A Difficulty: 3 Page: 116

63. Break-even analysis can provide all but which of the following types of information?
   A. Basis for sales goals
   B. Sales levels
   C. Volume of business needed
   D. Profit obtained

   Answer: D Difficulty: 3 Page: 117

64. A mathematical technique that solves resource allocation problems by attempting to minimize costs or maximize profits with limited resources and numerous options is known as which of the following?
   A. Linear programming
   B. Break-even analysis
   C. Queuing theory
   D. Regression analysis

   Answer: A Difficulty: 2 Page: 117

65. Which of the following should be used when a change in one variable is accompanied by an exactly proportional change in another variable?
   A. Linear programming
   B. Break-even analysis
   C. Queuing theory
   D. Regression analysis

   Answer: A Difficulty: 3 Page: 118

Chapter 4: Planning Tools and Techniques

66. You are the manager of a grocery store. One of the decisions you have to make is determining how many check-out registers to keep staffed at any given time. Which of the following are you using?
    A. Linear programming
    B. Break-even analysis
    C. Queuing theory
    D. Regression analysis

    Answer: C Difficulty: 1 Page: 119

67. The technique that balances the cost of having a waiting line of customers against the cost of service to maintain that line is called which of the following?
    A. Linear programming
    B. Break-even analysis
    C. Queuing theory
    D. Regression analysis

    Answer: C Difficulty: 1 Page: 119

68. All but which of the following are steps in the technique of managing time effectively?
    A. Identify objectives
    B. Prioritize objectives
    C. All objectives should be given equal priority
    D. List the activities necessary in order to accomplish the objectives

    Answer: C Difficulty: 1 Page: 121

69. Once you know your productivity schedule, when should you schedule your most important activities?
    A. Whenever they need to be completed
    B. During the morning
    C. During the afternoon
    D. During your most productive time period

    Answer: D Difficulty: 2 Page: 121

70. Meetings should be held when?
    A. Only in the afternoons
    B. When there is a reason
    C. Whenever the top manager feels like calling a meeting
    D. Only in the mornings

    Answer: B Difficulty: 2 Page: 124

71. Good time managers know how to minimize which of the following?
    A. Activities
    B. Expenses
    C. Disruptions
    D. Costs

    Answer: C Difficulty: 1 Page: 124

Scenario

Table 4-1
Samantha had just read a troubling report. They had lost 5% of their market share to their number one competitor last quarter and Samantha has no idea why. She had thought their company was doing fine. They provided day care services to middle-income beginning-level professionals in a town of approximately 100,000 people. Due to the high quality of care they provided and their low student to adult ratio, their company had been thriving. Samantha wondered what had changed. She decided to look at the competitor's advertisements in the local newspaper. Several advertisements were also offering older parent care as well as child care. Susan decided to call the local Chamber of Commerce to see if they knew what the trends for population growth were in the area. They reported that the median age was increasing to approximately 52 years of age and that this age group was also the age group that was moving into the area most regularly. There had been a dramatic decrease in younger families moving in during the last two years.

72. Referring to Table 4-1, which one of the following would have provided Samantha with information that would have allowed her to predict the emerging trend of an older age group moving to her town?
    A. Environmental scanning
    B. Competitive intelligence
    C. Revenue forecasting
    D. Historical analysis

    Answer: A Difficulty: 2

73. Referring to Table 4-1, when Samantha was reading the advertisements in the local paper, she was engaging in which of the following?
    A. Environmental scanning
    B. Competitive intelligence
    C. Revenue forecasting
    D. Historical analysis

    Answer: B Difficulty: 2

Chapter 4: Planning Tools and Techniques

74. Referring to Table 4-1, their reputation for high quality and their low student to adult ratio could be termed which of the following?
    A. Environmental scanning
    B. Competitive intelligence
    C. Revenue forecasting
    D. Competitive advantage

    Answer: D Difficulty: 3

75. Referring to Table 4-1, which of the following may help Samantha plan for what the future will be like for her business?
    A. Environmental scanning
    B. Competitive intelligence
    C. Scenarios
    D. Competitive advantage

    Answer: C Difficulty: 2

76. Referring to Table 4-1, all but which of the following are places Samantha would find information in helping her to conduct revenue forecasting for the next quarter?
    A. Demographic information from the Chamber of Commerce
    B. Economic reports from the Chamber of Commerce
    C. Last year's financial reports
    D. Next year's financial reports

    Answer: D Difficulty: 2

Table 4-2
Larry slammed the reports down on his desk. He had just come back from a very frustrating meeting with his manager. He had submitted next year's budget based on a percentage increase over last year's budget. The same thing he had done for the last five years. However, this afternoon, his manager told him he needed to redo the budget based on a technique where he would have to start from scratch, justifying every expenditure made by his department. Larry wondered if his manager realized the hours it would take him to compile a budget this way. His manager had told Larry that since they needed to cut expenses by 15% across the organization, this new budget would allow resources to be more efficiently allocated.

77. Referring to Table 4-2, Larry's budget from last year was which type of budget?
    A. Incremental budget
    B. Zero-based budget
    C. Profit budget
    D. Fixed budget

    Answer: A Difficulty: 2

78. Referring to Table 4-2, the new budget Larry was to prepare was which type of budget?
    A. Incremental budget
    B. Zero-based budget
    C. Profit budget
    D. Fixed budget

    Answer: B Difficulty: 2

79. Referring to Table 4-2, one of the major drawbacks of zero-based budgeting is which of the following?
    A. Lack of accuracy
    B. Increased accuracy
    C. Time involved in preparation
    D. Ease of preparation

    Answer: C Difficulty: 2

80. Referring to Table 4-2, one of the major advantages of zero-based budgeting is which of the following?
    A. Increased accuracy
    B. Ease of preparation
    C. More efficient allocation of scarce resources
    D. Lack of focus on unit objectives

    Answer: C Difficulty: 2

81. Referring to Table 4-2, if Larry were to prepare a budget based upon a fixed level of sales or production, he would be preparing which type of budget?
    A. Incremental budget
    B. Zero-based budget
    C. Profit budget
    D. Fixed budget

    Answer: D Difficulty: 3

Chapter 4: Planning Tools and Techniques

Table 4-3
Elise was excited. This was her first big project at her new job. Her manager had just left and on her desk was a pile of paperwork she would need to go through in order to start the project. She was in charge of planning the building of their new candy bar plant. Her first task was to determine which other people she would need to pull in order to help her with the project. Then she needed to start planning the construction of the plant itself.

82. Referring to Table 4-3, in determining the personnel Elise would need and the periods for which she would need them, which of the following planning techniques would be useful?
    A. Gantt chart
    B. Load chart
    C. PERT network analysis
    D. Break-even analysis

    Answer: A Difficulty: 3

83. Referring to Table 4-3, in determining the construction of the new candy bar plant, which of the following planning techniques would be useful?
    A. Gantt chart
    B. Load chart
    C. PERT network analysis
    D. Break-even analysis

    Answer: C Difficulty: 2

84. Referring to Table 4-3, which of the following is the longest or most time-consuming sequence of events that must happen in order for the candy bar plant to be completed in the shortest time possible?
    A. Activities
    B. Events
    C. Critical path
    D. Load path

    Answer: C Difficulty: 2

85. Referring to Table 4-3, if an event in the critical path is delayed by two weeks, what will be the delay in completing the entire project?
    A. It depends on what area was delayed
    B. One week
    C. Two weeks
    D. Four weeks

    Answer: C Difficulty: 3

86. Referring to Table 4-3, what is the first step Elise should take in determining the PERT network?
   A. Identify every significant activity
   B. Diagram the flow of activities
   C. Compute a time estimate
   D. Determine a schedule

   Answer: A Difficulty: 3

Essay

87. Compare and contrast the following three terms: environmental scanning, competitive intelligence, and scenarios.

    Answer:
    Environmental scanning - screening of large amounts of information to detect emerging trends and create a set of scenarios
    Scenarios - visualization of what the future will look like based upon the information obtained in environmental scanning
    Competitive intelligence - activity to identify competitors, what they are doing, and how their actions affect the focus organization

88. Explain how businesses today use benchmarking in their quest for quality.

    Answer:
    The search for the best practices among the competition or noncompetitors that lead to their superior performance
    A company can then use their competitor's ideas to better their own business

89. Describe two types of quantitative forecasting and two types of qualitative forecasting.

    Answer:
    Quantitative - time series analysis, regression model, econometric model, economic indicators, substitution-effect
    Qualitative - jury of opinion, sales-force composition, customer evaluation

90. Explain why budgets are such a popular planning tool. In your answer include the distinction between incremental budgets and zero-based budgets.

    Answer:
    Applicable to a wide variety of organizations
    Expressed in dollar amounts
    Incremental budgets - allocates funds based upon the allocation from a previous period
    Zero-based budgeting - budget request that starts from scratch regardless of prior appropriations

Chapter 4: Planning Tools and Techniques

91. Compare and contrast linear programming, break-even analysis and queuing theory.

    Answer:
    Linear programming - attempts to minimize costs or maximize profits with limited resources and numerous options
    Break-even analysis - identifies the point at which total revenue is sufficient to cover total costs
    Queuing theory - balances the cost of customers waiting in line to the cost of service of maintaining the line

Chapter 5: Foundations of Decision Making

True/False

1. Decision making is a process rather than a simple choice among alternatives.

    Answer: T Difficulty: 2 Page: 134

2. Problem identification is a key component of effective decision making.

    Answer: T Difficulty: 2 Page: 135

3. The process of decision making is as important to an individual's personal life as it is to businesses around the world.

    Answer: T Difficulty: 2 Page: 134

4. Decision criteria indicate the important factors in making a decision.

    Answer: T Difficulty: 1 Page: 136

5. Every decision maker has criteria that guide the decision making process.

    Answer: T Difficulty: 2 Page: 136

6. All criteria are equally important.

    Answer: F Difficulty: 1 Page: 136

7. Most decisions involve judgements that are reflected in the criteria, the weighting of the criteria and the evaluation of the alternatives.

    Answer: T Difficulty: 2 Page: 136

8. Most individuals make decisions based upon incomplete information.

    Answer: T Difficulty: 2 Page: 139

9. Few people actually behave rationally.

    Answer: T Difficulty: 2 Page: 141

10. Programmed decision making becomes decision making by precedent.

    Answer: T Difficulty: 3 Page: 144

11. Most managers possess only the characteristics of one decision making style.

    Answer: F Difficulty: 2 Page: 147

Chapter 5:   Foundations of Decision Making

12. Time limits are not important for meetings to abide by as long as something worthwhile is being accomplished.

    Answer: F Difficulty: 3 Page: 150

13. All participants in a meeting should have input.

    Answer: T Difficulty: 2 Page: 150

14. An agenda is an important component of a meeting.

    Answer: T Difficulty: 1 Page: 150

15. Managers need to remember to modify their decision styles to reflect the national culture of the country in which they are conducting business.

    Answer: T Difficulty: 3 Page: 154

Multiple Choice

16. Which of the following companies did Loida Nicolas Lewis begin managing upon the death of her husband?
    A. Nestle's
    B. Kellogg's
    C. Quaker
    D. Beatrice

    Answer: D Difficulty: 2 Page: 133

17. Loida Nicolas Lewis grew up in which of the following countries?
    A. United States
    B. England
    C. Philippines
    D. Singapore

    Answer: C Difficulty: 2 Page: 133

18. All but which of the following were goals Loida Nicolas Lewis was intent upon accomplishing?
    A. Raising a family
    B. Managing a major corporation
    C. Helping others
    D. Helping Filipinos enter the United States

    Answer: B Difficulty: 2 Page: 133

19. All but which of the following are major decisions made by Loida Nicolas Lewis in managing her business?
    A. Limiting the company to four core operations
    B. Selling of the company jet
    C. Downsizing corporate headquarters
    D. Expanding the company to include ice cream companies in Denmark and Italy

    Answer: D Difficulty: 3 Page: 133

20. The first step in the decision making process is which of the following?
    A. Develop the alternatives
    B. Analyze alternatives
    C. Identify decision criteria
    D. Identify the problem

    Answer: D Difficulty: 2 Page: 135

21. The discrepancy between an existing and a desired state of affairs is which of the following?
    A. A process
    B. A problem
    C. A scenario
    D. Criteria

    Answer: B Difficulty: 1 Page: 135

22. The factors that are relevant in making a decision are which of the following?
    A. The problem
    B. Decision criteria
    C. Scenarios
    D. Factor weights

    Answer: B Difficulty: 1 Page: 135

23. Price, size, gas mileage, color, options, and repair records are examples of which of the following when purchasing a new car?
    A. The problem
    B. Decision criteria
    C. Scenarios
    D. Factor weights

    Answer: B Difficulty: 2 Page: 135

Chapter 5:   Foundations of Decision Making

24. A simple approach to assigning weights to criteria is to assign the most important criteria the highest weight and then do which of the following?
    A. Disregard the rest of the criteria since they are not as important
    B. Assign weights to the rest based upon their degree of importance in comparison
    C. Assign equal weights to the rest of the criteria
    D. Weighting is not needed in developing criteria

    Answer: B Difficulty: 3 Page: 136

25. The strengths and weaknesses of each alternative become obvious in which step of the decision making process?
    A. Identify the problem
    B. Identify the decision criteria
    C. Analyze the alternatives
    D. Implement the alternative

    Answer: C Difficulty: 2 Page: 136

26. After all factors have been determined, weights have been assigned and alternatives have been identified, the next step is to do which of the following?
    A. Identify the problem
    B. Identify the decision criteria
    C. Analyze the alternatives
    D. Implement the alternative.

    Answer: D Difficulty: 2 Page: 137

27. Putting a decision into action and conveying the decision to the persons who will be affected by it is known as which of the following?
    A. Problem identification
    B. Decision implementation
    C. Rational decision making
    D. Irrational decision making

    Answer: B Difficulty: 2 Page: 137

28. The last step in the decision making process is which of the following?
    A. Evaluate the decision effectiveness
    B. Identify the decision criteria
    C. Analyze the alternatives
    D. Implement the alternative

    Answer: A Difficulty: 2 Page: 137

29. The fact that managers make consistent, value-maximizing choices within specified constraints is known as which of the following?
A. Implementation of the alternative
B. Decision implementation
C. Rational decision making
D. Irrational decision making

Answer: C Difficulty: 2 Page: 137

30. A manager would have a condition of which of the following if the outcome of every alternative was known?
A. Bounded rationality
B. Unbounded rationality
C. Certainty
D. Uncertainty

Answer: C Difficulty: 1 Page: 138

31. The process of assigning probabilities to outcomes that may occur is known as which of the following?
A. Uncertainty
B. Certainty
C. Risk
D. Bounded rationality

Answer: C Difficulty: 1 Page: 139

32. When decisions must be made with limited information because full knowledge of the problem is unavailable and the probability of outcomes is unknown, the condition of _____ exists.
A. Uncertainty
B. Certainty
C. Risk
D. Bounded rationality

Answer: A Difficulty: 2 Page: 139

33. Joe, the manager of Internet Made Easy, is concerned. He is trying, like all technological based companies to stay ahead of the competition by being the first to offer the new services available on the Internet. His business offers training to local businesses and so he must offer the latest available information; however, he must also advertise the classes and the content which means going to the publisher with that information six weeks before a class is to begin. What should his next series of classes offer? Joe is operating under the condition of which of the following?
A. Uncertainty
B. Certainty
C. Risk
D. Optimal decision making

Answer: A Difficulty: 2 Page: 138

Chapter 5: Foundations of Decision Making

34. Tim is the Department Chair of a local college. He is preparing the Fall schedule of classes. He knows approximately how many students will be in the classes from the preregistration that is required. He also knows how many faculty members are available and which classes they can teach. As he prepares the Fall schedule of classes, unless something extraordinary occurs, he is operating under the condition of which of the following?
    A. Uncertainty
    B. Certainty
    C. Risk
    D. Probability

    Answer: B Difficulty: 2 Page: 138

35. Managers often seek solutions that are satisfactory and sufficient. This is known as which of the following?
    A. Satisfactory decision making
    B. Satisficing
    C. Risk
    D. Optimal decision making

    Answer: B Difficulty: 2 Page: 139

36. The strap of John's backpack tears off as he starts to throw it over his shoulder. On the way to school, he stops at the first store that carries backpacks, walks in and purchases one off the front rack. John has just made what type of a decision?
    A. Satisfactory decision
    B. Satisficing decision
    C. Risky decision
    D. Optimal decision

    Answer: B Difficulty: 3 Page: 139

37. When decision makers construct simplified models that extract the essential features from a problem without capturing all the complexities of a problem, they are acting under which of the following?
    A. Bounded rationality
    B. Unbounded rationality
    C. Uncertainty
    D. Heuristics

    Answer: A Difficulty: 2 Page: 140

38. Because bounded rationality affects most managers, decisions made are strongly influenced by all but which of the following?
    A. Self-interest
    B. Organizational culture
    C. Politics
    D. Known outcomes

    Answer: D Difficulty: 3 Page: 140

Testbank

39. When a manager engages in behaviors that speed up the decision making process in order to avoid information overload, they are engaging in which of the following?
    A. Bounded rationality
    B. Unbounded rationality
    C. Uncertainty
    D. Heuristics

    Answer: D Difficulty: 2 Page: 140

40. Heuristics create which of the following in a decision maker's judgement?
    A. Certainty
    B. Uncertainty
    C. Biases
    D. Risk

    Answer: C Difficulty: 2 Page: 140

41. Jane just conducted the performance appraisals of five of her employees. Her appraisal was heavily influenced by the performance of the individuals during the last month. Jane's bias is an example of which of the following?
    A. Availability heuristic
    B. Representative heuristic
    C. Escalation of commitment
    D. Optimal decision making

    Answer: A Difficulty: 3 Page: 140

42. Kay based the forecasted sales figure of the new product on last year's sales figures from a previous product. Kay is engaging in which of the following?
    A. Availability heuristic
    B. Representative heuristic
    C. Escalation of commitment
    D. Optimal decision making

    Answer: B Difficulty: 3 Page: 141

43. The tendency for people to base their judgements on information that is readily available is known as which of the following?
    A. Availability heuristic
    B. Representative heuristic
    C. Escalation of commitment
    D. Optimal decision making

    Answer: A Difficulty: 1 Page: 140

Chapter 5: Foundations of Decision Making

44. The tendency for people to base judgements of probability on things with which they are familiar is known as which of the following?
    A. Availability heuristic
    B. Representative heuristic
    C. Escalation of commitment
    D. Optimal decision making

    Answer: B Difficulty: 1 Page: 141

45. An increased commitment to a previous decision despite negative information is known as which of the following?
    A. Availability heuristic
    B. Representative heuristic
    C. Escalation of commitment
    D. Optimal decision making

    Answer: C Difficulty: 1 Page: 142

46. In an effort to demonstrate that an initial decision was not wrong, instead of searching for new alternatives, managers engage in which of the following?
    A. Availability heuristic
    B. Representative heuristic
    C. Escalation of commitment
    D. Optimal decision making

    Answer: C Difficulty: 2 Page: 142

47. Lon authorizes an additional $100,000 for the production of the new product. The cost of the new product seems to be increasing far beyond what was planned or even forecast. However, Lon continues to support the project. Lon is engaging in which of the following?
    A. Availability heuristic
    B. Representative heuristic
    C. Escalation of commitment
    D. Optimal decision making

    Answer: C Difficulty: 3 Page: 142

48. Straightforward, familiar, easily defined problems where the information is easily defined and complete are which type of problem?
    A. Well-structured
    B. Ill-structured
    C. Programmed
    D. Nonprogrammed

    Answer: A Difficulty: 1 Page: 143

49. Problems where information is ambiguous or incomplete are which type of problem?
A. Well-structured
B. Ill-structured
C. Programmed
D. Nonprogrammed

Answer: B Difficulty: 1 Page: 143

50. When the petty cash in Elaine's drawer falls to less than $25, she places a request for additional funds to bring the total back to $100. This is an example of which of the following types of decision?
A. Well-structured
B. Ill-structured
C. Programmed
D. Nonprogrammed

Answer: C Difficulty: 2 Page: 143

51. A customer comes in with a request Jan has never heard before and she has been working for the hardware store for 15 years. Since it deals with the application of a new technology, Jan is not sure what to do? This is an example of which of the following types of problems?
A. Well-structured
B. Ill-structured
C. Programmed
D. Nonprogrammed

Answer: B Difficulty: 2 Page: 143

52. The supplier is late with the order of paper that is needed by the college during finals week. The secretary is sent to WalMart to pick up an extra case until the paper arrives. This is an example of which of the following types of problem?
A. Well-structured
B. Ill-structured
C. Programmed
D. Nonprogrammed

Answer: A Difficulty: 2 Page: 143

53. Jill has just been given the assignment of developing the marketing strategy for the company's new product to be released at Christmas. What type of decision making will be required of Jill?
A. Well-structured
B. Ill-structured
C. Programmed
D. Nonprogrammed

Answer: D Difficulty: 2 Page: 144

Chapter 5: Foundations of Decision Making

54. Decisions that must be custom-made to solve unique and nonrecurring problems are known as which of the following types of decisions?
    A. Well-structured
    B. Ill-structured
    C. Programmed
    D. Nonprogrammed

    Answer: D Difficulty: 1 Page: 144

55. "No smoking allowed" is an example of which of the following?
    A. Rule
    B. Procedure
    C. Policy
    D. Nonprogrammed decision

    Answer: A Difficulty: 2 Page: 144

56. Before being reimbursed for traveling expenses, the employee must file the following forms in the following order. This is an example of which of the following?
    A. Rule
    B. Procedure
    C. Policy
    D. Nonprogrammed decision

    Answer: B Difficulty: 2 Page: 144

57. "Whenever possible, we promote from within" is an example of which of the following?
    A. Rule
    B. Procedure
    C. Policy
    D. Nonprogrammed decision

    Answer: C Difficulty: 3 Page: 144

58. "We encourage the use of environmentally-safe materials" is an example of which of the following?
    A. Rule
    B. Procedure
    C. Policy
    D. Nonprogrammed decision

    Answer: C Difficulty: 3 Page: 144

59. "Before a health claim may be paid, the following steps must be taken", is an example of which of the following?
    A. Rule
    B. Procedure
    C. Policy
    D. Nonprogrammed decision

    Answer: B Difficulty: 3 Page: 144

60. Only employees with top-secret clearance may enter the sealed room", is an example of which of the following?
    A. Rule
    B. Procedure
    C. Policy
    D. Nonprogrammed decision

    Answer: A Difficulty: 2 Page: 144

61. Rules, procedures, and policies are most suitable for which types of problems?
    A. Well-structured
    B. Ill-structured
    C. Programmed
    D. Nonprogrammed

    Answer: A Difficulty: 3 Page: 144

62. A more realistic and much faster means of problem solving, developed by Michael F. Lamorte is which of the following?
    A. QUICK
    B. CLAMP
    C. CLIP
    D. CLAP

    Answer: B Difficulty: 2 Page: 145

63. Who has developed a decision making process that uses math and computer power to mimic nature with the potential to significantly impact our world?
    A. Galileo
    B. Lamorte
    C. Newton
    D. Hatten

    Answer: B Difficulty: 2 Page: 145

Chapter 5: Foundations of Decision Making

64. As managers move up the organizational hierarchy, problems are more likely to become
    A. Well-structured
    B. Ill-structured
    C. Programmed
    D. Nonprogrammed

    Answer: B Difficulty: 2 Page: 146

65. Lower-level managers are more likely to confront which type of problems?
    A. Well-structured
    B. Ill-structured
    C. Programmed
    D. Nonprogrammed

    Answer: A Difficulty: 1 Page: 146

66. Which of the following styles of decision making is characterized by low tolerance for ambiguity and a rational way of thinking which leads them to make fast decisions that focus on the short run?
    A. Analytic
    B. Conceptual
    C. Directive
    D. Behavioral

    Answer: C Difficulty: 2 Page: 147

67. Which of the following styles of decision making is characterized by individuals who prefer complete information and consider several alternatives?
    A. Analytic
    B. Conceptual
    C. Directive
    D. Behavioral

    Answer: A Difficulty: 2 Page: 147

68. Jay tends to always look at the broad picture and likes to look at many alternatives. He focuses on the long run and looks for creative solutions. He prefers which of the following styles of decision making?
    A. Analytic
    B. Conceptual
    C. Directive
    D. Behavioral

    Answer: B Difficulty: 2 Page: 147

69. Jane works well with others, is open to suggestions, and is concerned about her employees. She thinks intuitively and has a low tolerance for ambiguity. Which of the following describes her decision making style?
   A. Analytic
   B. Conceptual
   C. Directive
   D. Behavioral

   Answer: D Difficulty: 2 Page: 147

70. Managers spend what percentage of their time in meetings?
   A. 10%
   B. 25%
   C. 33%
   D. 40%

   Answer: D Difficulty: 1 Page: 150

71. Which of the following groups of people should participate in a meeting?
   A. Top management
   B. Middle management
   C. Employees only
   D. Everyone who has been invited to attend

   Answer: D Difficulty: 2 Page: 150

72. Which of the following defines the purpose of the meeting and the boundaries between relevant and irrelevant discussion topics?
   A. Minutes of the meeting
   B. Participant list
   C. Agenda
   D. Topic list

   Answer: C Difficulty: 2 Page: 150

73. All but which of the following are advantages of group decision making over individual decision making?
   A. Increased legitimacy
   B. More complete information
   C. Fewer alternatives due to group think
   D. Increased acceptance of the decision

   Answer: C Difficulty: 3 Page: 151

74. Many decisions fail after the final choice has been made because which of the following occurs?
   A. It was the wrong choice
   B. The decision criteria weights were incorrect
   C. People affected failed to accept the solution
   D. Satisficing occurred

   Answer: C Difficulty: 3 Page: 151

Chapter 5:   Foundations of Decision Making

75. All but which of the following are disadvantages of group decision making?
    A. More time taken to reach a solution
    B. Minority domination
    C. More alternatives
    D. Groupthink

    Answer: C Difficulty: 2 Page: 151

76. A form of conformity whereby group members withhold information or discussion in order to give the appearance of agreement is termed which of the following?
    A. Group conformity
    B. Groupthink
    C. Minority domination
    D. Group domination

    Answer: B Difficulty: 1 Page: 151

77. Group decisions tend to be
    A. Made more quickly
    B. More accurate
    C. Less creative
    D. More efficient

    Answer: B Difficulty: 3 Page: 151

78. Which of the following is the most effective number of people to have in a group?
    A. 5-7
    B. 2-10
    C. 3-7
    D. 3-12

    Answer: A Difficulty: 2 Page: 152

79. All but which of the following are methods by which group decision making can be improved?
    A. Brainstorming
    B. Nominal group technique
    C. Groupthink
    D. Electronic meetings

    Answer: C Difficulty: 2 Page: 153

80. A method that can be used to overcome the tendency toward conformity in group decision making is which of the following?
A. Brainstorming
B. Nominal group technique
C. Groupthink
D. Electronic meetings

Answer: A Difficulty: 2 Page: 153

81. All but which of the following is allowed in a brainstorming session?
A. Clear definition of the problem
B. Criticism of poor ideas
C. Large number of alternatives
D. Recording of all alternatives

Answer: B Difficulty: 3 Page: 153

82. Which of the following group techniques allows group members to meet together but allows independent thinking?
A. Brainstorming
B. Nominal group technique
C. Groupthink
D. Electronic meetings

Answer: B Difficulty: 2 Page: 153

83. The major advantages of which of the following group techniques allows for anonymity, honesty and speed?
A. Brainstorming
B. Nominal group technique
C. Groupthink
D. Electronic meetings

Answer: D Difficulty: 2 Page: 153

84. Experts claim that electronic meetings can be what percentage faster than traditional face-to-face meetings?
A. 25%
B. 33%
C. 50%
D. 55%

Answer: D Difficulty: 2 Page: 153

Chapter 5: Foundations of Decision Making

Scenario

Table 5-1
Sally leaves what she is doing and walks down the hall to the meeting room. One more meeting. As a manager, sometimes she feels like all she accomplishes is attending meetings. Furthermore, sometimes she has no idea why she needs to be at the meeting. She is not impacted by the topic being discussed nor are her comments asked for in the discussion. And last but not least, the meetings seem to last forever. Yesterday afternoon she sat in a meeting for three hours. Then she stayed two hours late in order to finish the work she needed to have been doing while she was in the meeting. As Sally walks in the door, she wonders what the purpose of this meeting will be.

85. Referring to Table 5-1, what percentage of time do managers like Sally spend in meetings?
    A. 10%
    B. 25%
    C. 40%
    D. 60%

    Answer: C Difficulty: 2

86. Referring to Table 5-1, what time frame should a meeting occupy?
    A. As long as is needed
    B. Meetings should start on time but do not need to end at any specific time
    C. Meetings should have a definite start and end time
    D. Meetings should always begin five minutes late to give everyone time to arrive

    Answer: C Difficulty: 2

87. Referring to Table 5-1, who should participate in the meeting?
    A. Top management
    B. Middle management
    C. Employees only
    D. Everyone invited to attend the meeting

    Answer: D Difficulty: 2

88. Referring to Table 5-1, who should be asked to attend a meeting?
    A. All employees
    B. Everyone impacted by the topic being discussed
    C. Anyone who has valuable information pertaining to the topic
    D. Those who are impacted by the topic and who have information to contribute

    Answer: D Difficulty: 2

9. Referring to Table 5-1, what would have helped Sally know the purpose of the meeting?
A. An agenda prepared and distributed in advance
B. An agenda distributed as people enter the meeting
C. No agenda is necessary
D. The introductory remarks of the meeting leader

Answer: A   Difficulty: 2

Table 5-2
Net income has fallen for the second quarter and Amanda is understandably worried. She knows at the Board of Directors meeting on Wednesday she will be closely questioned and be expected to have a plan to avoid any third quarter losses. Amanda begins to slowly read over the financial documents to try and ascertain areas that may be the cause. After much consideration, it appears that expenses have risen dramatically over the last few months. Amanda wonders why? She decides a meeting of the department heads is in order first thing tomorrow morning. At the meeting, Amanda would like to generate several possible solutions to the increased expenses. She wonders how to effectively explore all the options. At the meeting, the first option that is discussed is to downsize the research and development department since it is not essential to current operations. Several managers approve this plan. Amanda suggests that they need to look further at the issue. Several suggestions are made, many of which appear to be viable. Amanda wonders what to do next?

90. Referring to Table 5-2, what is the first step in the decision making process facing Amanda?
A. Identification of the decision criteria
B. Assignment of weights to the decision criteria
C. Identification of the real problem
D. Selection of an alternative that will solve the problem

Answer: C   Difficulty: 2

91. Referring to Table 5-2, what should Amanda do before the meeting in the morning in order to enable the participants to contribute the information that is needed?
A. Wait until the meeting and then discuss the situation
B. Prepare an agenda this afternoon and distribute it to all meeting participants
C. Send all participants a copy of only the financial reports
D. Invite all employees to the meeting as well as the department heads

Answer: B   Difficulty: 3

Chapter 5: Foundations of Decision Making

92. Referring to Table 5-2, which of the following would help Amanda develop a thorough list of alternative solutions to the problem?
    A. Groupthink
    B. Brainstorming
    C. Strategic planning
    D. Escalation of commitment

    Answer: B Difficulty: 2

93. Referring to Table 5-2, when several managers agree to the elimination of the research and development department, they are engaging in which of the following?
    A. Brainstorming
    B. Nominal technique
    C. Satisficing
    D. Optimal decision making

    Answer: C Difficulty: 2

94. Referring to Table 5-2, ultimately who must make the decision on which alternative to choose in the above scenario?
    A. A group decision of all managers and employees
    B. Amanda
    C. Board of Directors
    D. Employees

    Answer: B Difficulty: 3

Table 5-3
It seems like all Dave accomplishes is making decisions. Every time he turns around someone wants him to decide on one more thing. Just today the secretary came in and asked if she could reorder paper for the fax machine. Somehow that seemed like a decision that he really did not need to deal with. If he could avoid those types of decisions then when the foreman came in with the news of a major piece of equipment that needs repair, where the repair bill is almost as much as a new machine, John could focus more time and attention on the more complicated issues.

95. Referring to Table 5-3, the problem of whether or not to order more fax paper is an example of which of the following?
    A. Well-structured
    B. Ill-structured
    C. Programmed
    D. Nonprogrammed

    Answer: A Difficulty: 2

Testbank

96. Referring to Table 5-3, the problem of whether to repair the piece of equipment or to purchase a new machine is an example of which of the following?
    A. Well-structured
    B. Ill-structured
    C. Programmed
    D. Nonprogrammed

    Answer: B Difficulty: 2

97. Referring to Table 5-3, the decision on when to order fax paper could be determined by which of the following?
    A. Rule
    B. Procedure
    C. Policy
    D. Nonprogrammed decision

    Answer: A Difficulty: 2

98. Referring to Table 5-3, the decision on how to handle the equipment repair/replacement is an example of which of the following?
    A. Well-structured
    B. Ill-structured
    C. Programmed
    D. Nonprogrammed

    Answer: D Difficulty: 2

99. Referring to Table 5-3, John should be spending more time making _____ decisions and less time making _____ decisions.
    A. Nonprogrammed, programmed
    B. Programmed, nonprogrammed
    C. Rule, policy
    D. Programmed, policy

    Answer: A Difficulty: 3

Essay

100. Compare and contrast the types of problems and the differing types of decisions that are required at the three levels of management.

    Answer:
    Lower-management - Well-structured problems and programmed decision making
    Middle management - Less well-structured problems and less programmed decision making
    Top management - Ill-structured problems and nonprogrammed decision making

Chapter 5:   Foundations of Decision Making

101. Compare and contrast the biases of availability heuristics, representative heuristics, and escalation of commitment in the decision making process.

    Answer:
    Availability heuristics - the tendency to base judgements on information that is readily available
    Representative heuristics - tendency to base judgements on things that are familiar
    Escalation of commitment - an increased commitment to a decision despite negative information

102. Compare and contrast well-structured problems, ill-structured problems, programmed decision making and nonprogrammed decision making.

    Answer:
    Well-structured problems - straightforward, familiar, easily defined problems where a programmed decision can easily be made since it is a repetitive decision that can be handled routinely
    Ill-structured problems - New, unique problems that are ambiguous and where information is incomplete that require nonprogrammed decision making that is custom-made for that problem

103. Compare and contrast rules, procedures, and policies, giving an example of each.

    Answer:
    Rules - an explicit statement that leaves no room for interpretation
    Procedures - a series of interrelated sequential steps that must be used to address a problem
    Policy - a general guide that establishes parameters for a decision but leaves room for interpretation

104. Discuss three steps that can be taken in order to conduct an effective meeting.

    Answer:
    Prepare and distribute an agenda in advance of the meeting
    Consult with the participants before the meeting to ensure proper participation
    Establish specific time parameters
    Maintain a focused discussion
    Encourage participation by all members
    Encourage the difference of ideas
    Discourage personality clashes
    Bring closure by summarizing accomplishments

Chapter 6: Technology and the Design of Work Processes

True/False

1. The common feature of new technologies in the workplace is that they substitute human labor for machinery.

   Answer: F Difficulty: 2 Page: 164

2. Productivity is simply technology divided by labor, capital and materials.

   Answer: F Difficulty: 2 Page: 164

3. To improve productivity, technology is the primary focus of any manager's efforts.

   Answer: T Difficulty: 2 Page: 166

4. French Rags carries no accounts receivables because they have no inventory.

   Answer: T Difficulty: 3 Page: 166

5. Technology is redefining how the design of products is accomplished.

   Answer: T Difficulty: 1 Page: 166

6. The use of CAD has made the need for manual drafting even greater.

   Answer: F Difficulty: 2 Page: 166

7. The essence of just-in-time inventory systems is a computerized delivery code that is automatically sent whenever there are only three of a part remaining on the shelf.

   Answer: F Difficulty: 2 Page: 168

8. Robots are excellent at handling complicated tasks but less good at handling simple tasks.

   Answer: F Difficulty: 1 Page: 168

9. Flexible technologies are increasingly necessary in order to compete effectively.

   Answer: T Difficulty: 2 Page: 169

10. TQM argues that a 99.9 percent error-free performance standard is the highest standard of product/service excellence.

    Answer: F Difficulty: 3 Page: 171

Chapter 6: Technology and the Design of Work Processes

11. The PDCA cycle requires a linear approach to continuous improvement.

    Answer: F Difficulty: 2 Page: 172

12. The search for continuous improvement has a definite endpoint.

    Answer: F Difficulty: 2 Page: 172

13. The changing global environment and top heavy organizational structures are two reasons that reengineering has become so important to business today.

    Answer: T Difficulty: 2 Page: 173

14. The gathering and transferring of paper documents can take up to 90% of the time needed to finish typical office tasks.

    Answer: T Difficulty: 2 Page: 174

15. Wireless products are a major breakthrough in organizational communication.

    Answer: T Difficulty: 1 Page: 176

16. Expert systems are the next step beyond neural systems.

    Answer: F Difficulty: 3 Page: 176

17. New technologies are changing job demands and the skilled needed by employees.

    Answer: T Difficulty: 1 Page: 178

18. The redesign of work processes is achieving higher output with fewer workers.

    Answer: T Difficulty: 2 Page: 178

19. Even the knowledge of highly trained professionals can become obsolete in today's changing world.

    Answer: T Difficulty: 2 Page: 178

20. People who work in jobs with high core job dimensions are generally more motivated, satisfied, and productive than are those who do not.

    Answer: T Difficulty: 2 Page: 180

21. The JCM recommendations are as valid at the group level as they are at the individual level.

    Answer: T Difficulty: 2 Page: 183

22. Group composition is not critical to the success of the work group.

    Answer: F Difficulty: 2 Page: 185

23. The fastest growing trend in scheduling is temporary workers.

    Answer: F Difficulty: 2 Page: 187

Multiple Choice

24. Ross Operating Valve Company is producing which of the following?
    A. Valves sold through a catalog system
    B. Virtual products
    C. Irrigation equipment
    D. Complex fire preventive systems

    Answer: B Difficulty: 2 Page: 163

25. Technology used by Ross Operating Valve Company reduces the delivery time to which of the following?
    A. 1/100 of the time
    B. 1/75 of the time
    C. 1/60 of the time
    D. 1/50 of the time

    Answer: A Difficulty: 2 Page: 163

26. Prototypes of customized valves can be given to the customer by Ross Operating Valve Company in which of the following time periods?
    A. 36 hours
    B. 48 hours
    C. 72 hours
    D. 100 hours

    Answer: C Difficulty: 2 Page: 163

27. Which of the following describes how an organization transforms its inputs into outputs?
    A. Productivity
    B. Technology
    C. Computer aided design systems
    D. Computers

    Answer: B Difficulty: 1 Page: 163

Chapter 6: Technology and the Design of Work Processes

28. The common feature of new technologies is that they substitute _____ for human labor in transforming inputs into outputs?
    A. More productive manpower
    B. Computers
    C. Robots
    D. Machinery

    Answer: D Difficulty: 2 Page: 164

29. Technology can significantly increase which of the following?
    A. Sales
    B. Profits
    C. Productivity
    D. Number of personnel needed

    Answer: C Difficulty: 2 Page: 164

30. The formula for productivity is _____ divided by labor plus capital plus materials.
    A. Sales
    B. Profits
    C. Outputs
    D. Personnel

    Answer: C Difficulty: 2 Page: 164

31. French Rags produces which of the following?
    A. Exquisite French shawls
    B. Women's knitwear
    C. Elegant French evening gowns
    D. French scarves

    Answer: B Difficulty: 1 Page: 165

32. French Rags now sells their products to which of the following?
    A. Expensive clothing stores
    B. Discount outlets
    C. Directly to the customer
    D. Directly to retailers

    Answer: C Difficulty: 2 Page: 165

33. CAD allows engineers to develop new designs in as little as _____ of the time that is required for manual drafting.
    A. 1/4
    B. 1/3
    C. 1/2
    D. 2/3

    Answer: B Difficulty: 2 Page: 166

34. The use of computational and graphics software that allows the geometry of a product or component to be graphically displayed and manipulated on a video monitor is known as which of the following?
    A. CAT
    B. CAD
    C. GAD
    D. SWOT

    Answer: B Difficulty: 1 Page: 166

35. All but which of the following are components of operations technology?
    A. Distribution
    B. Continuous improvement processes
    C. Reengineering
    D. Downsizing

    Answer: D Difficulty: 2 Page: 167

36. Computer-controlled machines that manipulate materials and perform complex functions are known as which of the following?
    A. Robotics
    B. CAD
    C. JIT
    D. Flexible manufacturing systems

    Answer: A Difficulty: 1 Page: 168

37. Machines that act like human beings are called which of the following?
    A. Robotics
    B. CAD
    C. JIT
    D. Flexible manufacturing systems

    Answer: A Difficulty: 1 Page: 168

38. Robots were found to be good at handling simple jobs, but they failed when which of the following occurred?
    A. Conditions were too hot or too cold
    B. Tasks were too complicated
    C. Conditions were too hazardous
    D. Tasks were too repetitive

    Answer: B Difficulty: 1 Page: 168

39. Anything an organization can do to reduce the size of its _____ will improve productivity.
    A. Personnel department
    B. Accounts payable
    C. Inventory
    D. Sales

    Answer: C Difficulty: 2 Page: 168

Chapter 6: Technology and the Design of Work Processes

40. A system in which inventory items arrive as they are needed in production instead of being stored in stock is known as which of the following?
    A. Robotics
    B. CAD
    C. JIT
    D. Flexible manufacturing systems

    Answer: C Difficulty: 1 Page: 168

41. All but which of the following are benefits of just-in-time inventory systems?
    A. Reduced inventories
    B. Shorter manufacturing time
    C. Less space consumption
    D. Increased demand

    Answer: D Difficulty: 2 Page: 168

42. Systems that through the integration of computer-aided design, engineering, and manufacturing, can produce low-volume, customized products at a price comparable to that of high-volume, standardized products is known as which of the following?
    A. Robotics
    B. CAD
    C. JIT
    D. Flexible manufacturing systems

    Answer: D Difficulty: 2 Page: 169

43. The unique characteristic of flexible manufacturing systems is that by integrating computer-aided design, engineering, and manufacturing, they can produce products at which advantage?
    A. Higher quality but higher cost
    B. Low volume, comparable cost
    C. Lower cost and high volume
    D. High volume and low cost

    Answer: B Difficulty: 3 Page: 169

44. Using flexible manufacturing systems, when management wants to produce a new part, it changes which of the following?
    A. Personnel
    B. Machines
    C. Computer programs
    D. Assembly lines

    Answer: C Difficulty: 3 Page: 169

45. All but which of the following are ways that technology can improve customer service?
    A. Personalize service
    B. Augment service through providing additional support
    C. Depersonalize service
    D. Transform businesses to better suit the customer

    Answer: C Difficulty: 1 Page: 170

46. When a bookstore has your name, address, and phone number in their computer along with your favorite authors, a list of your purchases, and a list of the five best sellers you would like to read next, they are using technology for which of the following?
    A. Personalize service
    B. Augment service through providing additional support
    C. Depersonalize service
    D. Transform businesses to better suit the customer

    Answer: A Difficulty: 2 Page: 170

47. A hotel chain has your name, addresses, company and phone number on file along with the appropriate credit card number so that they can easily provide you with check-in. And they can also slide your bill under your door the morning that you check out so that all you have to do is slip your room card and bill in the drop box as you leave. They are using technology for which of the following?
    A. Personalize service
    B. Augment service through providing additional support
    C. Depersonalize service
    D. Transform businesses to better suit the customer

    Answer: B Difficulty: 2 Page: 170

48. All but which of the following are ways manufacturers can sell their products directly to the consumer through the use of distribution technology?
    A. Cable television channels
    B. Infomercials
    C. Retailers
    D. Internet

    Answer: C Difficulty: 2 Page: 171

49. The Home Shopping Network, Cable Value Network and QVC are examples of which of the following breakthroughs in distribution technology?
    A. Cable television channels
    B. Infomercials
    C. Retailers
    D. Internet

    Answer: A Difficulty: 2 Page: 171

Chapter 6:   Technology and the Design of Work Processes

50. Television programs that last half-an-hour where product testimonials are used to sell products in an entertainment format are known as which of the following?
    A. Cable television channels
    B. Infomercials
    C. Retailers
    D. Internet

    Answer: B Difficulty: 2 Page: 171

51. Which of the following is a relatively cheap way to reach 20 million consumers using the latest distribution channel made possible by computer technology?
    A. Cable television channels
    B. Infomercials
    C. Retailers
    D. Internet

    Answer: D Difficulty: 2 Page: 171

52. Continuous process improvements eliminate variability so that the uniformity of the product is increased which in turn leads to which of the following?
    A. Lower costs and higher quality
    B. Higher costs and higher quality
    C. Lower costs and lower quality
    D. Higher quality and increased sales

    Answer: A Difficulty: 3 Page: 172

53. The continuous search for product improvement requires which of the following?
    A. A linear approach
    B. A circular approach
    C. Only top management involvement
    D. Only employee involvement

    Answer: B Difficulty: 2 Page: 172

54. All but which of the following are components of the PDCA cycle?
    A. Planning
    B. Developing
    C. Checking
    D. Acting

    Answer: B Difficulty: 3 Page: 172

55. All but which of the following are key elements contained in reengineering?
   A. Identifying an organization's distinctive competencies
   B. Assessing core processes
   C. Reorganizing horizontally by process
   D. Reorganizing horizontally by department

   Answer: C Difficulty: 3 Page: 173

56. Superior store location, higher quality products, superior technical support and more-knowledgeable sales personnel are examples of which of the following?
   A. Distinctive competencies
   B. TQM
   C. Enhanced customer service
   D. Reengineering

   Answer: A Difficulty: 1 Page: 173

57. The analysis of the core processes that add value to an organization's distinctive competencies by transforming materials, capital, information, and labor into products and services that customers value is known as which of the following?
   A. Process value analysis
   B. CAD
   C. JIT
   D. Flexible manufacturing systems

   Answer: A Difficulty: 2 Page: 173

58. The reason that reengineering has become an issue in the 1990s, according to Hammer, is which of the following?
   A. Static business environment
   B. Changing global environment
   C. Need for more levels in the organizational structure
   D. Need for more middle managers

   Answer: B Difficulty: 2 Page: 173

59. Use of computer software to automatically process and route documents and information through an organization is known as which of the following?
   A. Workflow automation
   B. Internal communication
   C. Expert systems
   D. Neural networks

   Answer: A Difficulty: 1 Page: 174

Chapter 6:   Technology and the Design of Work Processes

60. Software that automates the movement of documents, eliminates the need for human involvement in determining who should get the information, collapse travel time and prevents misrouting is known as which of the following?
    A. Workflow automation
    B. Internal communication
    C. Expert systems
    D. Neural networks

    Answer: A Difficulty: 2 Page: 174

61. Organizations are converting internal information from _____ language to _____ language.
    A. Digital, analog
    B. Analog, wireless
    C. Wireless, digital
    D. Analog, digital

    Answer: D Difficulty: 3 Page: 175

62. By converting to a completely digital format, organizations will have a system in place whereby managers and employees can communicate by which of the following?
    A. Television
    B. Radio
    C. Computers
    D. Any form

    Answer: D Difficulty: 2 Page: 175

63. Which of the following signals is slower, less accurate, and prone to interruptions and distortions?
    A. Digital
    B. Analog
    C. Wireless
    D. Wireless and digital

    Answer: B Difficulty: 2 Page: 175

64. Which of the following are making it possible for people in organizations to be fully accessible to each other at any time regardless of where they are?
    A. Computers
    B. E-mail
    C. Wireless products
    D. Internet

    Answer: C Difficulty: 2 Page: 176

65. All but which of the following are examples of information technology that is providing support in the area of decision-making?
    A. Expert systems
    B. Neural networks
    C. Groupware
    D. Groupthink

    Answer: D Difficulty: 1 Page: 176

66. Software programs that use the encoded relevant experience of a human expert to analyze and solve ill-structured problems are known as which of the following?
    A. Expert systems
    B. Neural networks
    C. Groupware
    D. Superior systems

    Answer: A Difficulty: 2 Page: 176

67. Computer software that imitates the structure of brain cells and connections among them and that can distinguish patterns and trends too subtle or complex for human beings is known as which of the following?
    A. Expert systems
    B. Neural networks
    C. Groupware
    D. Superior systems

    Answer: B Difficulty: 2 Page: 176

68. A system that allows employees and lower-level managers to make high-quality decisions that previously could have been made by only senior managers is known as which of the following?
    A. Expert systems
    B. Neural networks
    C. Groupware
    D. Superior systems

    Answer: A Difficulty: 2 Page: 176

69. Which of the following has the ability to distinguish patterns and trends too subtle or complex for human beings?
    A. Expert systems
    B. Neural networks
    C. Groupware
    D. Superior systems

    Answer: B Difficulty: 2 Page: 176

Chapter 6: Technology and the Design of Work Processes

70. Computer software programs that facilitate group interaction and decision making by persons at different locations are known as which of the following?
    A. Expert systems
    B. Neural networks
    C. Groupware
    D. Superior systems

    Answer: C Difficulty: 1 Page: 177

71. Videoconferencing group meetings, disseminating presentations, augmenting face-to-face customer visits and conducting preliminary job candidate interviews are all examples of uses of which of the following?
    A. Expert systems
    B. Neural networks
    C. Groupware
    D. Superior systems

    Answer: C Difficulty: 2 Page: 177

72. All but which of the following new technologies are changing job demands and the skills that employees need in order to do those jobs?
    A. Reengineering
    B. TQM
    C. Flexible manufacturing systems
    D. Static business environment

    Answer: D Difficulty: 2 Page: 178

73. Offices characterized by open space, movable furniture, portable phones, laptop computers and electronic files are known as which of the following?
    A. Virtual workplace
    B. Modern offices
    C. Ergonomic offices
    D. Telecommuting

    Answer: A Difficulty: 2 Page: 179

74. A framework for analyzing and designing jobs and their interrelationships and impact on outcome variables is known as which of the following?
    A. Reengineering
    B. TQM
    C. Flexible manufacturing systems
    D. Job characteristics model

    Answer: D Difficulty: 2 Page: 180

75. All but which of the following are core job dimensions used in the job characteristics model?
    A. Skill variety
    B. Task identity
    C. Output
    D. Feedback

    Answer: C Difficulty: 2 Page: 180

76. The degree to which a job requires a variety of activities that call for different skills and talents is which of the following?
    A. Skill variety
    B. Task identity
    C. Autonomy
    D. Feedback

    Answer: A Difficulty: 1 Page: 180

77. The degree to which a job affects the lives or work of other people is known as which of the following?
    A. Skill variety
    B. Task identity
    C. Task significance
    D. Feedback

    Answer: C Difficulty: 1 Page: 180

78. The degree to which a job provides freedom, independence, and discretion to an individual in scheduling and carrying out his/her own work is known as which of the following?
    A. Skill variety
    B. Task identity
    C. Task significance
    D. Autonomy

    Answer: D Difficulty: 1 Page: 180

79. All but which of the following are needed in order for a person to view their job as combining to create meaningful work?
    A. Skill variety
    B. Task identity
    C. Task significance
    D. Autonomy

    Answer: D Difficulty: 3 Page: 181

Chapter 6:   Technology and the Design of Work Processes

80. A body shop worker who specializes in painting and who sprays paint eight hours a day would have which job characteristic?
    A. High variety
    B. Low variety
    C. High autonomy
    D. High identity

    Answer: B Difficulty: 3 Page: 182

81. A police telephone dispatcher who must handle calls as they come in according to a routine, highly specified procedure would have which job characteristic?
    A. High variety
    B. High identity
    C. Low autonomy
    D. High autonomy

    Answer: C Difficulty: 3 Page: 182

82. A cabinetmaker who designs a china cupboard, selects the wood, builds the cupboard and finishes the project to the customer's satisfaction would have which job characteristic?
    A. Low variety
    B. High identity
    C. Low significance
    D. Low feedback

    Answer: B Difficulty: 3 Page: 182

83. A pediatric nurse working in an intensive care unit would have which job characteristic?
    A. Low variety
    B. Low feedback
    C. High significance
    D. Low significance

    Answer: C Difficulty: 2 Page: 182

84. An electronics factory worker who assembles a computer and then routes it to a quality control inspector who tests it for proper operation and makes needed adjustments would have which job characteristic?
    A. High variety
    B. High identity
    C. High autonomy
    D. Low feedback

    Answer: D Difficulty: 2 Page: 182

85. A police detective who schedules his/her own work, makes contacts without supervision, and decides on the most effective techniques for solving cases would have which job characteristic?
    A. Low variety
    B. Low feedback
    C. High autonomy
    D. Low autonomy

    Answer: C Difficulty: 2 Page: 182

86. A framework for analyzing employee motivation and job satisfaction based upon the premise that employees adopt attitudes and behaviors in response to social cues provided by others is known as which of the following?
    A. SIP model
    B. SEP model
    C. JCM model
    D. Telecommuting

    Answer: A Difficulty: 1 Page: 182

87. Managers should give as much or more attention to employee _____ as they give to the actual job characteristics.
    A. Motivation
    B. Perceptions
    C. Skill level
    D. Task structure

    Answer: B Difficulty: 3 Page: 183

88. All but which of the following are conditions that should be met in order to have a successful work group?
    A. All members should have the expertise necessary for the task
    B. Group size is large enough to perform the task
    C. Members possess interpersonal skills as well as task skills
    D. Membership is similar in talents and perspectives in order to prevent differences

    Answer: D Difficulty: 2 Page: 185

89. Work hours arranged around six core hours that provide employees the freedom to decide for themselves when they will complete their remaining two hours of work each day is known as which of the following?
    A. Job sharing
    B. Flextime
    C. Telecommuting
    D. Temporary workers

    Answer: B Difficulty: 1 Page: 186

Chapter 6: Technology and the Design of Work Processes

90. Jane must be at the office between 9 am and 3 pm; however, when she works the other two hours is open to her choice as long as she puts in an eight-hour day sometime between 6 am and 6 pm. This is an example of which of the following?
    A. Job sharing
    B. Flextime
    C. Telecommuting
    D. Temporary workers

    Answer: B Difficulty: 2 Page: 186

91. All but which of the following are benefits obtained from the use of flextime?
    A. Increased motivation and morale
    B. Decreased absenteeism
    C. Ability to recruit higher-quality and more-diverse employees
    D. Decreased motivation and morale

    Answer: D Difficulty: 2 Page: 186

92. All but which of the following are steps in designing jobs in order to more effectively motivate employees?
    A. Establish client relationships
    B. Combine tasks
    C. Separate tasks
    D. Expand jobs vertically

    Answer: C Difficulty: 2 Page: 186

93. A special type of part-time work that allows two persons to split a traditional forty-hour-week job is known as which of the following?
    A. Job sharing
    B. Flextime
    C. Telecommuting
    D. Temporary workers

    Answer: A Difficulty: 1 Page: 187

94. The opportunity of acquiring the skills of two people while paying for only one is provided by which of the following?
    A. Job sharing
    B. Flextime
    C. Telecommuting
    D. Temporary workers

    Answer: A Difficulty: 2 Page: 187

95. The fastest growing trend in work scheduling is which of the following?
    A. Job sharing
    B. Flextime
    C. Telecommuting
    D. Temporary workers

    Answer: C Difficulty: 2 Page: 187

96. The ability to not commute, to have flexible hours, to dress as you please, and few interruptions from colleagues is known as which of the following?
    A. Job sharing
    B. Flextime
    C. Telecommuting
    D. Temporary workers

    Answer: C Difficulty: 1 Page: 187

97. Which of the following generates substantial savings for organizations through the ability to rent less space?
    A. Job sharing
    B. Flextime
    C. Telecommuting
    D. Temporary workers

    Answer: C Difficulty: 2 Page: 188

Scenario

Table 6-1
Brad's company is in need of additional employees. However, since his plant is open from 6 am until 7 pm, they have a wide variety of hours that must be staffed. Furthermore, all employees do not need to be at the plant the entire 13 hours. They had been running two eight hour shifts but management decided to cut back hours due to the strain running the equipment 16 hours a day was placing on the maintenance crew. Brad had no idea how to get employees to work the hours needed now. So when a consultant was hired to help with the new scheduling needs, he was ecstatic. The consultant and Brad determined that all employees were needed between the hours of 10:00 to 4:00. However, less employees were needed before and after those times. Furthermore, some of the planning and scheduling work did not need to be performed at the plant site.

98. Referring to Table 6-1, the hours of 10:00 to 4:00 would be considered which of the following?
    A. Main hours
    B. Core hours
    C. All employee hours
    D. Required hours

    Answer: B Difficulty: 2

Chapter 6:   Technology and the Design of Work Processes

99. Referring to Table 6-1, employees that work between 10:00 to 4:00 but then work their other two hours at their convenience would be utilizing which of the following?
    A. Flextime
    B. Job sharing
    C. Temporary workers
    D. Telecommuting

    Answer: A Difficulty: 2

100. Referring to Table 6-1, all but which of the following will give Brad the flexibility he may need in order to work with his new scheduling needs?
    A. Flextime
    B. Job sharing
    C. Groupthink
    D. Telecommuting

    Answer: C Difficulty: 2

101. Referring to Table 6-1, the employees that do not need to be on-site could utilize which of the following?
    A. Flextime
    B. Job sharing
    C. Groupthink
    D. Telecommuting

    Answer: D Difficulty: 2

102. Referring to Table 6-1, hiring two employees to fill one job would be another option that might allow Brad to gain additional employees. This is known as which of the following?
    A. Flextime
    B. Job sharing
    C. Groupthink
    D. Telecommuting

    Answer: B Difficulty: 2

Table 6-2
Janice is concerned. Her employees do not seem motivated or satisfied and productivity levels are falling in her department. She has just returned from a seminar on job design and is considering redesigning several of the jobs to see if that will help. Her plant produces lamps that are used in institutional settings. They customize the lamps to each order but they may do several hundred lamps for each order received. They had been using the traditional assembly line approach where the base was wired, the outer casing was put in place, the framework for the shade was added, the lightbulb was screwed in, the shade was placed on and the last step was plugging in the lamp to see if everything worked correctly. For each order, the plans were developed by middle management in consultation with the client. The plans were then given to the plant foreman who set up the assembly line for production. Janice wondered what could be done to redesign the jobs?

103. Referring to Table 6-2, what framework could Janice use to assist her in analyzing and redesigning the jobs?
    A. JCM
    B. JCT
    C. SWOT
    D. Job analysis

    Answer: A Difficulty: 2

104. Referring to Table 6-2, if each person is performing one task on the assembly line, using only one skill, which core job dimension is being described?
    A. Skill variety
    B. Task identity
    C. Task significance
    D. Feedback

    Answer: A Difficulty: 2

105. Referring to Table 6-2, which core job dimension would be affected if employees were allowed to follow a lamp down the assembly line and complete the lamp from beginning to end, doing the final testing themselves?
    A. Autonomy
    B. Task identity
    C. Task significance
    D. Feedback

    Answer: B Difficulty: 2

Chapter 6:   Technology and the Design of Work Processes

106. Referring to Table 6-2, which core job dimension would be affected if employees were placed on a team and worked with the client designing the plans and ended when the lamps were delivered to the client by the group of employees who actually set up the lamps and positioned them in the institution so that the lighting was most effective for the people using the lights in the institution?
    A. Autonomy
    B. Task identity
    C. Task significance
    D. Skill variety

    Answer: C Difficulty: 2

107. Referring to Table 6-2, all but which of the following are the most important core dimensions in the redesigning of jobs to create work that is more meaningful for the employee?
    A. Autonomy
    B. Task identity
    C. Task significance
    D. Skill variety

    Answer: A Difficulty: 3

Table 6-3
Sheldon is the chief operating officer of a manufacturing plant that produces valves. The plant has been in operation for years and until recently was moderately profitable. However sales have been falling due to the fact their expenses are higher than the competition and consequently their prices are higher. Sheldon is unsure where to start in evaluating the situation.

108. Referring to Table 6-3, which of the following may assist Sheldon in increasing the profitability of the business?
    A. Groupware
    B. Reengineering
    C. Downsizing
    D. Neural networks

    Answer: B Difficulty: 2

109. Referring to Table 6-3, if Sheldon chooses to use reengineering all but which of the following will be involved?
    A. Rethinking and redesigning processes
    B. Eliminating operations that are no longer needed
    C. Replacing antiquated machines
    D. Continuing to do things as they have been done

    Answer: D Difficulty: 2

110. Referring to Table 6-3, the first step in reengineering is extremely important because which of the following are determined?
    A. Profits
    B. Sales
    C. Distinctive competencies
    D. Management expertise

    Answer: C   Difficulty: 2

111. Referring to Table 6-3, as reengineering is begun, Sheldon discovers that several of the processes are adding little to the value of the product. Which reengineering element identified this?
    A. Identification of distinctive competencies
    B. Process value analysis
    C. Horizontal reorganization
    D. Lost value processes

    Answer: D   Difficulty: 2

112. Referring to Table 6-3, if Sheldon chooses to use self-managed teams, he would be doing which of the following?
    A. Identification of distinctive competencies
    B. Process value analysis
    C. Horizontal reorganization
    D. Vertical reorganization

    Answer: C   Difficulty: 2

Essay

113. Describe and explain the formula for productivity.

    Answer:
    Outputs divided by labor + capital + materials
    Output per labor hour is the most common measure of productivity
    Goal of management becomes increasing output while maintaining or reducing inputs

114. Explain the role technology plays in improving productivity.

    Answer:
    Technology is changing how inputs are transformed into outputs
    Human labor is being substituted for machines
    This frequently increases the amount of output that can be produced with fewer inputs
    The fact that technology can significantly increase productivity is the driving force behind the technological advances found in today's business world

Chapter 6: Technology and the Design of Work Processes

115. Explain the role of flexible manufacturing systems in business today.

    Answer:
    Provides management with a means by which they can respond in a global economy to rapidly changing conditions
    Allows management to maintain their competitive advantage
    Allows the production of nonstandardized products in low-volume at a cost comparable to mass production
    Flexible manufacturing systems are repealing the laws of economies of scale

116. Describe the three key elements of reengineering.

    Answer:
    Identify the distinctive competencies of the organization
    Assess core processes
    Reorganize horizontally by process

117. Compare and contrast three ways in which information technology assists in decision making.

    Answer:
    Expert system - allows lower-level managers to make high-quality decisions previously made only by senior-level managers
    Neural networks - allows the correlation of hundreds of variables at one time which a human cannot do
    Groupware - facilitate the meeting of people who are not necessarily at the same location which is increasingly important in today's global business world

118. Explain how telecommuting, job sharing and flextime are increasing the ability of an organization to remain flexible.

    Answer:
    Telecommuting is reducing the need for office space while allowing employees the ability to work from their homes which is beneficial for some
    Job sharing allows the organization to hire two people for the price of one person which gives them more employee input
    Flextime allows an employee to work during hours that fit their work schedules better which in turn decreases absenteeism and unsatisfied employees

Chapter 7: Basic Organization Designs

True/False

1. Organization design decisions are typically made by midlevel managers.

    Answer: F Difficulty: 2 Page: 198

2. Organization structure should always precede organization strategy.

    Answer: F Difficulty: 2 Page: 198

3. Early proponents of work specialization believed it could lead to infinitely increasing productivity.

    Answer: T Difficulty: 2 Page: 199

4. There is a point at which the diseconomies from division of labor exceed the economic advantage.

    Answer: T Difficulty: 2 Page: 199

5. Many organizations are increasing their span of control.

    Answer: T Difficulty: 2 Page: 200

6. The span of control today is increasingly being determined by analyzing contingency variables.

    Answer: T Difficulty: 3 Page: 201

7. No one should be held responsible for something over which he or she has no authority.

    Answer: T Difficulty: 3 Page: 201

8. Authority is related to one's position and has nothing to do with the individual.

    Answer: T Difficulty: 2 Page: 201

9. Authority is defined by one's vertical position in the hierarchy.

    Answer: T Difficulty: 2 Page: 204

10. Power is defined by one's vertical position and one's distance from the organization's center.

    Answer: T Difficulty: 2 Page: 204

Chapter 7: Basic Organization Designs

11. If an individual is low in the authority hierarchy they are also not close to the power core.

    Answer: F Difficulty: 3 Page: 205

12. In an organization that practices centralization in decision-making, all decisions are made by the CEO.

    Answer: T Difficulty: 2 Page: 206

13. Grouping activities by the following categories would be an example of functional departmentalization: men's clothing, women's clothing, tools, home decorations, and shoes.

    Answer: F Difficulty: 2 Page: 207

14. The most appropriate structure to use depends upon contingency factors.

    Answer: T Difficulty: 3 Page: 210

15. An organic structure has many rules with rigid hierarchical relationships and a tall structure.

    Answer: F Difficulty: 2 Page: 212

16. The organic organization is a highly adaptive form that is loose and flexible.

    Answer: T Difficulty: 1 Page: 212

17. If a company chooses to compete based upon cost-leadership strategies, then the organic structure will be the most effective.

    Answer: F Difficulty: 3 Page: 213

18. An organization with employees over 2,000 in number typically will have a very organic organizational structure.

    Answer: F Difficulty: 2 Page: 213

19. Environment is a major influence on structure.

    Answer: T Difficulty: 1 Page: 215

20. The simple structure is most widely used in small businesses where the owner and manager are the same person.

    Answer: T Difficulty: 2 Page: 216

Testbank

21. The strength of the functional structure lies in the advantages that accrue from work specialization.

    Answer: T Difficulty: 2 Page: 216

22. The chief advantage of the divisional structure is that it focuses on results.

    Answer: T Difficulty: 2 Page: 216

23. The unique characteristic of the matrix structure is that employees have only one boss.

    Answer: F Difficulty: 2 Page: 218

24. Boundaryless organizations are merely flatter organizations.

    Answer: F Difficulty: 3 Page: 219

25. An organization's culture can actually substitute for the rules and regulations that formally guide employees.

    Answer: T Difficulty: 2 Page: 221

Multiple Choice

26. St. Francis Regional Medical Center saw the same changes in their medical facility that were occurring across the country. These changes were which of the following?
    A. Increased hospital stays
    B. Decreased hospital stays
    C. More emphasis on technology
    D. Less emphasis on technology

    Answer: B Difficulty: 2 Page: 197

27. Which of the following had to change in order to meet the new direction St. Francis Regional Medical Center needed to take?
    A. Management
    B. Structure
    C. Technology
    D. Quality

    Answer: B Difficulty: 2 Page: 197

Chapter 7: Basic Organization Designs

28. Who was the impetus for change at St. Francis Regional Medical Center?
    A. Yoichi Morishita
    B. Sister M. Sylvia Egan
    C. Sister Mary Francis
    D. Bill Gates

    Answer: B Difficulty: 2 Page: 197

29. Yoichi Morishita has embarked upon changes in which of the following in order to improve white-collar productivity and simplify his organization?
    A. Technology
    B. Scheduling
    C. Organization design
    D. Management

    Answer: C Difficulty: 2 Page: 198

30. A process by which managers develop or change the structure of their company is known as which of the following?
    A. Technological design
    B. Organization design
    C. Management design
    D. Quality design

    Answer: B Difficulty: 1 Page: 198

31. Organization design decisions are typically made by which of the following?
    A. Senior management
    B. Midlevel management
    C. Lower-level management
    D. Operatives

    Answer: A Difficulty: 2 Page: 198

32. Organizational design should always _____ organizational strategy.
    A. Precede
    B. Occur at the same time as
    C. Follow
    D. Be independent

    Answer: C Difficulty: 3 Page: 198

33. All but which of the following are one of the six elements of structure?
    A. Work specialization
    B. Chain of command
    C. Span of control
    D. Technology

    Answer: D Difficulty: 1 Page: 199

34. A component of organization structure that involves having each discrete step of a job done by a different individual rather than having one individual do the whole job is known as which of the following?
    A. Work specialization
    B. Chain of command
    C. Span of control
    D. Departmentalization

    Answer: A Difficulty: 1 Page: 199

35. When five differing workers do one specific job preparing a Big Mac at McDonald's they are engaging in which of the following?
    A. Work specialization
    B. Chain of command
    C. Span of control
    D. Departmentalization

    Answer: A Difficulty: 2 Page: 199

36. All but which of the following are results of work that has become too specialized?
    A. Fatigue
    B. Low productivity
    C. Lower quality
    D. Lower turnover

    Answer: D Difficulty: 2 Page: 199

37. The management principle that no person should report to more than one boss is known as which of the following?
    A. Work specialization
    B. Chain of command
    C. Span of control
    D. Departmentalization

    Answer: B Difficulty: 1 Page: 200

38. Terri must constantly report to the Department Chair as well as her immediate Supervisor. Which of the following is being violated?
    A. Work specialization
    B. Chain of command
    C. Span of control
    D. Departmentalization

    Answer: B Difficulty: 2 Page: 200

Chapter 7: Basic Organization Designs

39. The number of employees a manager can direct efficiently and effectively is known as which of the following?
    A. Work specialization
    B. Chain of command
    C. Span of control
    D. Departmentalization

    Answer: C Difficulty: 1 Page: 200

40. Jayne has eight employees for whom she is directly responsible. This is known as which of the following?
    A. Work specialization
    B. Chain of command
    C. Span of control
    D. Departmentalization

    Answer: C Difficulty: 2 Page: 200

41. All but which of the following are contingency variables that determine the appropriate span of control for managers?
    A. Employee training
    B. Task complexity
    C. Management style preferences
    D. Expenses

    Answer: D Difficulty: 2 Page: 201

42. The rights inherent in a managerial position to give orders and expect them to be obeyed is known as which of the following?
    A. Responsibility
    B. Span of control
    C. Authority
    D. Accountability

    Answer: C Difficulty: 2 Page: 201

43. Jack has just been promoted to Line Manager for the assembling plant. Since Jack is now a manager which of the following automatically also goes with the title of manager?
    A. Respect
    B. Span of control
    C. Authority
    D. Acceptance by the employees

    Answer: C Difficulty: 2 Page: 201

44. The authority that entitles a manager to direct the work of an employee is known as which of the following?
    A. Span of control
    B. Line authority
    C. Staff authority
    D. Responsibility

    Answer: B Difficulty: 2 Page: 201

45. Positions that have some authority but that are created to support, assist, and advise the holders of line authority are known as which of the following?
    A. Span of control
    B. Line authority
    C. Staff authority
    D. Responsibility

    Answer: C Difficulty: 1 Page: 201

46. Those managers whose organizational function contribute directly to the achievement of organizational objectives have which of the following?
    A. Span of control
    B. Line authority
    C. Staff authority
    D. Responsibility

    Answer: B Difficulty: 2 Page: 201

47. A purchasing department may be created because the hospital administrator cannot effectively handle all purchasing. What type of position authority has been created?
    A. Span of control
    B. Line authority
    C. Staff authority
    D. Responsibility

    Answer: C Difficulty: 2 Page: 201

48. An individual's capacity to influence decisions is known as which of the following?
    A. Span of control
    B. Line authority
    C. Staff authority
    D. Power

    Answer: D Difficulty: 1 Page: 204

Chapter 7:   Basic Organization Designs

49. It is not necessary to have authority in order to wield power because an individual can move _____ toward the power core without moving up.
    A. Horizontally inward
    B. Directly upward
    C. Horizontally downward
    D. Directly downward

    Answer: A Difficulty: 3 Page: 204

50. Power based upon one's expertise, special skills, or knowledge is which of the following?
    A. Coercive power
    B. Reward power
    C. Expert power
    D. Referent power

    Answer: C Difficulty: 2 Page: 207

51. Power based upon identification with a person who has desirable resources or personal traits is known as which of the following?
    A. Coercive power
    B. Reward power
    C. Expert power
    D. Referent power

    Answer: D Difficulty: 2 Page: 207

52. Jim has the ability to "dock" paychecks of employees that arrive at work past 9:05. What kind of power does Jim possess?
    A. Coercive power
    B. Legitimate
    C. Expert power
    D. Referent power

    Answer: A Difficulty: 2 Page: 207

53. Harry is the only person that fully understands the new computer network in the office area. Whenever someone has questions, they go to Harry. Harry has which of the following?
    A. Coercive power
    B. Reward power
    C. Expert power
    D. Referent power

    Answer: C Difficulty: 2 Page: 207

54. All but which of the following are steps in building a power base?
    A. Build power relationships
    B. Develop associations
    C. Control important information
    D. Build your power base all at once

    Answer: D Difficulty: 2 Page: 206

55. One of the most crucial aspects of developing power is which of the following?
    A. Developing associations
    B. Controlling important information
    C. Respecting others
    D. Gaining seniority

    Answer: C Difficulty: 3 Page: 206

56. Groups of individuals who form to influence an event are called which of the following?
    A. Power groups
    B. Groupthink
    C. Coalitions
    D. Emerging groups

    Answer: C Difficulty: 2 Page: 206

57. The pushing down of decision-making authority to the lowest levels of an organization is known as which of the following?
    A. Centralization
    B. Decentralization
    C. Span of control
    D. Acceptance theory

    Answer: B Difficulty: 2 Page: 206

58. An organization where decisions are made by those employees closest to the problems are using which type of decision-making authority?
    A. Centralization
    B. Decentralization
    C. Span of control
    D. Acceptance theory

    Answer: B Difficulty: 2 Page: 207

59. The grouping of activities by functions performed is which of the following?
    A. Functional departmentalization
    B. Product departmentalization
    C. Customer departmentalization
    D. Geographic departmentalization

    Answer: A Difficulty: 1 Page: 208

Chapter 7:   Basic Organization Designs

60. A manager who organizes his or her plant by separating engineering, accounting, human resources, and purchasing is using which of the following types of departmentalization?
    A. Functional departmentalization
    B. Product departmentalization
    C. Customer departmentalization
    D. Geographic departmentalization

    Answer: A Difficulty: 2 Page: 207

61. The grouping of activities by product produced is which of the following?
    A. Functional departmentalization
    B. Product departmentalization
    C. Customer departmentalization
    D. Geographic departmentalization

    Answer: B Difficulty: 1 Page: 208

62. An organization that groups activities according to women's footwear, men's footwear, apparel, accessories, and leggings would use which of the following types of departmentalization?
    A. Functional departmentalization
    B. Product departmentalization
    C. Customer departmentalization
    D. Geographic departmentalization

    Answer: B Difficulty: 2 Page: 208

63. The grouping of activities by common customers would be which of the following?
    A. Functional departmentalization
    B. Product departmentalization
    C. Customer departmentalization
    D. Geographic departmentalization

    Answer: C Difficulty: 1 Page: 209

64. An office supply firm that has three departments based upon retail, wholesale and governmental customers is using which of the following types of departmentalization?
    A. Functional departmentalization
    B. Product departmentalization
    C. Customer departmentalization
    D. Geographic departmentalization

    Answer: C Difficulty: 2 Page: 209

65. The grouping of activities by territory is which of the following?
    A. Functional departmentalization
    B. Product departmentalization
    C. Customer departmentalization
    D. Geographic departmentalization

    Answer: D Difficulty: 1 Page: 209

66. An organization that has four sales regions, North, Midwest, South and Southwest is using which type of departmentalization?
    A. Functional departmentalization
    B. Product departmentalization
    C. Customer departmentalization
    D. Geographic departmentalization

    Answer: D Difficulty: 2 Page: 209

67. The grouping of activities by work or customer flow is which of the following?
    A. Functional departmentalization
    B. Process departmentalization
    C. Customer departmentalization
    D. Geographic departmentalization

    Answer: B Difficulty: 1 Page: 210

68. All but which of the following are contingency variables that affect the appropriate structure for an organization?
    A. Strategy
    B. Size
    C. Technology
    D. Sales

    Answer: D Difficulty: 2 Page: 211

69. A structure that is high in specialization, formalization, and centralization is which of the following?
    A. Strategic organization
    B. Mechanistic organization
    C. Organic organization
    D. Adhocracy

    Answer: B Difficulty: 2 Page: 212

Chapter 7:   Basic Organization Designs

70. Julie's organization has a very formal structure with strict lines of communication where there are many rules and duties are fixed. This is an example of which of the following?
    A. Strategic organization
    B. Mechanistic organization
    C. Organic organization
    D. Adhocracy

    Answer: B Difficulty: 2 Page: 212

71. A structure that is low in specialization, formalization and centralization is which of the following?
    A. Strategic organization
    B. Mechanistic organization
    C. Organic organization
    D. Bureaucracy

    Answer: C Difficulty: 1 Page: 212

72. Frederic works in an organization where a large amount of collaboration occurs and decision-making authority is decentralized. There are few rules and duties are adaptable. This is an example of which of the following?
    A. Strategic organization
    B. Mechanistic organization
    C. Organic organization
    D. Bureaucracy

    Answer: C Difficulty: 2 Page: 212

73. Which of the following structures is loose and flexible allowing it to change rapidly as the need arises?
    A. Strategic organization
    B. Mechanistic organization
    C. Organic organization
    D. Bureaucracy

    Answer: C Difficulty: 2 Page: 212

74. Strategy has what effect on structure?
    A. There is no relationship between structure and strategy
    B. Strategy has no effect on structure
    C. Strategy should follow structure
    D. Strategy should precede structure

    Answer: D Difficulty: 3 Page: 213

75. If the strategy of a company is to compete based on cost-leadership which requires stability and efficiency, which of the following structures will be most effective?
    A. Strategic organization
    B. Mechanistic organization
    C. Organic organization
    D. Adhocracy

    Answer: B Difficulty: 3 Page: 213

76. If a company is pursuing a differentiation strategy which requires flexibility and adaptability, which of the following structures will be most effective?
    A. Strategic organization
    B. Mechanistic organization
    C. Organic organization
    D. Bureaucracy

    Answer: C Difficulty: 3 Page: 213

77. Once an organization has approximately 2000 employees, what type of a structure will it probably be using?
    A. Strategic organization
    B. Mechanistic organization
    C. Organic organization
    D. Adhocracy

    Answer: B Difficulty: 2 Page: 213

78. An organization that uses technology which is nonroutine, will probably find which structure to be most effective?
    A. Strategic organization
    B. Mechanistic organization
    C. Organic organization
    D. Adhocracy

    Answer: C Difficulty: 2 Page: 213

79. If the environment in which the organization functions is relatively stable, which structure will be most effective?
    A. Strategic organization
    B. Mechanistic organization
    C. Organic organization
    D. Adhocracy

    Answer: B Difficulty: 2 Page: 213

Chapter 7:   Basic Organization Designs

80. Global competition which requires accelerated product innovation, and increased demands by consumers for higher quality and faster deliveries is requiring organizations to adapt which type of structure in order to be able to compete effectively?
    A. Strategic organization
    B. Mechanistic organization
    C. Organic organization
    D. Bureaucracy

    Answer: C Difficulty: 2 Page: 215

81. Asea Brown Boveri is a world leader in which of the following?
    A. High-quality paints
    B. High-speed trains and robotics
    C. Organically grown food
    D. Elegant evening gowns

    Answer: B Difficulty: 2 Page: 214

82. An organization that is low in specialization and formalization but high in centralization is known as which of the following?
    A. Simple structure
    B. Tall structure
    C. Decentralized structure
    D. Complex structure

    Answer: A Difficulty: 2 Page: 215

83. The strength of the functional structure is which of the following?
    A. It focuses on results
    B. It gains advantages due to work specialization
    C. Employees have more than one boss
    D. It is based solely on teams

    Answer: B Difficulty: 2 Page: 216

84. All but which of the following are advantages of the functional structure?
    A. Economies of scale
    B. Minimization of duplication
    C. Employee satisfaction
    D. Primary pursuit of functional goals

    Answer: D Difficulty: 3 Page: 216

85. The strength of the divisional structure is which of the following?
    A. It focuses on results
    B. It gains advantages due to work specialization
    C. Employees have more than one boss
    D. It is based solely on teams

    Answer: A Difficulty: 3 Page: 216

86. The major disadvantage of the divisional structure is which of the following?
    A. Economies of scale
    B. Minimization of duplication
    C. Employee satisfaction
    D. Duplication of activities and resources

    Answer: D Difficulty: 3 Page: 217

87. Which of the following structures combines the advantages of the functional specialization with the focus and accountability of product departmentalization?
    A. Team-based structure
    B. Boundaryless organizations
    C. Matrix structure
    D. Networking structure

    Answer: C Difficulty: 2 Page: 217

88. Which of the following is the primary strength of the matrix structure?
    A. Economies of scale and the ability to coordinate interdependent projects
    B. Propensity to foster power struggles
    C. Employee satisfaction
    D. Duplication of activities and resources

    Answer: A Difficulty: 2 Page: 218

89. The major disadvantage of the matrix structure is which of the following?
    A. Duplication of resources
    B. Lack of employee satisfaction
    C. Lack of economies of scale
    D. Confusion over who reports to whom

    Answer: D Difficulty: 2 Page: 218

90. In a team-based structure, who makes the decisions that affect the team?
    A. Top management
    B. Middle management
    C. First-line management
    D. Team members

    Answer: D Difficulty: 2 Page: 218

Chapter 7:   Basic Organization Designs

91. All but which of the following have contributed to the boundaryless organization?
    A. Technology
    B. Complex and dynamic environments
    C. Static environments
    D. Increases in telecommunication

    Answer: C Difficulty: 2 Page: 219

92. A system of shared meaning within an organization that determines, to a large degree, how employees act is which of the following?
    A. Boundaryless organization
    B. Span of control
    C. Culture
    D. Simple structure

    Answer: C Difficulty: 1 Page: 219

93. All but which of the following are characteristics of organizational culture?
    A. Member identity
    B. Control
    C. Risk tolerance
    D. Simple structure

    Answer: D Difficulty: 1 Page: 220

94. The system or patterns or values, symbols, rituals, myths and practices that have evolved over time are an organization's
    A. Control factors
    B. Culture
    C. History
    D. Characteristics

    Answer: B Difficulty: 2 Page: 220

95. The culture of an organization is largely determined by
    A. Top management
    B. Employees
    C. Stockholders
    D. The company founders

    Answer: D Difficulty: 2 Page: 220

96. Managers need less formal rules and regulations in an organization with which of the following?
    A. Weak culture
    B. Strong culture
    C. Tall structure
    D. Culture never impacts structure

    Answer: B Difficulty: 3 Page: 221

Testbank

Scenario

Table 7-1
Jerri is confused. She thought that once she had the title of manager, everyone would listen to her and accept her authority and power. However, she has noticed other employees that seem to have power. Whenever someone has a question on the computer system they always go to Helen who actually established the current system they are using. Usually Helen can get things up and running quicker than going to the support staff for help. Then there is Joe who has a remarkable amount of charm and charisma. He seems to have a power based simply upon himself. Then there is Jill, her secretary, who has a power entirely of her own. Jill turns in the timecards weekly and Jerri has seen her more than once override the timeclock and clock somebody in earlier than they actually arrived or clock out for them when the employee left work early. When Jerri questioned her about it, Jill just laughed and said that they had been doing it for years and the time all averaged out. The company allowed no overtime so any extra time employees spent at work was never compensated. Jerri sometimes wonders if she has any power at all.

97. Referring to Table 7-1, what type of power does Jerri actually possess?
    A. Legitimate power
    B. Reward power
    C. Expert power
    D. Referent power

    Answer: A Difficulty: 2

98. Referring to Table 7-1, what type of power does Helen possess?
    A. Coercive power
    B. Reward power
    C. Expert power
    D. Referent power

    Answer: C Difficulty: 2

99. Referring to Table 7-1, what type of power does Joe possess?
    A. Coercive power
    B. Reward power
    C. Expert power
    D. Referent power

    Answer: D Difficulty: 2

100. Referring to Table 7-1, what type of power does Jill possess?
    A. Coercive power
    B. Reward power
    C. Expert power
    D. Referent power

    Answer: B Difficulty: 2

Chapter 7: Basic Organization Designs

101. Referring to Table 7-1, what type of authority does Jerri possess?
    A. Span of control
    B. Line authority
    C. Staff authority
    D. Responsibility

    Answer: B Difficulty: 2

Table 7-2
John is aware that the structure of his organization must change in order to compete more effectively in today's global market. However, he is not sure which structure would work best for his company. His company is currently organized around an accounting department, human resource department, sales department, purchasing department and manufacturing department. However, there are other choices available. He has considered reorganizing around their primary products which are frames, silk flowers, dried flowers, art supplies, craft supplies and material. However, equally important are the differing clientele they serve which are homemakers who do arts/crafts, interior decorators, large institutions and professional consultants. Since the business is growing they now have stores across the United States primarily in the Northwest, Midwest, South and Southwest areas. Plus, his customers seldom shop for just one type of item. Frequently they purchase not only the flowers but the vases and other supplies that are needed in order to complete the arrangement which means oftentimes shopping in most of the areas in the store.

102. Referring to Table 7-2, the current structure that is being used is which of the following?
    A. Functional departmentalization
    B. Product departmentalization
    C. Customer departmentalization
    D. Geographic departmentalization

    Answer: A Difficulty: 2

103. Referring to Table 7-2, which of the following structures would be used if the grouping was done by frames, silk flowers, dried flowers, art supplies, craft supplies and materials?
    A. Functional departmentalization
    B. Product departmentalization
    C. Customer departmentalization
    D. Geographic departmentalization

    Answer: B Difficulty: 2

104. Referring to Table 7-2, which of the following structures would be used if the grouping of activities was centered around homemakers, interior decorators, institutions and consultants?
    A. Functional departmentalization
    B. Product departmentalization
    C. Customer departmentalization
    D. Geographic departmentalization

    Answer: C   Difficulty: 2

105. Referring to Table 7-2, which of the following departmental structures would be used if the grouping was based on the areas served in the United States?
    A. Functional departmentalization
    B. Product departmentalization
    C. Customer departmentalization
    D. Geographic departmentalization

    Answer: D   Difficulty: 2

106. Referring to Table 7-2, which of the following departmental structures would be used if the grouping was based on the flow of customers?
    A. Functional departmentalization
    B. Process departmentalization
    C. Customer departmentalization
    D. Geographic departmentalization

    Answer: B   Difficulty: 2

Table 7-3
Jim Johnson is the CEO of a major manufacturer of farming equipment. His company has been in business for the last 100 years and has been very profitable. The company is very formal and tall with formalized communication channels and rigid hierarchical relationships. All major decisions are made by Mr. Johnson. This has worked very well until lately. They have begun to have some major global competition. Companies overseas are bringing new products into the United States at a lower price. Furthermore, just yesterday, the new Vice-president had mentioned that he felt that there was a major market overseas for their products. As their strategy was beginning to change, Mr. Johnson also realized their structure too would need to change. But to what? The company was large and prior to these changes, the technology utilized while extensive, had been very routine. What was he to do?

107. Referring to Table 7-3, which organizational structure does the company currently utilize?
    A. Strategic organization
    B. Mechanistic organization
    C. Organic organization
    D. Adhocracy

    Answer: B   Difficulty: 2

Chapter 7:   Basic Organization Designs

108. Referring to Table 7-3, which type of decision-making authority is currently being used in the company?
    A. Centralization
    B. Decentralization
    C. Span of control
    D. Acceptance theory

    Answer: A Difficulty: 2

109. Referring to Table 7-3, Mr. Johnson's company probably needs to change from a _____ structure to a _____ structure.
    A. Mechanistic, organic
    B. Organic, mechanistic
    C. Organic, adhocracy
    D. Mechanistic, bureaucracy

    Answer: A Difficulty: 2

110. Referring to Table 7-3, the large size of the company and the use of routine technology are indicators that which type of structure would be most effective?
    A. Strategic organization
    B. Mechanistic organization
    C. Organic organization
    D. Adhocracy

    Answer: B Difficulty: 2

111. Referring to Table 7-3, which of the following contingency variables had the biggest impact on the need for changes in Mr. Johnson's organization?
    A. Size
    B. Technology
    C. Environment
    D. Management

    Answer: C Difficulty: 3

Essay

112. Describe the advantages and disadvantages of work specialization.

    Answer:
    Economies of scale
    Skills developed through repetition
    Pay workers for level of skill
    Training is easier and less expensive

    Can result in human diseconomies which lead to fatigue, stress, boredom, low productivity, higher turnover and increased absences

113. Compare and contrast authority and power.

    Answer:
    Authority comes from the position not the person

    Power is the ability of an individual to influence decisions which may not be reflected in their level of authority
    Five differing types of power; reward, coercive, legitimate, referent, and expert

114. Compare and contrast mechanistic versus organic organizations.

    Answer:
    Mechanistic
        Formal rules and regulations
        Rigid hierarchical relationships
        Fixed duties
        Centralized decision making
        Taller structure

    Organic
        Adaptable duties
        Few rules
        Decentralized decision making
        Flatter structure
        Increased collaboration

115. Describe the impact that strategy, size, technology and environment have on structure.

    Answer:
    Strategy should precede structure
    Structure must agree with the strategy chosen

    The larger the size of the organization the more formal the structure

    Nonroutine technology needs a more organic structure in order to be most effective

    Global, dynamic, ever-changing environment requires a more organic structure in order for organizations to retain their competitive advantage

116. Describe organizational culture.

    Answer:
    Basically the personality of the organization
    All values, symbols, rituals, myths, and practices that have evolved over time

    Strong culture can preclude the necessity of many rules and regulations
    Culture comes from the company founders and is relatively stable

Chapter 8: Staffing and Human Resource Management

True/False

1. The quality of an organization is determined by the quality of the people it hires and retains.

    Answer: T Difficulty: 2 Page: 230

2. Every manager is involved in human resource decisions.

    Answer: T Difficulty: 2 Page: 231

3. The employment process is dramatically influenced by the external environment.

    Answer: T Difficulty: 2 Page: 231

4. Management is not completely free to choose whom they hire, promote, or fire.

    Answer: T Difficulty: 3 Page: 233

5. Strategic human resource planning translates the organization's mission and objectives into the strategic plan that will allow the organization to achieve its goals.

    Answer: F Difficulty: 2 Page: 234

6. Demand for human resources is a result of demand for the products or services provided by the organization.

    Answer: T Difficulty: 3 Page: 235

7. Employee referrals may not increase the diversity and mix of employees.

    Answer: T Difficulty: 2 Page: 236

8. One of the major benefits of using internal searches for job candidates is that it builds employee morale.

    Answer: T Difficulty: 1 Page: 237

9. The selection process is essentially an exercise in prediction.

    Answer: T Difficulty: 2 Page: 237

10. The major point of any selection activity is to reduce the probability of making a reject error or an accept error.

    Answer: T Difficulty: 3 Page: 238

11. The burden lies with management to verify that any selection device it uses to differentiate applicants is related to job performance.

    Answer: T Difficulty: 3 Page: 239

12. Almost all organizations require an employee to complete a physical examination.

    Answer: F Difficulty: 2 Page: 239

13. Intelligence tests are reasonably good predictors for supervisory positions.

    Answer: T Difficulty: 2 Page: 240

14. Very few job applicants exaggerate or misrepresent data on application forms.

    Answer: F Difficulty: 2 Page: 241

15. The interview is most valid in determining an applicant's intelligence, level of motivation, and interpersonal skills.

    Answer: T Difficulty: 2 Page: 241

16. By asking predetermined structured questions during the interview, a better comparison of the job applicants can be made.

    Answer: T Difficulty: 2 Page: 242

17. Most job training takes place in the classroom.

    Answer: F Difficulty: 2 Page: 245

18. Training programs must be evaluated on some performance-based measure in order to ensure the training was actually effective.

    Answer: T Difficulty: 2 Page: 246

19. Employee development is more future-oriented than is employee training.

    Answer: T Difficulty: 2 Page: 246

20. Compensation administration attempts to design a cost-effective pay structure that will attract and retain competent employees.

    Answer: T Difficulty: 2 Page: 252

Chapter 8:   Staffing and Human Resource Management

21. Life, health and disability insurance are all examples of employee benefits.

    Answer: T Difficulty: 1 Page: 252

22. Businesses in the United States lose more than 90 million days yearly of lost productivity due to work-related accidents.

    Answer: T Difficulty: 2 Page: 253

23. OSHA places a very specific responsibility on managers for documenting employee injuries and illnesses.

    Answer: T Difficulty: 2 Page: 253

24. Maintaining a healthy work environment is strictly a legal consideration. It has no effect on worker productivity.

    Answer: F Difficulty: 2 Page: 253

25. Work force diversity is affecting the way employees are recruited, selected and oriented.

    Answer: T Difficulty: 2 Page: 254

26. If an employee who is guilty of sexual harassment is a manager or agent for an organization, the the organization is liable for sexual harassment.

    Answer: T Difficulty: 2 Page: 255

27. Sexual harassment policies should be reinforced by regular discussions with all employees.

    Answer: T Difficulty: 2 Page: 255

28. Companies that offer quality child and elder care can be said to offer family-friendly benefits.

    Answer: T Difficulty: 1 Page: 256

29. Only employees who have been downsized have emotions of frustration, guilt, and loss to deal with after the loss of their jobs.

    Answer: F Difficulty: 2 Page: 257

Multiple Choice

30. All but which of the following employers have had a difficult time finding a large pool of job applicants?
    A. Microsoft
    B. Oracle
    C. Sybase
    D. 3M

    Answer: D Difficulty: 2 Page: 230

31. Sybase has done all but which of the following in order to advertise new job positions that they have available?
    A. Television advertisements
    B. Bi-plane banners
    C. Finder's fees of up to $10,000 for current employees
    D. Bi-plane skywriting

    Answer: D Difficulty: 2 Page: 230

32. The management function that is concerned with getting, training, motivating, and keeping competent employees is known as which of the following?
    A. Human Resource Management
    B. Strategic management
    C. Personnel management
    D. Environmental management

    Answer: A Difficulty: 1 Page: 231

33. Which of the following most dramatically impacts the employment process?
    A. Internal environment
    B. External environment
    C. Culture
    D. Technology

    Answer: B Difficulty: 2 Page: 231

34. Which percentage of the United States private-sector work force is unionized?
    A. 2%
    B. 5%
    C. 11%
    D. 25%

    Answer: C Difficulty: 2 Page: 231

Chapter 8:   Staffing and Human Resource Management

35. A group of workers, acting together, seeking to promote and protect their mutual interests through collective bargaining is known as which of the following?
    A. Coalitions
    B. Groupthink
    C. Unions
    D. Employee organizations

    Answer: C Difficulty: 2 Page: 231

36. Which of the following contains the specific practices that management is required to implement when employees are represented by a union?
    A. Management rights
    B. Collective bargaining agreement
    C. Affirmative action programs
    D. Discrimination practices

    Answer: B Difficulty: 3 Page: 232

37. Programs that ensure that decisions and practices enhance the employment, upgrading, and retention of members of protected groups are known as which of the following?
    A. Management rights
    B. Collective bargaining agreement
    C. Affirmative action programs
    D. Discrimination practices

    Answer: C Difficulty: 1 Page: 233

38. Management's discretion over human resource decisions has been reduced due to which of the following?
    A. Management rights
    B. Technology
    C. Affirmative action programs
    D. Discrimination practices

    Answer: C Difficulty: 2 Page: 233

39. Which of the following prohibits pay differences based on sex for equal work?
    A. Civil Rights Act
    B. Age Discrimination Act
    C. Family and Medical Leave Act
    D. Equal Pay Act

    Answer: D Difficulty: 1 Page: 234

Testbank

40. Which of the following prohibits discrimination based on race, color, religion, national origin, or sex?
    A. Civil Rights Act
    B. Age Discrimination Act
    C. Family and Medical Leave Act
    D. Equal Pay Act

    Answer: A Difficulty: 2 Page: 234

41. Which of the following permits employees in organizations with 50 or more workers to take up to 12 weeks of unpaid leave each year for family or medical reasons?
    A. Civil Rights Act
    B. Age Discrimination Act
    C. Family and Medical Leave Act
    D. Equal Pay Act

    Answer: C Difficulty: 3 Page: 234

42. Which of the following requires employers to provide 60 days' notice before a facility closing or mass layoff?
    A. Civil Rights Act
    B. Worker Readjustment and Retraining
    C. Family and Medical Leave Act
    D. Equal Pay Act

    Answer: B Difficulty: 2 Page: 234

43. The process by which management ensures that it has the right personnel, who are capable of completing those tasks that will help the organization achieve its objectives is known as which of the following?
    A. Human resource management
    B. Human resource inventory report
    C. Personnel management
    D. Strategic human resource planning

    Answer: D Difficulty: 2 Page: 234

44. The process that allows management to assess what talents and skills are currently available in the organization is known as which of the following?
    A. Human resource management
    B. Human resource inventory report
    C. Personnel management
    D. Strategic human resource planning

    Answer: B Difficulty: 1 Page: 235

Chapter 8: Staffing and Human Resource Management

45. An assessment of the kinds of skills, knowledge, and abilities needed to successfully perform each job in an organization is which of the following?
   A. Job description
   B. Human resource inventory report
   C. Job analysis
   D. Job specification

   Answer: C Difficulty: 2 Page: 235

46. A written statement of what a jobholder does, how a job is done, and why a job is done is which of the following?
   A. Job description
   B. Human resource inventory report
   C. Job analysis
   D. Job specification

   Answer: A Difficulty: 2 Page: 235

47. A statement of the minimum acceptable qualifications that an applicant must possess to perform a given job successfully is which of the following?
   A. Job description
   B. Human resource inventory report
   C. Job analysis
   D. Job specification

   Answer: D Difficulty: 3 Page: 235

48. Which of the following focuses on job content, environment, and conditions of employment?
   A. Job description
   B. Human resource inventory report
   C. Job analysis
   D. Job specification

   Answer: A Difficulty: 2 Page: 235

49. The job requires a Bachelor's degree in Business Administration, four years of work experience, and the ability to use WordPerfect 6.1 and QuattroPro. This is an example of which of the following?
   A. Job description
   B. Human resource inventory report
   C. Job analysis
   D. Job specification

   Answer: D Difficulty: 2 Page: 235

50. Which of the following provides the major input used in determining the organization's human resource demands in the future?
    A. Revenue forecasts
    B. Profit forecasts
    C. Governmental regulations
    D. The competition

    Answer: A Difficulty: 2 Page: 235

51. The process of locating, identifying, and attracting capable applicants is known as which of the following?
    A. Decruitment
    B. Human resource inventory report
    C. Recruitment
    D. Strategic human resource planning

    Answer: C Difficulty: 1 Page: 236

52. The process of reducing the labor supply within an organization is known as which of the following?
    A. Decruitment
    B. Human resource inventory report
    C. Recruitment
    D. Strategic human resource planning

    Answer: A Difficulty: 1 Page: 236

53. The source that is used to find suitable candidates should be based upon all but which of the following?
    A. Local labor market
    B. Type or level of the position
    C. Size of the organization
    D. Location of the organization

    Answer: D Difficulty: 3 Page: 236

54. Which of the following produces the best job candidates?
    A. Internal searches
    B. Advertisements
    C. School placement
    D. Employee referrals

    Answer: D Difficulty: 3 Page: 236

55. All but which of the following are traditional recruiting sources?
    A. Internal searches
    B. Advertisements
    C. School placement
    D. Early retirements

    Answer: D Difficulty: 2 Page: 237

Chapter 8: Staffing and Human Resource Management

56. The process of screening job applicants to ensure that the most appropriate candidates are hired is known as which of the following?
    A. Selection process
    B. Human resource inventory report
    C. Recruitment
    D. Strategic human resource planning

    Answer: A Difficulty: 2 Page: 237

57. All but which of the following are decruitment options?
    A. Layoffs
    B. Transfers
    C. Reduced workweeks
    D. School placement

    Answer: D Difficulty: 2 Page: 238

58. Which of the following essentially attempts to determine which applicant, if hired, will be successful?
    A. Selection process
    B. Human resource inventory report
    C. Recruitment
    D. Strategic human resource planning

    Answer: A Difficulty: 1 Page: 238

59. The primary goal of any selection activity is to reduce the probability of which of the following?
    A. Reject errors
    B. Accept errors
    C. Reject errors and accept errors
    D. Forecasting errors

    Answer: C Difficulty: 3 Page: 238

60. To be effective, selection devices need to measure the same variable consistently. This is known as which of the following?
    A. Reject errors
    B. Reliability
    C. Validity
    D. Recruitment

    Answer: B Difficulty: 2 Page: 239

61. Terri has taken the same typing test four times on four different days. She has scored approximately the same score each time. This test has
    A. High reliability
    B. Low reliability
    C. High validity
    D. Low validity

    Answer: A Difficulty: 2 Page: 239

62. Terri has taken an inventory assessment test six differing times and has received six differing evaluations of where her job strengths are greatest. This test has
    A. High reliability
    B. Low reliability
    C. High validity
    D. Low validity

    Answer: B Difficulty: 2 Page: 239

63. The proven relationship between a selection device and some relevant criteria is know as which of the following?
    A. Reject errors
    B. Reliability
    C. Validity
    D. Recruitment

    Answer: C Difficulty: 1 Page: 239

64. Jayne was required to take a dictation test and receive a score of 75 words per minute on the test. The job she is applying for no longer requires the use of dictation. This test has
    A. High reliability
    B. Low reliability
    C. High validity
    D. Low validity

    Answer: D Difficulty: 2 Page: 239

65. Who must prove that the selection device used to differentiate job applicants is related to job performance?
    A. The employee that resists taking the test
    B. Management
    C. The courts
    D. Unions

    Answer: B Difficulty: 3 Page: 239

66. Almost all organizations required candidates to complete which of the following?
    A. Performance-simulation tests
    B. Background investigations
    C. Physical examinations
    D. Application forms

    Answer: D Difficulty: 2 Page: 239

Chapter 8:   Staffing and Human Resource Management

67. Tests of intellectual ability, spatial and mechanical ability, perceptual accuracy and motor abilities are moderately valid predictors of which jobs?
    A. Semiskilled
    B. Unskilled operative jobs in industrial organizations
    C. Supervisory positions
    D. Semiskilled and unskilled operative jobs in industrial organizations

    Answer: D Difficulty: 3 Page: 240

68. Intelligence tests are reasonably good predictors of which jobs?
    A. Semiskilled
    B. Unskilled operative jobs in industrial organizations
    C. Supervisory positions
    D. Semiskilled and unskilled operative jobs in industrial organizations

    Answer: C Difficulty: 3 Page: 240

69. Selection devices that are based upon actual job behaviors are known as which of the following?
    A. Performance-simulation tests
    B. Background investigations
    C. Physical examinations
    D. Application forms

    Answer: A Difficulty: 2 Page: 240

70. The best-known performance-simulation tests are which of the following?
    A. Work sampling
    B. Assessment centers
    C. Written tests
    D. Work sampling and assessment centers

    Answer: D Difficulty: 2 Page: 240

71. Which of the following can be valid and reliable selection devices when they are structured, well-organized and held to common questioning?
    A. Performance-simulation tests
    B. Written tests
    C. Physical examinations
    D. Interviews

    Answer: D Difficulty: 1 Page: 240

72. All but which of the following are potential biases that can affect the interview process?
    A. Interviewer has a stereotype of what a good applicant should look like
    B. Negative information is given undue weight
    C. Decisions may be made within the first few minutes of the interview
    D. Answers to the questions asked are carefully listened to by the interviewer

    Answer: D Difficulty: 2 Page: 241

73. The interview is most valid in determining all but which of the following?
    A. Applicant's intelligence
    B. Level of motivation of the applicant
    C. Interpersonal skills of applicant
    D. Productivity level of the applicant

    Answer: D Difficulty: 3 Page: 241

74. Since a significant percentage of job applicants exaggerate or misrepresent data on job applications, which of the following may prove beneficial?
    A. Performance-simulation tests
    B. Written tests
    C. Physical examinations
    D. Background investigations

    Answer: D Difficulty: 2 Page: 241

75. All but which of the following are steps that will increase the validity and reliability of the interview process?
    A. Review the job description and the job specification
    B. Prepare a set of structured questions
    C. Ask only questions that seem appropriate for each individual candidate
    D. Write down your evaluation of the candidates as soon as possible

    Answer: C Difficulty: 2 Page: 242

76. All but which of the following are major objectives of the orientation process?
    A. Reduce the initial anxiety of the new employee
    B. Familiarize new employees with the job
    C. Complete all training required for the job
    D. Facilitate the outsider-insider transition

    Answer: C Difficulty: 2 Page: 243

Chapter 8:   Staffing and Human Resource Management

77. Businesses in the United States spend _____ a year on training programs to build workers' skills.
    A. $20 million
    B. $40 million
    C. $40 billion
    D. $80 billion

    Answer: C Difficulty: 2 Page: 243

78. A learning experience that seeks to improve employees' job performance by changing their skills, knowledge, attitudes, or behavior is known as which of the following?
    A. Orientation
    B. Job training
    C. Human resource management
    D. Strategic human resource planning

    Answer: B Difficulty: 1 Page: 243

79. All but which of the following questions are involved when determining if training is needed for employees?
    A. What are the organization's goals?
    B. What tasks must be completed to achieve the goals?
    C. What behaviors are necessary in order for each jobholder to complete their job
    D. What is the percentage increase in sales from last year?

    Answer: D Difficulty: 2 Page: 244

80. All but which of the following may be indicators that job training may be needed?
    A. Decreases in production
    B. Decrease in accidents
    C. Increase in accidents
    D. Lower quality

    Answer: B Difficulty: 2 Page: 244

81. What information is provided in a realistic job preview (RJP)?
    A. Only positive information about the job
    B. Only negative information about the job
    C. Opportunities for advancement
    D. Both positive and negative information about the job

    Answer: D Difficulty: 2 Page: 244

82. Which of the following should be the basis for evaluation of a training program?
    A. Difficulty level of the training
    B. Instructor personality
    C. Entertainment value
    D. Improvement in actual employee job performance

    Answer: D Difficulty: 1 Page: 246

83. All but which of the following are typical training methods?
    A. Job rotation
    B. Classroom lectures
    C. Simulation exercises
    D. Assessment centers

    Answer: D Difficulty: 2 Page: 246

84. Which of the following training methods involve learning tasks on the same equipment that is actually used on the job but in a simulated work environment?
    A. Job rotation
    B. Classroom lecture
    C. Simulation exercises
    D. Vestibule training

    Answer: D Difficulty: 2 Page: 246

85. Which of the following training methods uses lateral transfers which provide employees the opportunity to work at different jobs and provides exposure to a variety of tasks?
    A. Job rotation
    B. Classroom lecture
    C. Simulation exercises
    D. Vestibule training

    Answer: A Difficulty: 2 Page: 246

86. Jake is being sent to a two-week seminar to explore new uses of technology in his industry. It is hoped that the information that he obtains will help prepare him for a future position in strategic development. Jake is involved in which of the following?
    A. Employee training
    B. Employee development
    C. Human resource management
    D. Classroom lectures

    Answer: B Difficulty: 3 Page: 246

Chapter 8: Staffing and Human Resource Management

87. The process of establishing performance standards and evaluating performance in order to arrive at objective human resource decisions and to provide documentation to support personnel decisions is known as which of the following?
    A. Human resource management
    B. Strategic human resource planning
    C. Performance management system
    D. Evaluation system

    Answer: C Difficulty: 1 Page: 247

88. All but which of the following are types of performance appraisal methods?
    A. Written essay
    B. MBO
    C. Critical incidents
    D. SWOT

    Answer: D Difficulty: 1 Page: 247

89. Which of the following performance appraisal methods requires little training and no complex forms but may be more of a measure of the evaluator's writing ability than the performance of the employee?
    A. Written essay
    B. MBO
    C. Critical incidents
    D. BARS

    Answer: A Difficulty: 2 Page: 250

90. Which of the following performance appraisal methods focuses on specific and measurable job behaviors but is time-consuming and difficult to develop?
    A. Written essay
    B. MBO
    C. Critical incidents
    D. BARS

    Answer: D Difficulty: 2 Page: 250

91. Which of the following compares employees with one another?
    A. Written essay
    B. MBO
    C. Critical incidents
    D. Multiperson

    Answer: D Difficulty: 2 Page: 250

92. All but which of the following are examples of multiperson comparisons?
    A. Group order ranking
    B. Individual ranking
    C. Paired comparison
    D. Ranked comparison

    Answer: D Difficulty: 2 Page: 250

93. Which of the following performance appraisal methods is the preferred method for evaluating managers and professional employees based upon the accomplishment of a specific set of objectives?
    A. Written essay
    B. MBO
    C. Critical incidents
    D. Multiperson

    Answer: B Difficulty: 2 Page: 251

94. All but which of the following are discipline measures a manager can use?
    A. Verbal warnings
    B. Written warnings
    C. Promotion
    D. Suspension

    Answer: C Difficulty: 1 Page: 251

95. A process designed to help employees overcome performance-related problems is which of the following?
    A. Discipline
    B. Strategic human resource planning
    C. Employee counseling
    D. Remediation

    Answer: C Difficulty: 1 Page: 251

96. The primary determination of pay level is which of the following?
    A. Equity
    B. Minimum wage
    C. Type of job performed
    D. Educational level

    Answer: C Difficulty: 2 Page: 252

97. Nonfinancial rewards designed to enrich employees' lives are known as which of the following?
    A. Compensation administration
    B. Employee benefits
    C. Salary
    D. Wages

    Answer: B Difficulty: 1 Page: 252

Chapter 8: Staffing and Human Resource Management

98. The process of determining a cost-effective pay structure that will attract and retain competent employees, provide an incentive for them to work hard, and ensure that pay levels will be perceived as fair is known as which of the following?
    A. Compensation administration
    B. Employee benefits
    C. Salary
    D. Wages

    Answer: A Difficulty: 1 Page: 252

99. Life insurance, disability insurance, retirement programs, and health insurance are all examples of which of the following?
    A. Compensation administration
    B. Employee benefits
    C. Salary
    D. Wages

    Answer: B Difficulty: 2 Page: 253

100. How many days of lost productivity occur each year in the United States due to work-related injuries?
    A. 1 million
    B. 10 million
    C. 50 million
    D. 90 million

    Answer: D Difficulty: 2 Page: 253

101. Which of the following federal laws is designed to assure that workers experience safe and healthful working conditions?
    A. Occupational Safety and Health Act
    B. Environmental Protection Agency
    C. Securities and Exchange Commission
    D. Agency of Health and Safety

    Answer: A Difficulty: 1 Page: 253

102. The best sexual harassment training involves which of the following?
    A. Lectures
    B. Videos
    C. Letting participants talk to each other
    D. Letting participants talk to the trainer

    Answer: C Difficulty: 2 Page: 255

103. Flextime, child care, summer camp, parental leave and adoption benefits are all examples of which of the following?
    A. Employee benefits
    B. Compensation administration
    C. Family-friendly benefits
    D. Wages

    Answer: C Difficulty: 2 Page: 256

104. A set of attitudes, perceptions, and behaviors of employees who remain after involuntary employee reductions is known as which of the following?
    A. Employee benefits
    B. Compensation administration
    C. Family-friendly benefits
    D. Layoff-survivor sickness

    Answer: D Difficulty: 1 Page: 257

Scenario

Table 8-1
Sally is preparing for a day of interviewing job applicants for the foreman's position on the assembly line. Interviewing is always an interesting process but it takes so much time and the outcome is so important. The company really needs a good person in this position. Though Sally was an operative before being promoted to plant supervisor, she never actually worked that part of the assembly line. She is unsure what types of questions will be the best to ask during the interview. Sally has also not had a chance to review the applicant's resumes and application forms. Sally is also wondering how much time to spend recording the interviews. She could just conduct all the interviews and then spend an hour or so writing down her observations at the end of the day.

105. Referring to Table 8-1, what is the first thing that Sally should do in order to prepare for the job interview?
    A. Prepare a set of questions
    B. Review the job description and the job specification
    C. Prepare questions based upon the job application form
    D. Review the applicant's resume

    Answer: B Difficulty: 3

106. Referring to Table 8-1, all but which of the following are reasons why Sally should review the job application forms and resumes?
    A. To know which areas she needs more information about
    B. To avoid asking questions for which she already has answers
    C. To get a complete picture of the candidate and their abilities
    D. To make some pre-judgements about which candidates will be best-suited for the job

    Answer: B Difficulty: 2

Chapter 8: Staffing and Human Resource Management

107. Referring to Table 8-1, what types of questions should Sally ask during the interview?
    A. Structured
    B. Unstructured
    C. Close-ended
    D. Questions over information found on the application form and resume

    Answer: A Difficulty: 2

108. Referring to Table 8-1, how should Sally begin the interview?
    A. With small talk
    B. With the first structured interview question
    C. With an easy interview question
    D. It does not matter

    Answer: A Difficulty: 2

109. Referring to Table 8-1, when should Sally write down her observations about the candidates?
    A. At the end of the day
    B. She does not need to write anything down
    C. At the end of the first three
    D. After each interview

    Answer: D Difficulty: 2

Table 8-2
Johanna has just returned from conference on performance appraisal methods. It was an interesting conference and one that was needed. Johanna knew that the company method of evaluating employees needed some drastic revision. The current method in use was to simply have the immediate supervisor write out an evaluation of each individual employee. The method was time-consuming for the supervisors and as much a test of their writing skills as it was an evaluation of performance. Johanna was leaning toward three choices. The first choice involved one of the oldest and most popular performance appraisals. This involved listing a set of performance factors such as quantity of work, quality of work, cooperation, etc. and then rating each factor on an incremental scale. The second choice involved a system that would focus on specific and measurable job behaviors. The third choice was very results-oriented and used extensively with managers and professional employees.

110. Referring to Table 8-2, what is the current performance appraisal method being used?
    A. Written essay
    B. Graphic rating scales
    C. BARS
    D. MBO

    Answer: A Difficulty: 1

111. Referring to Table 8-2, what is the first choice that Johanna is considering known as?
    A. Written essay
    B. Graphic rating scales
    C. BARS
    D. MBO

    Answer: B Difficulty: 2

112. Referring to Table 8-2, what would be the primary advantage of using the first choice?
    A. Rich example of behaviorally based data
    B. Provide quantitative data
    C. Focuses on end goals
    D. Compares employees with one another

    Answer: B Difficulty: 2

113. Referring to Table 8-2, what would be the major disadvantage of the second choice?
    A. Difficult to develop
    B. Depends on evaluator's writing skills
    C. Unwieldy with large numbers of employees
    D. Provides information on only critical behaviors that foster ineffective job performance

    Answer: A Difficulty: 3

114. Referring to Table 8-2, what is the third choice that Johanna is considering?
    A. Written essay
    B. Graphic rating scales
    C. BARS
    D. MBO

    Answer: D Difficulty: 2

Chapter 8:   Staffing and Human Resource Management

Table 8-3
Jo sighed. Productivity levels were down by 5% this month. After just spending $150,000 on new equipment, she was not quite sure how to explain this to top management. She had been so sure that new equipment would increase productivity levels. In fact all the research she had done before purchasing the equipment had substantiated just that. What was the problem? She decided a trip to the assembly line floor was in order. Talking to the assembly line supervisor provided Jo with some new insights. The equipment manufacturer had said the new equipment would be easier to run than the old equipment. Jo had felt the equipment was similar enough that no training on the new equipment was necessary. Evidently that was not the case. The assembly line supervisor said there had been many down hours while people tried to figure out how to run the new machines. Furthermore these machines were much more interrelated. One job tied into the next job so if one person did something incorrectly, the next person on the line could not easily step in and fix the problem. Furthermore, these machines were much more technical and computer-like than the old machines had been. Evidently, they were not as easy to use as the manufacturer had stated.

115. Referring to Table 8-3, which of the following may be a first step in solving Jo's problem?
    A. Employee development
    B. Employee training
    C. Strategic human resource planning
    D. Compensation administration

    Answer: B Difficulty: 1

116. Referring to Table 8-3, what may be a necessary first step in order to introduce all employees to the new system and convey some specific technical information to everyone at the same time?
    A. Job rotation
    B. Classroom lectures
    C. Simulation exercises
    D. Vestibule training

    Answer: B Difficulty: 2

117. Referring to Table 8-3, which of the following would be most effective in training people on how to use the new equipment properly?
    A. Job rotation
    B. Classroom lectures
    C. Simulation exercises
    D. Vestibule training

    Answer: D Difficulty: 2

118. Referring to Table 8-3, since the machines are so interrelated, which training method may help employees understand each of the differing jobs better?
    A. Job rotation
    B. Classroom lectures
    C. Simulation exercises
    D. Vestibule training

    Answer: A   Difficulty: 2

119. Referring to Table 8-3, what is probably the main reason for the decrease in productivity?
    A. Lack of employee development
    B. Lack of employee motivation
    C. Lack of management motivation
    D. Lack of employee training

    Answer: D   Difficulty: 2

Essay

120. Describe the strategic human resource management process.

    Answer:
    The process seeks to find the best personnel to accomplish the job in the most efficient and effective manner
    Planning, recruiting, selecting, orientation, training, performance appraisals, compensation, safety and health issues as well as current issues must all be effectively dealt with

121. Compare and contrast job analysis, job description, and job specification.

    Answer:
    Job analysis - the process of determining exactly what is involved in performing a job
    Job description - a detailed description of the duties required in a specific job
    Job specification - the qualifications, skills, knowledge, education, abilities a person must possess in order to be able to perform the job

122. Compare and contrast validity and reliability in relationship to employment selection.

    Answer:
    Any selection process must be both valid and reliable
    It is management's responsibility to demonstrate that all selection devices are both reliable and valid
    Reliability demonstrates that a selection device will obtain the same results consistently
    Validity demonstrates that there is a relationship between the selection device and the relevant job criteria

Chapter 8: Staffing and Human Resource Management

123. Describe the selection devices that work best with various kinds of jobs.

    Answer:
    Work sampling works best with low-level and middle to low-skilled jobs
    Assessment centers work well with managerial positions
    Intelligence tests work well with managerial positions
    Interviews work well to measure intelligence and interpersonal skills and consequently also are good predictors for management positions

124. Describe two techniques that can be used to evaluate employee performance.

    Answer:
    Written essay
    Critical incidents
    Graphic rating scales
    BARS
    Multiperson
    MBO

125. Describe two types of training methods that can be used.

    Answer:
    Job rotation
    Understudy assignments
    Classroom lectures
    Films and videos
    Simulation exercises
    Vestibule training

126. Discuss three current issues in human resource management today.

    Answer:
    Compensation
    Employee benefits
    OSHA
    Work force diversity
    Sexual harassment
    Family-friendly benefits
    Layoff-survivor sickness

Chapter 9: Managing Change and Innovation

True/False

1. Although change has always been a part of a manager's job, it has become more so in recent years.

   Answer: T Difficulty: 2 Page: 267

2. Decision-making would be dramatically simplified for managers if no changes occurred.

   Answer: T Difficulty: 1 Page: 268

3. Technology and competition are examples of sources of internal forces that dictate a need for change.

   Answer: F Difficulty: 2 Page: 268

4. A new or modified strategy is an internal source of change for an organization.

   Answer: T Difficulty: 2 Page: 271

5. The calm waters metaphor envisions a trip over unfamiliar waters with a crew that has never before worked together.

   Answer: F Difficulty: 2 Page: 273

6. The white water rapids metaphor has dominated the thinking of managers and academics until recently.

   Answer: F Difficulty: 2 Page: 273

7. Lewin's three-step process treats change as a break in the equilibrium of the organization.

   Answer: T Difficulty: 3 Page: 273

8. Many of today's managers face constant change, bordering on chaos.

   Answer: T Difficulty: 2 Page: 274

9. Senior employees resist change more than do new employees.

   Answer: T Difficulty: 2 Page: 277

10. Covert attempts to influence others through twisting or distorting facts to make the change look more attractive is called coercion.

    Answer: F Difficulty: 2 Page: 277

Chapter 9: Managing Change and Innovation

11. The primary focus on technological change in TQM is directed at developing flexible processes to support continuous improvement.

    Answer: T Difficulty: 3 Page: 279

12. The effort to assist organizational members with a planned change is referred to as organizational design.

    Answer: F Difficulty: 2 Page: 279

13. When OD efforts are planned, organization leaders are, in essence, attempting to change the culture of the organization.

    Answer: T Difficulty: 3 Page: 279

14. George has a chronic sense of urgency and a high desire to compete. George has a Type B personality.

    Answer: F Difficulty: 2 Page: 282

15. The goal of every manager is to reduce all stress.

    Answer: F Difficulty: 2 Page: 283

16. Being creative means seeing usual things in the usual way.

    Answer: F Difficulty: 1 Page: 284

17. An organization that stimulates creativity is one that develops novel approaches to things or unique solutions to problems.

    Answer: T Difficulty: 2 Page: 284

18. The innovative organization is characterized by its ability to channel its creative abilities into useful outcomes.

    Answer: T Difficulty: 3 Page: 284

19. The incubation period in the process of innovation may take years to complete.

    Answer: T Difficulty: 2 Page: 285

20. Organic structures positively influence innovation.

    Answer: T Difficulty: 2 Page: 285

21. Frequent interunit communication helps to facilitate innovation.

    Answer: T Difficulty: 2 Page: 286

22. Creative people stay within their comfort zone and become experts in one area.

    Answer: F Difficulty: 3 Page: 286

23. An organizational culture that fosters innovation accepts ambiguity and has a low tolerance for risk.

    Answer: F Difficulty: 3 Page: 287

24. New idea champions are extremely self-confident, persistent, energetic and have a tendency to take risks.

    Answer: T Difficulty: 2 Page: 287

Multiple Choice

25. Galia Maor, CEO of Bank Leumi Le-Israel, foresees a world in the not-too-distant future where what will occur?
    A. Fewer bank defaults
    B. No bank service fees
    C. Technobanking
    D. More women in bank management

    Answer: C Difficulty: 2 Page: 267

26. First Direct is a system that does which of the following?
    A. Monitors all banking activities
    B. Helps women network in the banking industry
    C. Allows home banking from the living room easy chair
    D. Allows for automatic loans to qualifying women

    Answer: C Difficulty: 2 Page: 267

27. An alteration of an organization's environment, structure, technology or people is which of the following?
    A. Innovation
    B. Creativity
    C. Change
    D. Technology

    Answer: C Difficulty: 1 Page: 268

28. A manager has basically three options when handling change. They include all but which of the following?
    A. Altering structures
    B. Altering technology
    C. Altering natural resources
    D. Altering people

    Answer: C Difficulty: 2 Page: 268

Chapter 9:   Managing Change and Innovation

29. All but which of the following are external sources of change for an organization?
    A. New competition
    B. Redefined or modified strategy
    C. Government laws and regulations
    D. Technology

    Answer: B Difficulty: 2 Page: 268

30. All but which of the following are internal sources of change?
    A. Redefined or modified strategy
    B. Technology
    C. Employee attitudes
    D. New personnel

    Answer: B Difficulty: 2 Page: 271

31. A person who initiates and assumes the responsibility for managing a change in an organization is known as which of the following?
    A. Innovation agent
    B. Creativity agent
    C. Change agent
    D. Technology agent

    Answer: C Difficulty: 1 Page: 271

32. Susan has just attended a conference on new office technology that will dramatically impact the jobs of all administrative assistants. Workloads should be drastically reduced but extensive training will be required. Susan is enthusiastic about the new technology and assumes the responsibility for the implementation of the equipment and the resulting training. Susan is which of the following?
    A. Innovation agent
    B. Creativity agent
    C. Change agent
    D. Technology agent

    Answer: C Difficulty: 2 Page: 271

33. Patrick Purcell is the publisher of which of the following?
    A. Omaha World Herald
    B. Boston Herald
    C. Denver Post
    D. Saturday Evening Post

    Answer: B Difficulty: 2 Page: 272

34. Patrick Purcell realized that his organization desperately needed which of the following?
    A. New technology
    B. New suppliers
    C. Changes
    D. New management

    Answer: C Difficulty: 2 Page: 272

35. The metaphor that likens an organization to a sea captain and crew that knew exactly where they were going because they had been there many times before is which of the following?
    A. Calm water metaphor
    B. White water rapids
    C. A dynamic environment
    D. A static environment

    Answer: A Difficulty: 2 Page: 272

36. The metaphor that likens an organization to a group who are totally unfamiliar with each other and are traveling in unknown waters where their destination is not even certain is which of the following?
    A. Calm water metaphor
    B. White water rapids
    C. A dynamic environment
    D. A static environment

    Answer: B Difficulty: 2 Page: 273

37. Until recently which metaphor dominated the thinking of practicing managers and academics?
    A. Calm water metaphor
    B. White water rapids
    C. A dynamic environment
    D. A static environment

    Answer: A Difficulty: 3 Page: 272

38. All but which of the following are steps in Kurt Lewin's change process?
    A. Unfreezing the status quo
    B. Changing to a new state
    C. Disrupting the equilibrium
    D. Refreezing the new change

    Answer: C Difficulty: 3 Page: 273

Chapter 9: Managing Change and Innovation

39. According to Kurt Lewin, change can be accomplished in all but which of the following ways?
    A. Driving forces can be increased
    B. Driving forces can be decreased
    C. Restraining forces can be decreased
    D. Driving forces and restraining forces can be combined

    Answer: B Difficulty: 3 Page: 273

40. The white water metaphor takes into consideration that environments are
    A. Certain and static
    B. Uncertain and dynamic
    C. Certain and dynamic
    D. Uncertain and static

    Answer: B Difficulty: 3 Page: 274

41. Most competitive advantages last less than
    A. Three months
    B. Six months
    C. Twelve months
    D. Eighteen months

    Answer: D Difficulty: 2 Page: 275

42. Change is affecting what number of managers today?
    A. A few
    B. Some
    C. Many
    D. The majority

    Answer: D Difficulty: 1 Page: 275

43. All but which of the following are reasons people resist change?
    A. Uncertainty
    B. Concern over personal loss
    C. Concern over personal gain
    D. The belief that the change is not in the organization's best interest

    Answer: C Difficulty: 2 Page: 275

44. For permanent change to occur without extensive resistance, based on the Coch and French study, what must happen?
    A. Top management involvement
    B. Stockholder involvement
    C. Employee participation
    D. Stakeholder participation

    Answer: C Difficulty: 3 Page: 276

45. The Coch and French study occurred in a plant where which of the following was made?
    A. Skirts and blouses
    B. Coats and suits
    C. Pajamas
    D. Evening gowns

    Answer: C Difficulty: 2 Page: 276

46. All but which of the following are techniques that managers can use to reduce resistance to change?
    A. Coercion
    B. Facilitation and support
    C. Top management dictates the change
    D. Education and communication

    Answer: C Difficulty: 2 Page: 277

47. Which of the following is used to reduce resistance to change when resistance comes from a powerful group and commitment must be bought?
    A. Coercion
    B. Facilitation and support
    C. Negotiation
    D. Education and communication

    Answer: C Difficulty: 3 Page: 278

48. Which of the following can be used to reduce resistance to change when the resistance is due to misinformation?
    A. Coercion
    B. Facilitation and support
    C. Negotiation
    D. Education and communication

    Answer: D Difficulty: 2 Page: 278

49. Changes in authority relationships, coordination mechanisms, job design or degree of centralization fall under which category of options that a manager can change?
    A. Structure
    B. Technology
    C. People
    D. Management

    Answer: A Difficulty: 2 Page: 278

Chapter 9: *Managing Change and Innovation*

50. Changes in the way work is processed or the methods and equipment used falls under which category of options that a manager can change?
    A. Structure
    B. Technology
    C. People
    D. Management

    Answer: B Difficulty: 1 Page: 278

51. Changes in employee attitudes, expectations, perceptions or behaviors falls under which category of options that a manager can change?
    A. Structure
    B. Technology
    C. People
    D. Management

    Answer: C Difficulty: 2 Page: 279

52. The focus on which of the following is to constructively change the attitudes and values of organizational members so they can more readily adapt to, and be more effective in achieving the new directions of the organization?
    A. Organization culture
    B. Strategic human resource planning
    C. Organizational development
    D. Process consultation

    Answer: C Difficulty: 2 Page: 279

53. One of the fundamental issues behind organizational development is its reliance on _____ in an effort to foster an environment in which open communication and trust exists.
    A. Top management participation
    B. Middle management participation
    C. Supervisory participation
    D. Employee participation

    Answer: D Difficulty: 3 Page: 279

54. All but which of the following are the more popular OD efforts used in organizations?
    A. Survey feedback
    B. Process consultation
    C. Team building
    D. Employee assistance programs

    Answer: D Difficulty: 2 Page: 280

55. The OD technique where efforts are designed to assess employee attitudes and perceptions of the change by responding to a specific set of questions is which of the following?
    A. Survey feedback
    B. Process consultation
    C. Team building
    D. Employee assistance programs

    Answer: A Difficulty: 2 Page: 280

56. When an outside consultant helps managers perceive, understand and act upon process events, they are using which OD technique?
    A. Survey feedback
    B. Process consultation
    C. Team building
    D. Employee assistance programs

    Answer: B Difficulty: 1 Page: 280

57. Helping different work groups to become more cohesive involves using which OD technique?
    A. Survey feedback
    B. Process consultation
    C. Team building
    D. Intergroup development

    Answer: D Difficulty: 2 Page: 280

58. The force or influence a person feels when faced with an opportunity, constraint, or demand that they perceive to be both uncertain and important is called which of the following?
    A. Culture
    B. Change
    C. Stress
    D. Karoshi

    Answer: C Difficulty: 1 Page: 280

59. Stress is said to be _____ when the situation offers someone an opportunity to gain something.
    A. Negative
    B. Positive
    C. Irrelevant
    D. Overwhelming

    Answer: B Difficulty: 2 Page: 281

Chapter 9:   Managing Change and Innovation

60. Regardless of the situation, a stressful condition exists when all but which of the following occurs?
    A. When there is doubt or uncertainty regarding an opportunity to be seized
    B. When there is doubt or uncertainty regarding a removal of a constraint
    C. When there is doubt or uncertainty regarding avoidance of a loss
    D. When there is doubt or uncertainty regarding the importance of the outcome

    Answer: D Difficulty: 3 Page: 281

61. If winning or losing is not important, stress
    A. Is highest
    B. Is lowest
    C. Does not exist
    D. Is ever present

    Answer: C Difficulty: 2 Page: 281

62. All but which of the following are examples of organizational stressors?
    A. Role ambiguity
    B. Role clarity
    C. Technological advancements
    D. Reengineering

    Answer: B Difficulty: 2 Page: 281

63. All but which of the following are examples of personal stressors?
    A. Personality type
    B. Family matters
    C. Financial problems
    D. Downsizing

    Answer: D Difficulty: 2 Page: 281

64. Surveys indicate that up to _____ of the workers in the United States experience high job stress.
    A. 10%
    B. 25%
    C. 60%
    D. 75%

    Answer: D Difficulty: 2 Page: 281

65. In Japan, which of the following is the term used to refer to a sudden heart attack caused by overworking?
    A. Kaiban
    B. Karoshi
    C. Kazaam
    D. Overworked

    Answer: B Difficulty: 2 Page: 282

66. A person who is characterized by a chronic sense of urgency and an excessive competitive drive has which of the following?
    A. Type A personality
    B. Type B personality
    C. Hyperactivity
    D. Karoshi

    Answer: A Difficulty: 1 Page: 282

67. George constantly strives to exceed. He must always get the highest grade in the class and has a sense of urgency about him at all times. George probably has which of the following?
    A. Type A personality
    B. Type B personality
    C. Hyperactivity
    D. Karoshi

    Answer: A Difficulty: 2 Page: 282

68. A person with a relaxed and easy-going personality who easily accepts change would have which of the following?
    A. Type A personality
    B. Type B personality
    C. Hyperactivity
    D. Karoshi

    Answer: B Difficulty: 2 Page: 282

69. Kevin is a very relaxed, easy-going person who appears to have all the time in the world. He is never too busy to stop and chat for a moment. Kevin has which of the following?
    A. Type A personality
    B. Type B personality
    C. Hyperactivity
    D. Karoshi

    Answer: B Difficulty: 2 Page: 282

Chapter 9:   Managing Change and Innovation

70. All but which of the following are ways stress reveals itself?
    A. Physiological
    B. Psychological
    C. Behavioral
    D. Type B personality

    Answer: D Difficulty: 2 Page: 282

71. A program offered by an organization to help a formerly productive employee who now has a problem get back on the job as quickly as possible is which of the following?
    A. Employee Assistance Programs
    B. Wellness Programs
    C. Stress Reduction Programs
    D. Human Resource Management

    Answer: A Difficulty: 1 Page: 283

72. A local college offers its employees reduced rates when they use the physical fitness facilities, offers weight control seminars and nutrition education and provides incentives for employees who stop smoking. The college has which of the following?
    A. Employee Assistance Programs
    B. Wellness Programs
    C. Stress Reduction Programs
    D. Human Resource Management

    Answer: B Difficulty: 2 Page: 283

73. Campbell Soup Company offers a program for employees seeking the first step in psychiatric or substance-abuse help. They are offering which of the following?
    A. Employee Assistance Programs
    B. Wellness Programs
    C. Stress Reduction Programs
    D. Human Resource Management

    Answer: A Difficulty: 2 Page: 283

74. A manager's goal is to reduce which amount/type of stress?
    A. All stress
    B. All organizational stress
    C. Dysfunctional stress
    D. All personal stress

    Answer: C Difficulty: 2 Page: 283

75. 3M has generated more than 30% of its $13 billion in revenues from products introduced during the previous
    A. 10 years
    B. 5 years
    C. 2 years
    D. 1 year

    Answer: B Difficulty: 3 Page: 284

76. The process of taking a new idea and turning it into a useful product is known as which of the following?
    A. Creativity
    B. Innovation
    C. New products
    D. Entrepreneurship

    Answer: B Difficulty: 2 Page: 284

77. The moment when all prior efforts in the innovative process successfully come together is known as which of the following?
    A. Perception
    B. Incubation
    C. Inspiration
    D. Innovation

    Answer: C Difficulty: 2 Page: 285

78. Which of the following involves taking the inspiration and turning it into a useful product, service, or way of doing things?
    A. Perception
    B. Incubation
    C. Inspiration
    D. Innovation

    Answer: D Difficulty: 1 Page: 285

79. Which of the following may take years before the idea finally "gels" and the next step occurs?
    A. Perception
    B. Incubation
    C. Inspiration
    D. Innovation

    Answer: B Difficulty: 2 Page: 285

Chapter 9:   Managing Change and Innovation

80. All but which of the following are variables that a manager can foster in order to stimulate innovation?
    A. Structure variables
    B. Culture variables
    C. Human resource practices
    D. Management practices

    Answer: D Difficulty: 2 Page: 285

81. All but which of the following are true statements concerning the effect of structural variables on innovation?
    A. Organic structures positively influence innovation
    B. Mechanistic structures positively influence innovation
    C. Plentiful resources encourage innovation
    D. Interunit communication facilitates innovation

    Answer: B Difficulty: 3 Page: 285

82. All but which of the following are ways a person can increase their creativity?
    A. Think of yourself as creative
    B. Keep a notepad near your bed to write down ideas
    C. Brainstorm with others
    D. Stay within your comfort zone

    Answer: D Difficulty: 3 Page: 286

83. All but which of the following are ways a person can increase their creativity?
    A. Do things differently
    B. Find several right answers
    C. Turn creative ideas into action
    D. Engage in activities in your comfort zone

    Answer: D Difficulty: 3 Page: 286

84. An innovative culture is apt to have all but which of the following characteristics?
    A. Low external controls
    B. Tolerance of the practical
    C. Focus on ends rather than means
    D. Tolerance for risk

    Answer: B Difficulty: 2 Page: 287

Scenario

Table 9-1
The company Frank works for currently has a mechanistic organizational structure. It has worked very well for the company for the last 75 years since its founding. However, in order to compete in the global marketplace, Frank knows a more organic structure with many less levels and work groups based upon teams across departmental functions is desperately needed. However, his preliminary discussions of such a change had met with much resistance. Nobody seemed to understand the need for the change. In fact, one group of senior managers was openly hostile about the change. Frank was relatively sure the rest of the employees would accept the change if they understood the reasons why. In fact, he was sure several of the employees had the expertise to make the new structure work well for the company.

85. Referring to Table 9-1, which group is more likely to resist the changes?
    A. New employees
    B. Senior employees
    C. New managers
    D. Stockholders

    Answer: B Difficulty: 2

86. Referring to Table 9-1, which technique to reduce the resistance to changing the organizational structure may be a good first step?
    A. Coercion
    B. Facilitation and support
    C. Participation
    D. Education and communication

    Answer: D Difficulty: 2

87. Referring to Table 9-1, which technique to reduce resistance to change may be necessary in order to get the senior managers to accept the change?
    A. Manipulation and co-optation
    B. Facilitation and support
    C. Participation
    D. Education and communication

    Answer: A Difficulty: 3

88. Referring to Table 9-1, which technique may help the operatives accept the changes?
    A. Manipulation and co-optation
    B. Facilitation and support
    C. Participation
    D. Education and communication

    Answer: C Difficulty: 2

Chapter 9: Managing Change and Innovation

89. Referring to Table 9-1, which of the following is probably the primary reason the senior managers are resisting the change?
    A. Uncertainty
    B. Concern over personal loss
    C. Concern over personal gain
    D. The belief that the change is not in the organization's best interest

    Answer: B Difficulty: 3

Table 9-2
Krista is unsure what to do next. The company that she works for is about to implement a radical new technology transformation that will affect every person in the organization. They are basically updating their plant to the 21st century and almost everything is changing. Krista is in charge of assisting the members of the company with the planned changes. Since it is a long-term change that is organization-wide, management felt that someone needed to facilitate the change since in essence it was changing the culture of the company. The first thing Krista had done was to ask employees a specific set of questions about the perceived changes. From this data, then Krista needed to decide what to do next. An outside consultant had been hired to help Krista diagnose the interpersonal processes that needed improvement. The move from functional departmentalization to work teams was a change that the new technology was necessitating. This was a major change for employees who had worked in specific departments for most of their careers. Furthermore, the teams will then have to interact with each other as they use the new technology. Krista feels like her task is almost overwhelming.

90. Referring to Table 9-2, Krista is in charge of which of the following?
    A. Human resource management
    B. Strategic human resource planning
    C. Organizational development
    D. Cultural change

    Answer: C Difficulty: 2

91. Referring to Table 9-2, the first step that Krista had taken was which of the following?
    A. Survey feedback
    B. Process consultation
    C. Team building
    D. Intergroup development

    Answer: A Difficulty: 2

92. Referring to Table 9-2, the outside consultant was performing which of the following?
    A. Survey feedback
    B. Process consultation
    C. Team building
    D. Intergroup development

    Answer: B Difficulty: 2

93. Referring to Table 9-2, due to the fact teams are a new component of this organization, which of the following may help develop positive interpersonal relationships, and clarify the roles and responsibilities of each team member?
    A. Survey feedback
    B. Process consultation
    C. Team building
    D. Intergroup development

    Answer: C Difficulty: 1

94. Referring to Table 9-2, since the work groups ultimately will be required to work together fairly closely, which of the following may be necessary?
    A. Survey feedback
    B. Process consultation
    C. Team building
    D. Intergroup development

    Answer: D Difficulty: 2

Table 9-3
Kevin is a very relaxed, easy-going employee. When the new technological processes were implemented last month he was able to easily accept the changes and start working through learning the new techniques necessary to use the new processes. George, on the other hand, was concerned about the new technology long before it was ever implemented. He was afraid he would no longer be able to be the top performer in his department. He has had several problems adapting to the new situation.

95. Referring to Table 9-3, which of the following categories of stress does the new technology fall under?
    A. Personal stressors
    B. Organizational stressors
    C. Type A personalities
    D. Type B personalities

    Answer: B Difficulty: 2

96. Referring to Table 9-3, which of the following best describes Kevin?
    A. Type A personality
    B. Type B personality
    C. Hyperactivity
    D. Karoshi

    Answer: B Difficulty: 2

Chapter 9:   Managing Change and Innovation

97. Referring to Table 9-3, which of the following best describes George?
    A. Type A personality
    B. Type B personality
    C. Type C personality
    D. Karoshi

    Answer: A Difficulty: 2

98. Referring to Table 9-3, which of the following symptoms are George's fellow employees and supervisors most apt to notice indicating he is suffering from stress?
    A. High blood pressure
    B. Changes in metabolism
    C. Sleep problems
    D. Increased tension and anxiety

    Answer: D Difficulty: 3

99. Referring to Table 9-3, which type of employee is most likely to show signs of stress even if their organizational and personal stressors are low?
    A. Type A personality
    B. Type B personality
    C. Hyperactivity
    D. Karoshi

    Answer: A Difficulty: 3

Essay

100. Describe how organizations can stimulate innovation.

     Answer:
     Structures that are flexible, fewer rules, plentiful resources, interunit communication
     Culture that encourages experimentation, rewards for both success and failure, and promotes risk-taking
     Human resources that focus on employee training and development
     Product champions who are allowed decision-making discretion and autonomy

101. Identify external versus internal forces of change.

     Answer:
     External sources - competition, governmental laws and regulations, technology, and economic changes
     Internal sources - redefinition or modification of strategy, new equipment, changing work force, compensation packages, employee attitudes and management policies

102. Compare and contrast the following two metaphors: calm waters versus white water rapids.

    Answer:
    Calm waters - change is an unnatural break in the equilibrium that occurs infrequently while the organization sails through waters it knows to a certain destination with a crew that has worked together for years
    White water rapids - change is constant, unpredictable, and uncertain so the small canoe is moving through waters that are constantly changing towards a destination that is unknown with a crew that is unfamiliar with each other

103. Explain the three primary reasons people are apt to resist change.

    Answer:
    Fear of personal loss
    The uncertainty created
    The belief the change is not in the organization's best interest

104. Differentiate between creativity and innovation

    Answer:
    Creativity is the ability to look at things in a new and unique way
    Innovation is the ability to take an idea and turn it into a useful product, service, or operation method

Chapter 10: Foundations of Individual and Group Behavior

True/False

1. Individuals in groups behave differently than individuals acting alone.

   Answer: T Difficulty: 2 Page: 298

2. Organizational behavior focuses primarily on two areas, individual and group behavior.

   Answer: T Difficulty: 1 Page: 298

3. The goals of OB are to explain and alter behavior.

   Answer: F Difficulty: 3 Page: 299

4. The statement, "I hate my job" is an example of an attitude.

   Answer: T Difficulty: 2 Page: 299

5. The affective component of an attitude is the emotional, or feeling segment of the attitude.

   Answer: T Difficulty: 2 Page: 299

6. An employee's general attitude toward his or her job is job involvement.

   Answer: F Difficulty: 2 Page: 299

7. Individuals will seek a stable state where there is a maximum of dissonance.

   Answer: F Difficulty: 2 Page: 300

8. The degree of influence that individuals believe they have over the elements will have an impact on how they react to the dissonance felt.

   Answer: T Difficulty: 2 Page: 301

9. If the issues causing the dissonance are of great importance, the individual will not be under great tension to reduce the dissonance.

   Answer: F Difficulty: 3 Page: 301

10. Dissonance can be managed.

    Answer: T Difficulty: 3 Page: 302

11. Recent research is providing renewed support that happy workers are productive workers.

    Answer: T Difficulty: 2 Page: 302

12. One of the most widely-used methods of identifying personalities is the Big-Five model.

    Answer: F Difficulty: 2 Page: 302

13. Proponents of personality instruments believe that it is important to know personality types because personality influences the way people interact and solve problems.

    Answer: T Difficulty: 3 Page: 304

14. Emotional stability was the factor that predicted job performance for all five groups in the study cited in your text.

    Answer: F Difficulty: 3 Page: 304

15. If an individual blames their boss for a poor performance evaluation, they have an internal locus of control.

    Answer: F Difficulty: 3 Page: 305

16. A person that believes the end justifies the means has a high Mach perspective.

    Answer: T Difficulty: 2 Page: 305

17. People low in self-esteem believe they possess the ability to succeed at work.

    Answer: F Difficulty: 2 Page: 305

18. Low self-monitors have a high behavioral consistency between who they are and what they do.

    Answer: T Difficulty: 2 Page: 307

19. Managers who are high risk-takers make more rapid decisions but require more information.

    Answer: F Difficulty: 3 Page: 309

20. Holland's model argues that satisfaction is highest and turnover lowest when personality and occupation are in agreement.

    Answer: T Difficulty: 2 Page: 310

Chapter 10: Foundations of Individual and Group Behavior

21. A country's culture should influence the dominant personality characteristics of its population.

    Answer: T Difficulty: 2 Page: 310

22. Research on perception consistently demonstrates that individuals who look at the same thing will see it in the same way.

    Answer: F Difficulty: 2 Page: 311

23. When Jane blames her failure to get the Emerson account on the advertising department's lack of creativity but sees acquiring the Ninson account as her personal success even though the advertising department was also an important factor, she is using fundamental attribution theory.

    Answer: F Difficulty: 3 Page: 313

24. The statement older workers are less productive is an example of selectivity.

    Answer: F Difficulty: 2 Page: 314

25. Employees react to perceptions not reality.

    Answer: T Difficulty: 2 Page: 315

26. When attempting to shape behavior, a manager should identify all behaviors that need to be molded.

    Answer: F Difficulty: 2 Page: 317

27. The behavior of individuals in a group is the same as individual behavior.

    Answer: F Difficulty: 1 Page: 318

28. Achieving some level of prestige from belonging to a group is a security reason for joining a group.

    Answer: F Difficulty: 2 Page: 319

29. The dress code of a company can be enforced very effectively through the use of norms.

    Answer: T Difficulty: 2 Page: 320

30. Anything can have status value if others in the group admire it.

    Answer: T Difficulty: 3 Page: 321

31. Large groups are good for taking action while smaller groups are good for gaining diverse input.

    Answer: F   Difficulty: 2   Page: 323

Multiple Choice

32. Alexander Panikin never gave up hope of doing which of the following?
    A. Becoming a CEO of a major U.S. company
    B. Changing the Russian political system
    C. Owning his own company
    D. Becoming a millionaire

    Answer: C   Difficulty: 2   Page: 297

33. Panikin pays his employees which of the following amounts?
    A. Minimum wage
    B. The state wage
    C. Twice the state wage
    D. Triple the state wage

    Answer: C   Difficulty: 2   Page: 297

34. The study of actions of people specifically at work is known as which of the following?
    A. Organizational development
    B. Organizational behavior
    C. Organizational training
    D. Human resource management

    Answer: B   Difficulty: 1   Page: 297

35. All but which of the following are visible aspects of organizational behavior?
    A. Strategies
    B. Technology
    C. Group norms
    D. Formal authority

    Answer: C   Difficulty: 2   Page: 298

36. All but which of the following are hidden aspects of organizational behavior?
    A. Attitudes
    B. Perceptions
    C. Interpersonal and intergroup conflicts
    D. Objectives

    Answer: D   Difficulty: 2   Page: 298

Chapter 10: Foundations of Individual and Group Behavior

37. When topics such as attitudes, personality, perceptions, learning and motivation are considered, OB is looking at which of the following?
    A. Group behavior
    B. Individual behavior
    C. Stress management
    D. Creativity

    Answer: B Difficulty: 1 Page: 298

38. When topics such as norms, roles, team building and conflict are considered, OB is looking at which of the following?
    A. Group behavior
    B. Individual behavior
    C. Stress management
    D. Creativity

    Answer: A Difficulty: 1 Page: 298

39. The goals of OB are to do which of the following?
    A. Explain and predict behavior
    B. Explain and alter behavior
    C. Alter and predict behavior
    D. Simply observe behavior

    Answer: A Difficulty: 3 Page: 298

40. All but which of the following are components of attitudes?
    A. The cognitive component
    B. The affective component
    C. The behavioral component
    D. The emotional component

    Answer: D Difficulty: 2 Page: 299

41. The part of an attitude that is comprised of beliefs, opinions, knowledge and information is which of the following?
    A. The cognitive component
    B. The affective component
    C. The behavioral component
    D. The emotional component

    Answer: A Difficulty: 2 Page: 299

42. The part of an attitude that is an intention to behave in a certain way toward someone or something is which of the following?
    A. The cognitive component
    B. The affective component
    C. The behavioral component
    D. The emotional component

    Answer: C Difficulty: 2 Page: 299

43. "I will not work with Jim any more" is an example of which of the following?
    A. The cognitive component
    B. The affective component
    C. The behavioral component
    D. The emotional component

    Answer: C Difficulty: 2 Page: 299

44. "I dislike making cold calls" said the insurance sales producer. This is an example of which of the following?
    A. The cognitive component
    B. The affective component
    C. The behavioral component
    D. The emotional component

    Answer: B Difficulty: 2 Page: 299

45. All but which of the following are the most important and most studied job-related attitudes?
    A. Job satisfaction
    B. Job involvement
    C. Organizational development
    D. Organizational commitment

    Answer: C Difficulty: 2 Page: 299

46. Which of the following is concerned with the degree to which an employee identifies with his or her job, actively participates in it, and considers his or her performance important to his or her self-worth?
    A. Job satisfaction
    B. Job involvement
    C. Organizational development
    D. Organizational commitment

    Answer: B Difficulty: 2 Page: 299

47. Jill has been teaching for 18 years. Each day she arrives at work smiling and ready to teach another room full of students. She loves her job. This describes which of the following?
    A. Job satisfaction
    B. Job involvement
    C. Organizational development
    D. Organizational commitment

    Answer: A Difficulty: 2 Page: 299

Chapter 10: Foundations of Individual and Group Behavior

48. Research has concluded that people seek consistency between which of the following?
    A. Attitudes and perceptions
    B. Perceptions and behaviors
    C. Attitudes and behaviors
    D. Beliefs and attitudes

    Answer: C Difficulty: 3 Page: 300

49. All but which of the following are steps that can be taken when there is inconsistency between their attitudes and behaviors?
    A. Alter their attitudes
    B. Alter their behavior
    C. Develop a rationalization for the discrepancy
    D. Alter their perceptions

    Answer: D Difficulty: 2 Page: 300

50. Any incompatibility between two or more attitudes or between behavior and attitudes is known as which of the following?
    A. Cognitive dispersion
    B. Cognitive dissonance
    C. Organizational behavior
    D. Organizational development

    Answer: B Difficulty: 1 Page: 300

51. All but which of the following affects the desire of an individual to reduce dissonance?
    A. The degree of influence the individual has over the elements involved
    B. The rewards that may be involved
    C. The importance of the elements involved
    D. The ability of the individual

    Answer: D Difficulty: 2 Page: 300

52. If the factors creating the dissonance are relatively important, the pressure to reduce the dissonance is
    A. Greater
    B. Less
    C. Stays the same
    D. Is not affected

    Answer: A Difficulty: 3 Page: 299

53. If the dissonance-producing behavior is required due to a supervisor's direct order over which the individual has little control, then the pressure to reduce the dissonance is
    A. Greater
    B. Less
    C. Stays the same
    D. Is not affected

    Answer: B Difficulty: 3 Page: 301

54. If the rewards are high, even though the dissonance is high, the tension caused by the dissonance tends to be
    A. Greater
    B. Less
    C. Stays the same
    D. Is not affected

    Answer: B Difficulty: 3 Page: 301

55. When people are described with terms such as quiet, passive, loud, aggressive, loyal, tense, and sociable, which of the following is being described?
    A. Cognitive dissonance
    B. Attitudes
    C. Values
    D. Personality

    Answer: D Difficulty: 1 Page: 302

56. One of the more widely-used indicators of identifying personalities is which of the following?
    A. Five-factor model of personality
    B. Myers-Briggs type indicator
    C. Machiavellianism inventory
    D. Personality inventory

    Answer: B Difficulty: 2 Page: 302

57. All but which of the following are the dimensions of personality used by the Myers-Briggs type indicator?
    A. Extroverts
    B. Introverts
    C. Sensing
    D. Informational

    Answer: D Difficulty: 2 Page: 303

Chapter 10: Foundations of Individual and Group Behavior

58. The major criticism of the MBTI is which of the following?
    A. It lacks popularity
    B. It lacks evidence to support its validity
    C. It lacks evidence to support its reliability
    D. It lacks acceptance by the business community

    Answer: B Difficulty: 3 Page: 304

59. All but which of the following are factors in the Big-Five model?
    A. Extroversion
    B. Agreeableness
    C. Conscientiousness
    D. Introversion

    Answer: D Difficulty: 2 Page: 304

60. When determining the degree to which someone is sociable, talkative, and assertive, which factor of the Big-Five model would be discussed?
    A. Extroversion
    B. Agreeableness
    C. Conscientiousness
    D. Openness to experience

    Answer: A Difficulty: 2 Page: 304

61. The degree to which someone is imaginative, artistically sensitive and intellectual would be which of the Big-Five model factors?
    A. Openness to experience
    B. Agreeableness
    C. Conscientiousness
    D. Emotional stability

    Answer: A Difficulty: 2 Page: 304

62. Which factor predicted job performance for all five occupational groups in the study cited in the text?
    A. Openness to experience
    B. Agreeableness
    C. Conscientiousness
    D. Emotional stability

    Answer: C Difficulty: 3 Page: 304

63. All but which of the following have proven powerful in explaining individual behavior in organizations?
    A. Locus of control
    B. Machiavellianism
    C. Self-esteem
    D. Personality

    Answer: D Difficulty: 2 Page: 305

64. An employee who blames his supervisor for a poor performance evaluation has which of the following?
    A. Internal locus of control
    B. External locus of control
    C. Low self-esteem
    D. High Machiavellianism

    Answer: B Difficulty: 3 Page: 305

65. "If it works, use it" is an example of someone with which of the following?
    A. Internal locus of control
    B. External locus of control
    C. Low self-esteem
    D. High Machiavellianism

    Answer: D Difficulty: 3 Page: 305

66. People that believe they possess the ability needed in order to succeed on the job have which of the following?
    A. Internal locus of control
    B. External locus of control
    C. High self-esteem
    D. High Machiavellianism

    Answer: C Difficulty: 3 Page: 305

67. Carol is able to adjust her behavior depending on external, situational factors. She is highly sensitive to external cues and behaves differently in differing situations. She has which of the following?
    A. High self-monitoring
    B. Low self-monitoring
    C. Low self-esteem
    D. High Machiavellianism

    Answer: A Difficulty: 3 Page: 307

68. Joe is always Joe. No matter where he is he is the same loud, obnoxious, outgoing person. Joe has which of the following?
    A. High self-monitoring
    B. Low self-monitoring
    C. Low self-esteem
    D. High Machiavellianism

    Answer: B Difficulty: 3 Page: 307

Chapter 10: Foundations of Individual and Group Behavior

69. Managers who make rapid decisions and require less information have which of the following?
    A. High self-monitoring
    B. Low self-monitoring
    C. High risk-takers
    D. High Machiavellianism

    Answer: C Difficulty: 3 Page: 309

70. A lawyer or real estate agent should have which of the following personality types?
    A. Realistic
    B. Social
    C. Conventional
    D. Enterprising

    Answer: D Difficulty: 2 Page: 309

71. A corporate manager or an accountant should have which of the following personality types?
    A. Realistic
    B. Social
    C. Conventional
    D. Enterprising

    Answer: C Difficulty: 2 Page: 309

72. The theory based on Holland's research argues that satisfaction is highest and turnover is lowest when
    A. Personality and occupation are in disagreement
    B. Personality and occupation are in agreement
    C. There is no relationship between personality and occupation
    D. Job involvement is low

    Answer: B Difficulty: 2 Page: 310

73. All but which of the following are key points in Holland's model?
    A. There are different types of jobs
    B. There are different types of personalities
    C. People in job environments congruent with their personality types should be more satisfied and less likely to voluntarily resign
    D. People in job environments congruent with their personality types should be less satisfied and more likely to voluntarily resign

    Answer: D Difficulty: 3 Page: 310

74. The major value of a manager understanding personality differences lies in which of the following?
   A. It helps in the selection process of matching jobs with employees
   B. It is always interesting
   C. It provides a basis to fire employees
   D. It is important information to record for performance evaluations

   Answer: A Difficulty: 3 Page: 310

75. The process of organizing and interpreting sensory impressions in order to give meaning to the environment is known as which of the following?
   A. Attribution theory
   B. Perception
   C. Personality
   D. Organizational behavior

   Answer: B Difficulty: 2 Page: 311

76. All but which of the following factors operate to shape and sometimes distort our perceptions?
   A. The context of the situation
   B. The personal characteristics of the individual
   C. The relationship of the target to its background
   D. The personal characteristics of the individual do not affect perception

   Answer: D Difficulty: 2 Page: 311

77. The theory used to develop an explanation of how we judge people differently depending on the meaning we attribute to a given behavior is known as which of the following?
   A. Attribution theory
   B. Perception
   C. Personality
   D. Organizational behavior

   Answer: A Difficulty: 2 Page: 312

78. All but which of the following determine whether a behavior was internally or externally controlled?
   A. Distinctiveness
   B. Consensus
   C. Halo effect
   D. Consistency

   Answer: C Difficulty: 2 Page: 312

Chapter 10: *Foundations of Individual and Group Behavior*

79. John arrived ten minutes late for work which is his usual routine. This is an example of which of the following?
    A. High consistency
    B. Low consistency
    C. High consensus
    D. Low distinctiveness

    Answer: A Difficulty: 3 Page: 312

80. Jill's sales for last month were 15% less than usual. Ordinarily she meets her sales goal every month. This is an example of which of the following?
    A. High consistency
    B. Low consistency
    C. High consensus
    D. High distinctiveness

    Answer: D Difficulty: 3 Page: 312

81. John arrives ten minutes late for work which is his normal routine. The cause is which of the following?
    A. Internal
    B. External
    C. Consensus
    D. Distinctiveness

    Answer: A Difficulty: 3 Page: 313

82. Last month no one in the department met their sales goal with the new product. The cause is which of the following?
    A. Internal
    B. External
    C. Consistency
    D. Distinctiveness

    Answer: B Difficulty: 3 Page: 313

83. When managers evaluate their employees' performance, they have a tendency to underestimate the influence of external factors and overestimate the influence of internal or personal factors. This is known as which of the following?
    A. Self-serving bias
    B. Fundamental attribution theory
    C. Attribution theory
    D. Perception

    Answer: B Difficulty: 2 Page: 313

84. All but which of the following are shortcuts people use in perceiving and interpreting the behavior of others?
    A. Selectivity
    B. Stereotyping
    C. Self-fulfilling prophecy
    D. Assume differences

    Answer: D Difficulty: 2 Page: 314

85. Susan expects her employees to meet their sales goals each month. She holds high expectations for all her employees. This is an example of which of the following?
    A. Selectivity
    B. Stereotyping
    C. Self-fulfilling prophecy
    D. Assume differences

    Answer: C Difficulty: 3 Page: 314

86. Lane likes to try different jobs and to be challenged by every task with which he is involved. He assumes everyone else wants the same things. This is an example of which of the following?
    A. Selectivity
    B. Stereotyping
    C. Self-fulfilling prophecy
    D. Assumed similarity

    Answer: D Difficulty: 3 Page: 314

87. Helen is a very pleasant person to work with. She is consistently very positive and enthusiastic about her work. Her supervisor rated her high in every area on her performance evaluation based upon this characteristic. This is an example of which of the following?
    A. Selectivity
    B. Stereotyping
    C. Self-fulfilling prophecy
    D. Halo effect

    Answer: D Difficulty: 3 Page: 314

88. "Most women will not relocate for a promotion." This statement is an example of which of the following?
    A. Selectivity
    B. Stereotyping
    C. Self-fulfilling prophecy
    D. Halo effect

    Answer: B Difficulty: 2 Page: 314

Chapter 10:   Foundations of Individual and Group Behavior

89. Which theory argues that behavior is a function of its consequences?
    A. Fundamental attribution theory
    B. Self-serving bias
    C. Operant conditioning
    D. Social learning theory

    Answer: C Difficulty: 2 Page: 315

90. Which of the following strengthens a behavior and increases the likelihood that it will be repeated?
    A. Punishment
    B. Positive reinforcement
    C. Halo effect
    D. Extinction

    Answer: B Difficulty: 2 Page: 315

91. If your performance appraisal reflects the extra hours you spent on your job, which was a considerable amount of overtime, what are you likely to do for your next performance appraisal, according to operant conditioning?
    A. Spend less hours on the job - no overtime
    B. Spend more hours on the job - many hours of overtime
    C. Spend the same amount of hours - no overtime
    D. How many hours of overtime you put in will have nothing to do with your performance appraisal

    Answer: B Difficulty: 3 Page: 316

92. The theory that people can learn through observation and direct experience is which of the following?
    A. Fundamental attribution theory
    B. Self-serving bias
    C. Operant conditioning
    D. Social learning theory

    Answer: D Difficulty: 1 Page: 316

93. Destiny has watched her supervisor run the machine for two hours. Now it is time for her to try the process. This is an example of which of the following?
    A. Attentional processes
    B. Retention processes
    C. Motor reproduction processes
    D. Reinforcement processes

    Answer: C Difficulty: 2 Page: 317

94. Every time Destiny does the process correctly, her supervisor tells her she did a good job. This is an example of which of the following?
   A. Attentional processes
   B. Retention processes
   C. Motor reproduction processes
   D. Reinforcement processes

   Answer: D Difficulty: 2 Page: 317

95. Systematically reinforcing behavior each successive step that moves an individual closer to a desired behavior is which of the following?
   A. Fundamental attribution theory
   B. Shaping behavior
   C. Operant conditioning
   D. Social learning theory

   Answer: B Difficulty: 1 Page: 317

96. All but which of the following are steps a manager can take in shaping the behavior of an employee?
   A. Identify the critical behaviors
   B. Establish a baseline for performance
   C. Measure the change that has occurred
   D. Identify all behaviors

   Answer: D Difficulty: 2 Page: 317

97. Suspending an employee for a week without pay for arriving at work intoxicated would be an example of which of the following?
   A. Positive reinforcement
   B. Negative reinforcement
   C. Punishment
   D. Extinction

   Answer: C Difficulty: 1 Page: 318

98. Which of the following strengthen a desired response and increase the probability of repetition?
   A. Punishment and extinction
   B. Extinction and negative reinforcement
   C. Negative reinforcement and positive reinforcement
   D. Punishment and positive reinforcement

   Answer: C Difficulty: 3 Page: 318

99. Informal groups tend to form around which of the following?
   A. Friendships and common interests
   B. Common interests and directed organizational goals
   C. Social contacts and organizational goals
   D. Organizational goals and friendships

   Answer: A Difficulty: 2 Page: 319

Chapter 10: Foundations of Individual and Group Behavior

100. All but which of the following are reasons why people join groups?
    A. Status
    B. Security
    C. Goal achievement
    D. Desire to be independent

    Answer: D Difficulty: 1 Page: 319

101. Jason joined the newcomers club at work the first day on the job in order to make friends in his new environment. This fulfilled which need?
    A. Self-esteem
    B. Affiliation
    C. Goal achievement
    D. Status

    Answer: B Difficulty: 2 Page: 319

102. Kathy joined the highly-esteemed women's club in order to achieve the prestige that came from belonging to that group. This fulfilled which need?
    A. Self-esteem
    B. Affiliation
    C. Goal achievement
    D. Status

    Answer: D Difficulty: 2 Page: 319

103. Jessica knew that the only way to build the new park was to get a large group of community people behind the project. She organized a group to fulfill which need?
    A. Self-esteem
    B. Affiliation
    C. Goal achievement
    D. Status

    Answer: C Difficulty: 2 Page: 319

104. Since Jessie is now a manager she is expected to wear professional attire, take her breaks in the manager's lounge and eat lunch at the restaurants where the other managers eat. This is an example of which of the following?
    A. Roles
    B. Norms
    C. Status systems
    D. Group cohesiveness

    Answer: A Difficulty: 2 Page: 320

105. After wearing blue jeans to work for three days and getting harassed by fellow coworkers who were wearing slacks or skirts, Janice decided to go buy slacks for work and leave her blue jeans for the weekend. This is an example of which of the following?
    A. Roles
    B. Norms
    C. Status systems
    D. Group cohesiveness

    Answer: B Difficulty: 2 Page: 321

106. An office with a window or a reserved parking space are a sign of which of the following?
    A. Roles
    B. Norms
    C. Status systems
    D. Group cohesiveness

    Answer: C Difficulty: 2 Page: 322

107. All but which of the following statements is true?
    A. Small groups are faster at solving problems
    B. Large groups provide more of a diverse input
    C. Groups of approximately 5-7 members tend to more effective for taking action
    D. As groups get larger, the contribution of individual members grows larger

    Answer: D Difficulty: 2 Page: 323

108. All but which of the following are true statements?
    A. Highly cohesive groups are more effective than less cohesive groups
    B. The more cohesive a group, the more members will follow its goals
    C. If cohesiveness is high and attitudes are unfavorable, productivity increases
    D. If cohesiveness is low and goals are supported, productivity increases but at a reduced level

    Answer: C Difficulty: 3 Page: 323

Chapter 10: Foundations of Individual and Group Behavior

Scenario

Table 10-1
Marjorie has always believed that the most effective way to manage people is to be caring and compassionate. She felt the workplace should be a pleasant environment where people could enjoy coming to work. That worked fine for 15 years until the recent hiring of a new vice-president. Not only does he want the work environment changed so that "people spend more time working and less time on social issues" but he has informed Marjorie she must layoff ten employees in her department in order to cut costs.

109. Referring to Table 10-1, Marjorie spent time in developing which job-related attitude?
    A. Organizational behavior
    B. Job satisfaction
    C. Job involvement
    D. Organizational commitment

    Answer: B Difficulty: 2

110. Referring to Table 10-1, Marjorie is probably suffering which of the following due to the directives issued by the vice-president?
    A. Cognitive dispersion
    B. Cognitive dissonance
    C. Organizational behavior
    D. Organizational development

    Answer: B Difficulty: 2

111. Referring to Table 10-1, all but which of the following will affect the amount of dissonance Marjorie experiences in this situation?
    A. The degree of influence she has over the elements involved
    B. The rewards that may be involved
    C. The importance of the elements involved
    D. The ability of the individual

    Answer: D Difficulty: 2

112. Referring to Table 10-1, since the decision to layoff 10 people is a directive over which Marjorie has little control, her dissonance level will be
    A. Greater
    B. Less
    C. The same
    D. There is no relationship between her dissonance level and the control she has over the directive

    Answer: B Difficulty: 2

113. Referring to Table 10-1, all but which of the following are the choices that Marjorie has in order to deal with her dissonance?
    A. Alter her attitudes
    B. Alter her behavior
    C. Develop a rationalization for the discrepancy
    D. Alter her perceptions

    Answer: D Difficulty: 2

Table 10-2
Talk about personalities. Samantha is sure she has one of everything in her very diverse workforce. Sometimes she wonders if her 20 employees have anything in common. Yesterday Jon came in complaining and blaming her for his poor performance evaluation. He seemed to forget the five differing times during the last six months he and Samantha had sat down and discussed the fact that his continual tardiness and absences were going to affect his evaluation. Then there was Joe, who was always Joe. He was a likable enough person but he was always loud and outspoken and bordered on being rude. Even when the President of the company had been in the office last week, he was still the same Joe. Then there was Cassie who daily made the statement that the end justifies the means. Samantha, more than once, had to remind Cassie of the company code of ethics. Finally, though, there was Sam who quietly and efficiently did her work on a regular consistent basis. She was always ready for a new assignment and trusted that she had the abilities needed in order to succeed on the next project. For Samantha, she was a safety net in times of crisis.

114. Referring to Table 10-2, why should Samantha be concerned about the differing personalities in her workforce?
    A. It helps her in the selection process of matching jobs with employees
    B. It is always interesting
    C. It gives her a basis to fire employees
    D. It is important information to record for performance evaluations

    Answer: A Difficulty: 3

115. Referring to Table 10-2, Jon has which of the following?
    A. Internal locus of control
    B. External locus of control
    C. Low self-esteem
    D. High Machiavellianism

    Answer: B Difficulty: 3

116. Referring to Table 10-2, Joe demonstrates which of the following?
    A. High self-monitoring
    B. Low self-monitoring
    C. Low self-esteem
    D. High Machiavellianism

    Answer: B Difficulty: 3

Chapter 10: Foundations of Individual and Group Behavior

117. Referring to Table 10-2, Cassie demonstrates which of the following?
    A. High self-monitoring
    B. Low self-monitoring
    C. Low self-esteem
    D. High Machiavellianism

    Answer: D Difficulty: 3

118. Referring to Table 10-2, Sam has which of the following?
    A. High self-monitoring
    B. Low self-monitoring
    C. High self-esteem
    D. High Machiavellianism

    Answer: C Difficulty: 3

Table 10-3
Frederic has 15 sales employees for which he is responsible. In the next month, he must conduct performance evaluations for all of his employees. His employees are all so different, sometimes it seems to Frederic there is no way to give an honest appraisal of each individual. Just this morning for example, two employees were late for the weekly sales meeting. Frederic can never remember Carol being late before but Jake is late every week. Jake's constant tardiness for their weekly meeting is the primary characteristic that comes to mind when Frederic sits down to do Jake's performance appraisal. Carol, on the other hand, is always on time, always has her reports in by their due date and always meets all deadlines. Then there is George. George is his outstanding salesperson. Each month Frederic expects more business to be written by George than the previous month and George never lets him down. At least Frederic knows he can depend on George.

119. Referring to Table 10-3, the behavior of Carol is _____ while the tardy behavior of Jake is probably _____.
    A. Externally caused, internally caused
    B. Internally caused, externally caused
    C. Distinctive behavior, consensus behavior
    D. Consensus behavior, consistent behavior

    Answer: A Difficulty: 3

120. Referring to Table 10-3, if Frederic evaluates Jake primarily on his late arrival at the weekly meetings, which distortion will have occurred?
    A. Halo effect
    B. Stereotyping
    C. Self-fulfilling prophecy
    D. Assumed similarity

    Answer: A Difficulty: 2

121. Referring to Table 10-3, when Jake blames Frederic for his poor performance appraisal it is an example of which of the following?
A. Fundamental attribution theory
B. Self-serving bias
C. Perception
D. Attribution theory

Answer: B Difficulty: 3

122. Referring to Table 10-3, if Carol's evaluation is primarily based on her consistency in timeliness, which of the following will have occurred?
A. Halo effect
B. Stereotyping
C. Self-fulfilling prophecy
D. Assumed similarity

Answer: A Difficulty: 2

123. Referring to Table 10-3, Frederic's expectations of George is an example of which of the following?
A. Halo effect
B. Stereotyping
C. Self-fulfilling prophecy
D. Assumed similarity

Answer: C Difficulty: 2

Essay

124. Explain the goals of organizational behavior and its importance.

Answer:
Explain behavior
Predict behavior
Involves looking at individual behavior and group behavior
Managers must accomplish goals through others so in order to be most effective they must understand behavior both of individuals and groups

125. Explain the three components of attitudes.

Answer:
Cognitive - the beliefs, opinion, knowledge or information held by a person
Affective - the emotional or feeling part of a person
Behavioral - the intent to behave in a certain manner toward something or someone

Chapter 10: Foundations of Individual and Group Behavior

126. Describe cognitive dissonance.

   Answer:
   Explains the relationship between attitudes and behavior
   An incompatibility an individual has is uncomfortable and thus an individual will try to lessen the dissonance
   The degree of importance, the degree of influence, and the rewards involved all affect the amount of dissonance experienced

127. Compare and contrast the following: locus of control, Machiavellianism, self-esteem, self-monitoring and risk propensity.

   Answer:
   These five personality traits have proven most powerful in explaining individual behavior in an organization
   Locus of control - the degree to which people believe they are masters of their own fate
   Machiavellianism - the belief that the ends justify the means
   Self-esteem - the degree of like or dislike an individual has for himself/herself
   Self-monitoring - the ability of an individual to adjust his/her behavior to external/situational factors
   Risk propensity - the ability/desire of a person for taking risks

128. Describe three reasons people join groups.

   Answer:
   Security - strength in numbers
   Status - attaining a level of prestige
   Self-esteem - enhancing one's feelings of self-worth
   Affiliation - social needs
   Power - achieving something through a group action not possible individually
   Goal achievement - accomplishing something together that could not be accomplished alone

Chapter 11: Understanding Work Teams

True/False

1. Teams can serve as a source of job satisfaction.

   Answer: T Difficulty: 2 Page: 333

2. Work groups and work teams are the same thing.

   Answer: F Difficulty: 2 Page: 335

3. A work team generates no positive synergy, that is the overall level of performance is no greater than the sum of the individual inputs.

   Answer: F Difficulty: 2 Page: 335

4. A work team that meets regularly to discuss quality problems and solutions but has no authority to implement decisions is a problem-solving team.

   Answer: F Difficulty: 2 Page: 336

5. A self-managed team can result in a decreased importance for supervisory positions.

   Answer: T Difficulty: 1 Page: 338

6. A cross-functional team can be difficult to manage.

   Answer: T Difficulty: 2 Page: 338

7. The positive contribution that diversity makes to teams will probably decline over time and the group will become more cohesive.

   Answer: T Difficulty: 2 Page: 339

8. Teams are automatic productivity enhancers.

   Answer: T Difficulty: 2 Page: 339

9. High-performing teams have members who possess both technical and interpersonal skills.

   Answer: T Difficulty: 2 Page: 340

10. Effective team leaders are increasingly taking the role of coach or facilitator.

    Answer: T Difficulty: 3 Page: 340

Chapter 11: Understanding Work Teams

11. The infrastructure should support team members and reinforce behaviors that lead to high levels of performance.

    Answer: T Difficulty: 2 Page: 341

12. Everyone can be a team player.

    Answer: F Difficulty: 2 Page: 342

13. The challenge of creating team players will be greatest where the national culture has strong collectivism values.

    Answer: F Difficulty: 2 Page: 342

14. Team members need to be reminded of the importance of patience since teams can take longer to do things.

    Answer: T Difficulty: 2 Page: 346

15. Promotions, pay raises, and other forms of recognition should be given to employees for how effective they are as a collaborative team member.

    Answer: T Difficulty: 3 Page: 346

16. Effective teams can become stagnant.

    Answer: T Difficulty: 2 Page: 346

17. Mature teams are prone to groupthink.

    Answer: T Difficulty: 2 Page: 346

18. Historically the relationship between management and labor has been one of cooperation.

    Answer: F Difficulty: 1 Page: 347

19. Labor laws such as the National Labor Relations Act are now working against cooperation between management and labor.

    Answer: T Difficulty: 2 Page: 348

20. The current legal environment does not prohibit labor and management teams in the United States.

    Answer: T Difficulty: 2 Page: 348

21. One of the central characteristics of TQM is the use of teams.

    Answer: T Difficulty: 2 Page: 348

22. Teams are an effective way to provide the continuous improvement the TQM necessitates.

    Answer: T Difficulty: 2 Page: 349

Multiple Choice

23. Ken Ball had what time period to prove to top management that his plan for Imperial Oil Refinery would work?
    A. Six months
    B. 12 months
    C. 18 months
    D. 24 months

    Answer: B Difficulty: 2 Page: 332

24. Ball's analysis of Imperial Oil Refinery showed that which of the following was the main problem?
    A. Technology
    B. Equipment
    C. Management
    D. Employees

    Answer: D Difficulty: 2 Page: 332

25. Teams typically outperform individuals when the tasks being done require all but which of the following?
    A. Multiple skills
    B. Judgement
    C. Quick decisions
    D. Experience

    Answer: C Difficulty: 2 Page: 333

26. All but which of the following are stages in group development?
    A. Storming
    B. Forming
    C. Adjourning
    D. Developing

    Answer: D Difficulty: 2 Page: 333

27. The stage in group development when members are determining what behaviors are acceptable and a great amount of uncertainty occurs is which of the following?
    A. Storming
    B. Forming
    C. Adjourning
    D. Performing

    Answer: B Difficulty: 2 Page: 333

Chapter 11:   Understanding Work Teams

28. Which stage in group development is characterized by conflict over leadership and the controls that the group places on individuals?
    A. Storming
    B. Forming
    C. Adjourning
    D. Performing

    Answer: A Difficulty: 2 Page: 333

29. Which stage in group development is characterized by performing the tasks for which the group was established?
    A. Storming
    B. Forming
    C. Adjourning
    D. Performing

    Answer: D Difficulty: 2 Page: 334

30. In which stage do groups prepare for disbandment?
    A. Storming
    B. Forming
    C. Adjourning
    D. Performing

    Answer: C Difficulty: 1 Page: 334

31. A group that interacts primarily to share information and to make decisions that will help each group member perform within his/her area of responsibility is
    A. A work group
    B. A work team
    C. A quality circle
    D. A functional team

    Answer: A Difficulty: 2 Page: 335

32. A group that engages in collective work that requires joint effort and generates a positive synergy is
    A. A work group
    B. A work team
    C. A quality circle
    D. A functional team

    Answer: B Difficulty: 2 Page: 335

33. A group where the overall level of performance is no greater than the sum of the individual's inputs is which of the following?
   A. A work group
   B. A work team
   C. A quality circle
   D. A functional team

   Answer: A Difficulty: 2 Page: 335

34. All but which of the following are the most common forms of teams?
   A. Functional teams
   B. Problem-solving teams
   C. Self-managed teams
   D. Cross-matrix teams

   Answer: D Difficulty: 2 Page: 336

35. Which of the following types of teams are involved in efforts to improve work activities or to solve specific problems within a particular unit of the company?
   A. Functional teams
   B. Problem-solving teams
   C. Self-managed teams
   D. Cross-matrix teams

   Answer: A Difficulty: 2 Page: 336

36. Teams that meet weekly to discuss ways of improving quality, efficiency, and the work environment are called which of the following?
   A. Functional teams
   B. Problem-solving teams
   C. Self-managed teams
   D. Quality circles

   Answer: B Difficulty: 2 Page: 336

37. Teams that meet regularly to discuss quality problems, investigate the causes of the problems, recommend solutions but do not have the authority to make a final decision are called
   A. Functional teams
   B. Problem-solving teams
   C. Self-managed teams
   D. Quality circles

   Answer: D Difficulty: 2 Page: 336

Chapter 11:   Understanding Work Teams

38. Which of the following did Mei-Lin Cheng and her team tackle at Hewlett-Packard?
    A. Computer viruses
    B. Development of a new data base that would cover customer orders to inventory control
    C. Restructuring the organization
    D. Development of a new computer

    Answer: B Difficulty: 2 Page: 337

39. A formal group who operates without a manager and are responsible for a complete work process or segment that delivers a product or service to an internal or external customer is known as which of the following?
    A. Functional teams
    B. Problem-solving teams
    C. Self-managed teams
    D. Quality circles

    Answer: C Difficulty: 2 Page: 338

40. Which of the following types of teams results in supervisory positions taking on a decreased importance and even being eliminated?
    A. Functional teams
    B. Problem-solving teams
    C. Self-managed teams
    D. Quality circles

    Answer: C Difficulty: 2 Page: 338

41. A work team that is brought together to accomplish a particular task is which of the following?
    A. Functional teams
    B. Problem-solving teams
    C. Self-managed teams
    D. Cross-functional teams

    Answer: D Difficulty: 2 Page: 338

42. Which of the following types of teams is an effective way to exchange information, develop new ideas, solve problems and coordinate complex tasks?
    A. Functional teams
    B. Problem-solving teams
    C. Self-managed teams
    D. Cross-functional teams

    Answer: D Difficulty: 2 Page: 338

Testbank

43. Which of the following types of teams can be very difficult to manage?
    A. Functional teams
    B. Problem-solving teams
    C. Self-managed teams
    D. Cross-functional teams

    Answer: D Difficulty: 2 Page: 338

44. Individuals who are capable of readjusting their work skills are able to do which of the following?
    A. Job-morph
    B. Change jobs
    C. Work on interpersonal skills
    D. Be a team leader

    Answer: A Difficulty: 2 Page: 340

45. High-performing teams have members who possess both technical skills and _____ skills.
    A. Managerial
    B. Technological
    C. Interpersonal
    D. Nonconformity skills

    Answer: C Difficulty: 2 Page: 340

46. Which of the following is strongly influenced by organizational culture and management actions?
    A. Clear understanding of the goal
    B. Job-morphing
    C. Communication
    D. Trust

    Answer: D Difficulty: 3 Page: 340

47. The willingness of team members to do anything that has to be done to help the team succeed is known as
    A. Unified commitment
    B. Job-morphing
    C. Communication
    D. Trust

    Answer: A Difficulty: 2 Page: 340

48. Since teams tend to be flexible and continuously making adjustments, team members also need _____ skills?
    A. Technological
    B. Technical
    C. Negotiating
    D. Groupthink

    Answer: C Difficulty: 2 Page: 340

Chapter 11:   Understanding Work Teams

49. Effective team leaders today can best be described by which of the following terms?
    A. The boss
    B. The team leader
    C. A coach or facilitator
    D. Dictatorial

    Answer: C Difficulty: 2 Page: 341

50. All but which of the following are ways a manager can build trust among teams?
    A. Be a team player
    B. Keep confidences
    C. Practice disclosing only the information that is needed by the group
    D. Demonstrate competence

    Answer: C Difficulty: 3 Page: 341

51. Which of the following is the one substantial barrier to using work teams?
    A. Lack of creativity
    B. Lack of diversity
    C. Individual resistance
    D. Open communication

    Answer: C Difficulty: 2 Page: 342

52. In order to perform well as team members, individuals must be able to do all but which of the following?
    A. Communicate openly and honestly
    B. Confront differences and resolve conflicts
    C. Place a high priority on personal goals
    D. Place a lower priority on personal goals for the good of the team

    Answer: C Difficulty: 1 Page: 342

53. The challenge of creating team players will be greatest when all but the following occurs?
    A. The national culture is highly individualistic
    B. The national culture is values collectivism
    C. Teams are used in established organizations that have traditionally valued individual achievement
    D. Teams are not used in the original organizational infrastructure

    Answer: B Difficulty: 2 Page: 342

212

54. All but which of the following are options when managers are trying to turn individuals into team players?
    A. Proper selection
    B. Employee training
    C. Rewarding the appropriate team behaviors
    D. Rewarding the appropriate individual behaviors

    Answer: D Difficulty: 2 Page: 344

55. When hiring team members, in addition to technical skills individuals should also possess?
    A. Technological skills
    B. Interpersonal skills
    C. Environmental skills
    D. Groupthink skills

    Answer: B Difficulty: 2 Page: 344

56. The research by Margerison and McCann suggests that which roles are needed in order for teams to be successful?
    A. All roles are needed
    B. Creator-innovator
    C. Linkers
    D. Upholders-maintainers

    Answer: A Difficulty: 2 Page: 345

57. A team player who is concerned with establishing operating procedures that turn ideas into reality and get things done is which of the following?
    A. Thruster-organizers
    B. Creator-innovator
    C. Linkers
    D. Upholders-maintainers

    Answer: A Difficulty: 2 Page: 345

58. A team player who is a good listener and encourage team members to seek additional information before making decisions is which of the following?
    A. Thruster-organizers
    B. Creator-innovator
    C. Reporter-advisors
    D. Upholders-maintainers

    Answer: C Difficulty: 2 Page: 345

Chapter 11:   Understanding Work Teams

59. A team player who tries to understand all views and try to build cooperation among all team members is which of the following?
    A. Thruster-organizers
    B. Creator-innovator
    C. Linkers
    D. Upholders-maintainers

    Answer: C Difficulty: 2 Page: 345

60. All but which of the following are topics that a training specialist may cover when training teams?
    A. Team problem solving
    B. Communication
    C. Negotiation
    D. Environmental scanning

    Answer: D Difficulty: 2 Page: 346

61. Reward systems for teams should focus on which of the following?
    A. Individual contribution
    B. Effectiveness as a team member
    C. Individual contribution to the team goals
    D. Reward systems should not be tied to team behavior

    Answer: B Difficulty: 3 Page: 346

62. Mature teams are particularly prone to
    A. High levels of performance
    B. Continuing innovative solutions
    C. Groupthink
    D. Effective communication

    Answer: C Difficulty: 3 Page: 347

63. All but which of the following are techniques a manager can use to reinvigorate mature work teams?
    A. Offer refresher training
    B. Offer advanced training
    C. Encourage team members to treat their development as a constant learning experience
    D. Do not address maturity problems until they arise

    Answer: D Difficulty: 1 Page: 347

64. The key theme that labor laws appear to be conveying is that where work teams are introduced, which of the following must occur?
    A. Work teams must have power to make decisions and act independent of management
    B. Work teams must have power to make decisions in cooperation with management
    C. Work teams must be independent of direct management control although management has final authority on decisions made
    D. Work teams must constantly work in cooperation with management

    Answer: A Difficulty: 3 Page: 348

65. Answering yes to any but which of the following questions may indicate the team may be illegal in a unionized setting?
    A. Does management dominate the team?
    B. Is the team independent?
    C. Does the team deal with traditional bargaining issues?
    D. Does the team deal with management on any issues?

    Answer: B Difficulty: 3 Page: 348

66. One of the central characteristics of TQM is
    A. Communication
    B. Teams
    C. Management support
    D. Large, sweeping improvements

    Answer: B Difficulty: 2 Page: 348

67. The essence of TQM is process improvement and which of the following is the key to process improvement?
    A. Communication
    B. Top management
    C. Employee participation
    D. Technology

    Answer: C Difficulty: 2 Page: 349

Chapter 11: Understanding Work Teams

Scenario

Table 11-1
Sairah has just returned from a seminar dealing with the research of Margerison and McCann where the roles of work team members was discussed. She is enthusiastic as she sets down to select members for the new team she is developing. Hopefully she can avoid some problems of past teams by selecting individuals to fill the roles needed by the work team. Jim comes to mind immediately. He is one of the most imaginative people Sairah knows. He continuously comes up with new and novel ideas; however, he is very independent and likes to work at his own pace. Ruby, on the other hand, has an extreme concern for following policies and rules. He is excellent at examining details and making sure all the facts and figures will work. Putting those two together on a team, though, may pose some interpersonal problems since they are so different. Then there is Shane. He always has such strong convictions about how things should be done. However, he will protect the group from outsiders and go to battle for them. He will help provide team stability.

68. Referring to Table 11-1, which team role will Jim effectively play?
    A. Linkers
    B. Creator-innovators
    C. Controller-inspectors
    D. Reporter-advisors

    Answer: B

69. Referring to Table 11-1, which team role will Ruby play?
    A. Linkers
    B. Creator-innovators
    C. Controller-inspectors
    D. Reporter-advisors

    Answer: C

70. Referring to Table 11-1, what role needs to be fulfilled in order to enable Jim and Ruby to effectively work together?
    A. Linkers
    B. Assessor-developers
    C. Controller-inspectors
    D. Reporter-advisors

    Answer: A

71. Referring to Table 11-1, what team role will Shane play?
    A. Upholder-maintainers
    B. Assessor-developers
    C. Controller-inspectors
    D. Reporter-advisors

    Answer: A

72. Referring to Table 11-1, which role is the most important role to have filled in order for the team to be effective?
    A. Linkers
    B. Concluder-producers
    C. Upholder-maintainers
    D. All roles are needed in order for the team to be most effective

Answer: D

Table 11-2
Shannon had never been a member of a team before. Her organization had always highly valued individual effort. Consequently, the switch to teams had been difficult. Furthermore, there had been no training in team development. And right now, Shannon was not certain they were ever going to get past this current stage of continuous intragroup conflict. There was a lot of conflict over who was going to lead the team. Once everyone had thought of themselves as part of the team, not just a group of individuals, Shannon had thought things would start to get better. That first stage had been very difficult but now the second stage seemed no better. Shannon wondered if they would ever reach a stage of cohesiveness where close relationships would start to develop. Furthermore, at this point she was not sure they would ever get to the point of actually performing the task they had been set up for, which was to work across functions to develop a new piece of surgical equipment. Since the team was to be disbanded in two years, Shannon was afraid they were going to spend their whole two years becoming a team and never actually develop the new equipment.

73. Referring to Table 11-2, which stage is the group currently in?
    A. Adjourning
    B. Performing
    C. Norming
    D. Storming

Answer: D

74. Referring to Table 11-2, the first stage the group worked through was which of the following?
    A. Adjourning
    B. Performing
    C. Forming
    D. Storming

Answer: C

75. Referring to Table 11-2, which stage is Shannon afraid the group will never reach?
    A. Adjourning
    B. Performing
    C. Forming
    D. Storming

Answer: B

Chapter 11: Understanding Work Teams

76. Referring to Table 11-2, which stage is characterized by cohesiveness and close relationships?
    A. Adjourning
    B. Performing
    C. Norming
    D. Storming

    Answer: C

77. Referring to Table 11-2, which of the following best describes this group of individuals?
    A. Work group
    B. Work team
    C. Problem-solving team
    D. Quality circle

    Answer: B

Table 11-3
Richard knew that just switching to teams was not going to necessarily increase productivity. He knew that there were some characteristics he needed to ensure that the group possessed in order for the group to be most effective. He knew that the group members needed the requisite technical skills but he wondered if there were any other skills he needed to ensure every group member also had. He knew the group was going to have to be willing to put aside individual goals and focus on the success of the team goals. He knew the group would need to be characterized by dedication to the team's goals and a willingness to expend extraordinary amounts of energy in order to achieve the goals. He also knew that some individual work skills would have to be readjusted in order to benefit the team.

78. Referring to Table 11-3, all but which of the following are characteristics the group needs in order to be effective?
    A. Clear understanding of the goal
    B. Unified commitment
    C. Groupthink
    D. Effective leadership

    Answer: C

79. Referring to Table 11-3, what other skills/skill is needed by the group members besides the requisite technical skills?
    A. Technological skills
    B. Interpersonal skills
    C. Environmental skills
    D. Nonconformity skills

    Answer: B

80. Referring to Table 11-3, Richard also knew that effective leadership could help a team through difficult situations by doing which of the following?
    A. Making the decision for the group
    B. Representing top management in having final authority over all group actions
    C. Clarifying goals
    D. Job-morphing

    Answer: C

81. Referring to Table 11-3, the willingness of the group to do what it takes to help the group succeed is known as which of the following?
    A. Unified commitment
    B. Team commitment
    C. Goal attainment
    D. Team loyalty

    Answer: A

82. Referring to Table 11-3, when team members can readjust their work skills to fit the needs of the team, it is referred to as which of the following?
    A. Unified commitment
    B. Team loyalty
    C. Job-morphing
    D. Goal attainment

    Answer: C

Essay

83. Explain why work teams are growing in popularity today.
    They typically outperform individuals when the tasks require multiple skills, judgement and experiences which is ever needed today
    They are more flexible and adaptable to the changing environment
    They also enhance employee involvement, increase employee morale, and promote work force diversity

    Answer:
    Compare and contrast the five stages of team development.
    Forming - people join the team and define its purpose
    Storming - intragroup conflict arises
    Norming - close relationships develop and cohesiveness develops
    Performing - the tasks for which the group was developed actually get accomplished
    Adjourning - the group disbands

Chapter 11:   Understanding Work Teams

84. Describe three common types of work teams.

    Answer:
    Functional teams - involved in efforts to improve work activities or to solve specific problems within a particular functional unit
    Problem-solving teams - meets weekly to discuss ways of improve quality, efficiency and the work environment
    Quality circles - meets regularly to discuss quality problems, investigate the causes of problems, recommends solutions, but has no authority to implement decisions
    Self-managed teams - group without a manager who is responsible for a complete work process or segment that delivers a product/service to an internal/external customers
    Cross-functional teams - employees from different work areas who are brought together to accomplish a particular task

85. Discuss four characteristics of high-performing work teams

    Answer:
    Clear goals
    Members who have the necessary technical and interpersonal skills
    Mutual trust
    Unified commitment
    Good communication
    Effective leadership
    Adequate negotiating skills

86. Explain the role of teams in TQM.

    Answer:
    Teams are one of the central characteristics
    Employee participation is the key to process improvement and teams are an effective way to involve employees
    TQM requires employees to share ideas and then have those ideas enacted

Chapter 12: Motivating and Rewarding Employees

True/False

1. Motivation is a personal trait, that is some people are motivated and some people are not motivated.

    Answer: F

2. The level of motivation stays the same both between individuals and within individuals at different times.

    Answer: F

3. McGregor developed the hierarchy of needs theory.

    Answer: F

4. A Theory X manager would believe that people dislike work.

    Answer: T

5. A Theory Y manager would believe that people seek out responsibility.

    Answer: T

6. The most effective managers use only Theory Y.

    Answer: F

7. Working conditions and salary are examples of hygiene factors, according to Herzberg.

    Answer: T

8. Recognition and growth are examples of motivation factors, according to Herzberg.

    Answer: T

9. The need to make others behave in a way that they would not have behaved otherwise is known as the need for achievement, according to McClelland.

    Answer: F

10. Employees with a high need for achievement will avoid what they perceive to be very easy or very difficult tasks.

    Answer: T

Chapter 12: Motivating and Rewarding Employees

11. When inequities occur, according to Adams, employees attempt to correct the situation.

    Answer: T

12. A state of inequity exists when employees perceive their ratio of inputs-outcomes to be equal to those of their relevant others.

    Answer: F

13. Whenever employees perceive inequity, they will seek to correct the situation.

    Answer: T

14. Currently, the most comprehensive explanation of motivation is McClelland's three-need theory.

    Answer: F

15. In Vroom's expectancy theory, the degree to which the individual believes that performing at a particular level will lead to attainment of the desired outcome is the attractiveness variable.

    Answer: F

16. Expectancy theory emphasizes payoff or rewards.

    Answer: T

17. Managers need to reward employees with those things that they value most positively, according to expectancy theory.

    Answer: T

18. Understanding motivation is maximized when each theory is looked at independently.

    Answer: F

19. Using expectancy theory, a person's perception of the outcome is more important than the reality of the outcome.

    Answer: T

20. Managers must change motivational techniques to fit the cultural differences in their diverse work force.

    Answer: T

21. In collectivist nations, such as Japan and Mexico, motivation focused on self-interest will be effective.

    Answer: F

22. The fear of being fired in Japan and Mexico is less effective than in the United States, when considering motivation.

    Answer: T

23. Recognizing and embarrassing the worst sales clerk by giving them an award may be effective in the United States but it will not work in China.

    Answer: F

24. To motivate employees, a manager should choose a method that motivates a majority of his or her employees

    Answer: F

25. Pay-for-performance programs focus on paying an employee for time on the job not a specific performance measure.

    Answer: F

26. The growing popularity of pay-for-performance can be explained in terms of motivation and cost control.

    Answer: T

27. Pay based upon leadership skills, problem solving skills, or strategic planning skills would be pay-for-performance compensation.

    Answer: F

28. Employee Stock Ownership Programs positively affect productivity and employee satisfaction.

    Answer: T

29. Organizations should not expect immediate increases in employee motivation and productivity using ESOPs, but over time increases in these areas should occur.

    Answer: T

30. Employees are motivated only by money.

    Answer: F

Chapter 12:   Motivating and Rewarding Employees

31. Praise, employee recognition, and empowerment are motivational techniques that managers can use to motivate minimum-wage workers.

    Answer: T

Multiple Choice

32. FormPac Corporation produces which of the following?
    A. Custom plastic products
    B. Packing forms for fine china
    C. Packing forms for rare art
    D. Cookies packaged so that they do not crumble

    Answer: A   357

33. What did William Duff of FormPac Corporation change that increased company profits by 25%?
    A. The product
    B. Strategic planning
    C. The method by which bonuses were awarded
    D. The structure of the organization to include functional teams

    Answer: C

34. The willingness to exert high levels of effort to reach organizational goals, conditioned by the effort's ability to satisfy some individual need is known as which of the following?
    A. Team work
    B. Motivation
    C. Needs
    D. Theory X

    Answer: B   p.358

35. All but which of the following are key components in the definition of motivation?
    A. Effort
    B. Organizational goals
    C. Wants
    D. Needs

    Answer: C   p.358

36. High levels of effort are unlikely to lead to favorable job performance unless
    A. Technology is also considered
    B. Quality of the effort is also considered
    C. Team work is also considered
    D. Management efforts are also considered

    Answer: B

224

Testbank

37. An internal state that makes certain outcomes appear attractive is which of the following?
   A. Team work
   B. Motivation
   C. Needs
   D. Theory X

   Answer: C   p.358

38. Motivated employees are in a state of
   A. Chaos
   B. Equilibrium
   C. Tension
   D. Serenity

   Answer: C

39. The greater the tension level of the motivated employee, the _____ the effort level.
   A. Lower
   B. Higher
   C. Same
   D. There is no relationship between tension level and effort level

   Answer: B

40. The best-known theory of motivation is which of the following?
   A. Maslow's hierarchy of needs
   B. McGregor's theory X and theory Y
   C. Herzberg's motivation-hygiene theory
   D. McClelland's three-needs theory

   Answer: A   p.359

41. All but which of the following are needs in Maslow's hierarchy of needs theory?
   A. Physiological needs
   B. Safety needs
   C. Environmental needs
   D. Esteem needs

   Answer: C   p.359

42. A person who is looking for affection, belongingness, acceptance and friendship is at which need level, according to Maslow?
   A. Physiological needs
   B. Safety needs
   C. Social needs
   D. Esteem needs

   Answer: C   359

225

Chapter 12: *Motivating and Rewarding Employees*

43. John has a job that pays well, desires to make a contribution to the organization, has an active social life and his overpowering drive now is to become all the he is capable of becoming. At which level is John?
    A. Self-actualization
    B. Safety
    C. Social
    D. Esteem

    Answer: C

44. At the top of Maslow's hierarchy of needs is which of the following?
    A. Esteem needs
    B. Social needs
    C. Self-actualization needs
    D. Safety needs

    Answer: C p 360

45. According to Maslow, when does a need stop motivating?
    A. When it is substantially satisfied
    B. A need never stops motivating
    C. When an individual returns to a lower level need
    D. When the next level of needs is achieved

    Answer: A

46. Which of the following statements would a Theory Y manager consider to be true?
    A. Employees dislike work
    B. Employees must be coerced, controlled or threatened
    C. Employees view work as being as natural as rest or play
    D. Employees will shirk responsibilities whenever possible

    Answer: C   p.360

47. Which of the following statements would a Theory X manager consider to be true?
    A. Employees view work as being as natural as play
    B. Employees will exercise self-direction if they are committed to the objectives
    C. The average person can learn to accept, even seek, responsibility
    D. Employees will shirk responsibility

    Answer: D

48. Mangers who use which of the following theories will be most successful?
    A. Theory X
    B. Theory Y
    C. Neither theory is effective
    D. Both theories can be used successfully

    Answer: D

49. Who developed the motivation-hygiene theory?
    A. Victor Vroom
    B. Douglas McGregor
    C. Frederick Herzberg
    D. Abraham Maslow

    Answer: C   p. 364

50. The theory that intrinsic factors are related to job satisfaction and extrinsic factors are related to job dissatisfaction is which of the following?
    A. Maslow's hierarchy of needs
    B. McGregor's theory x and theory y
    C. Vroom's expectancy theory
    D. Herzberg's motivation-hygiene theory

    Answer: D   p. 364

51. Salary, working conditions and security are examples of which of the following?
    A. Theory X
    B. Theory Y
    C. Motivators
    D. Hygiene factors

    Answer: D   p 366

52. Achievement, recognition, and growth are examples of which of the following?
    A. Theory X
    B. Theory Y
    C. Motivators
    D. Hygiene factors   p. 364

    Answer: C

53. Those factors that increase job satisfaction are which of the following?
    A. Theory X
    B. Theory Y
    C. Motivators
    D. Hygiene factors

    Answer: C   364

54. When these factors are present, people will not be dissatisfied but neither will they be satisfied.
    A. Theory X
    B. Theory Y
    C. Motivators
    D. Hygiene factors

    Answer: D

Chapter 12: Motivating and Rewarding Employees

55. Which of the following is not a major relevant need in work situations, according to McClelland?
    A. Need for achievement
    B. Need for power
    C. Need for recognition
    D. Need for affiliation

    Answer: C

56. Which of the following needs, according to McClelland, focuses on the need to make others behave in a way that they would not have behaved otherwise?
    A. Need for achievement
    B. Need for power
    C. Need for recognition
    D. Need for affiliation

    Answer: B   p.346

57. People with this need will avoid what they perceive to be very easy or very difficult tasks.
    A. Need for achievement
    B. Need for power
    C. Need for recognition
    D. Need for affiliation

    Answer: A

58. People with this need prefer to be in competitive and status-oriented situations.
    A. Need for achievement
    B. Need for power
    C. Need for recognition
    D. Need for affiliation

    Answer: B   346

59. Jessica strives to develop friendships, prefers to work in cooperative situations and works toward a high degree of mutual understanding in her relationships. She is demonstrating which need?
    A. Need for achievement
    B. Need for power
    C. Need for recognition
    D. Need for affiliation

    Answer: D

60. Which theory focuses on employee perceptions of what they get from a job situation in relation to what they put into it and then compare their inputs-outcomes ratio with the inputs-outcomes ratios of relevant others?
    A. Vroom's expectancy theory
    B. Adam's equity theory
    C. Herzberg's motivation-hygiene theory
    D. McClelland's three-need theory

    Answer: B

61. If employees perceive their input-outcomes ratio to be equal to the relevant others which they compare themselves to, then
    A. A state of equity exists
    B. A state of inequity exists
    C. A state of dissatisfaction is present
    D. A state of disequilibrium is present

    Answer: A   p.367
    A
    Moderate

62. When inequities exist, employees
    A. Do not mind
    B. Do not notice
    C. Attempt to correct the inequities
    D. Disregard the information obtained

    Answer: C

63. The three referent categories that employees choose to compare themselves to are all but which of the following?
    A. Other
    B. System
    C. Self
    D. Management

    Answer: D

64. All but which of the following statements is true concerning equity pay propositions?
    A. Given payment by time, overrewarded employees will produce more than equitably paid employees
    B. Given payment by quantity, overrewarded employees will produce fewer but high-quality units
    C. Given payment by time, underrewarded employees will produce more units or poorer-quality units
    D. Given payment by time, underrewarded employees will produce less units or poorer-quality units

    Answer: C

Chapter 12: Motivating and Rewarding Employees

65. The theory that an individual tends to act in a certain way in the expectation that the act will be followed by a given outcome and according to the attractiveness of the outcome is which of the following?
    A. Vroom's expectancy theory
    B. Adam's equity theory
    C. Herzberg's motivation-hygiene theory
    D. McClelland's three-needs theory

    Answer: A

66. Currently, the most comprehensive explanation of motivation is which of the following?
    A. Vroom's expectancy theory
    B. Adam's equity theory
    C. Herzberg's motivation-hygiene theory
    D. McClelland's three-needs theory

    Answer: A

67. All but which of the following are the three variables that are central to Vroom's expectancy theory?
    A. Effort-performance
    B. Performance-reward
    C. Effort-reward
    D. Attractiveness

    Answer: C

68. If the producers meet their sales goals for the month, they are given an all-expense paid trip to a Denver Bronco football game. Football is not one of Houston's favorite sports and the Denver Broncos are definitely not his favorite team. Using Vroom's expectancy theory, which variable would this fall under?
    A. Effort-performance
    B. Performance-reward
    C. Effort-reward
    D. Attractiveness

    Answer: D

69. Sabrina's supervisor just told her if she works overtime this weekend she can have two days off next week as comp time. Last month Sabrina worked one weekend and still has not received her promised two days off. This is an example of which variable using Vroom's expectancy theory?
    A. Effort-performance
    B. Performance-reward
    C. Effort-reward
    D. Attractiveness

    Answer: B

70. Katina has just been asked to type up a report in two days using a software program she has never seen before. Furthermore, 15 graphs, bar charts, and pie charts are an integral part of the report. She will have to use a color printer in a different department because their department does not have a color printer. Katina wonders she will get the project accomplished on time and in the format wanted by her manager. This is an example of which variable using Vroom's expectancy theory?
    A. Effort-performance
    B. Performance-reward
    C. Effort-reward
    D. Attractiveness

    Answer: A

71. All but which of the following statements is true concerning Vroom's expectancy theory?
    A. It is based on self-interest where each employee seeks to maximize personal satisfaction
    B. Managers must understand which rewards employees will positively value
    C. The employee must see the connection between performance and rewards
    D. The theory is concerned with reality not with perceptions

    Answer: D

72. An understanding of motivation is maximized when all theories are
    A. Looked at independently
    B. Looked at interdependently
    C. Looked at individually
    D. None of the theories in the chapter are relevant today

    Answer: B Difficulty: 3 Page: 373

73. To maximize motivation in today's diverse work force, management must focus on
    A. Using the same techniques for everyone
    B. Regularly using the same techniques
    C. Being flexible
    D. Any motivational theory will work with any individual

    Answer: C Difficulty: 2 Page: 374

74. Steps a manager can use to motivate employees include all but which of the following?
    A. Match people to jobs
    B. Use goals
    C. Make all rewards the same
    D. Link rewards to performance

    Answer: C Difficulty: 2 Page: 375

Chapter 12:   Motivating and Rewarding Employees

75. Steps a manager can use to motivate employees include all but which of the following?
    A. Check the system for equity
    B. Individualize rewards
    C. Ensure that the goals are a stretch for the employee and even unattainable for the best employees
    D. Do not ignore the motivational impact of money

    Answer: C Difficulty: 2 Page: 375

76. All but which of the following countries place value on the self-interest concept and individualism?
    A. United States
    B. Great Britain
    C. Singapore
    D. Australia

    Answer: C Difficulty: 3 Page: 376

77. Employees in all but which of the following countries should be more receptive to team-based job design, group goals, and group-performance evaluations?
    A. Venezuela
    B. Japan
    C. Singapore
    D. Australia

    Answer: D Difficulty: 3 Page: 376

78. Compensation plans, such as piece-rate plans, and profit sharing, that pay employees on the basis of some performance measure are which of the following?
    A. Competency-based compensation
    B. Employee stock ownership programs
    C. Wages
    D. Pay-for-performance programs

    Answer: D Difficulty: 1 Page: 376

79. Under pay-for-performance programs, employees are compensated for
    A. How hard they try
    B. Performance on the job
    C. Time on the job
    D. Seniority

    Answer: B Difficulty: 2 Page: 377

80. A program that pays and rewards employees on the basis of skills, knowledge or behavior that they possess is which of the following?
    A. Competency-based compensation
    B. Employee stock ownership programs
    C. Wages
    D. Pay-for-performance programs

    Answer: A Difficulty: 1 Page: 377

81. Fifteen percent of Johanna's salary is based upon retail sales, profits and customer satisfaction. This is an example of which of the following?
    A. Competency-based compensation
    B. Employee stock ownership programs
    C. Wages
    D. Pay-for-performance programs

    Answer: D Difficulty: 2 Page: 377

82. A compensation program in which employees become part owners of the organization by receiving stock as a performance incentive is which of the following?
    A. Competency-based compensation
    B. Employee stock ownership programs
    C. Wages
    D. Pay-for-performance programs

    Answer: B Difficulty: 1 Page: 377

83. Sally receives shares of stock in the company she works for as a part of her compensation package. This is an example of which of the following?
    A. Competency-based compensation
    B. Employee stock ownership programs
    C. Wages
    D. Pay-for-performance programs

    Answer: B Difficulty: 1 Page: 378

84. Besides money, all but which of the following are other rewards managers can use to motivate minimum-wage employees?
    A. Employee recognition
    B. Crew member of the month
    C. Praise used for manipulative purposes only
    D. Empowerment

    Answer: C Difficulty: 1 Page: 379

Chapter 12: Motivating and Rewarding Employees

Scenario

Table 12-1
Jericho has several employees with a wide range of behaviors. He has been having a difficult time understanding where some of his employees are at as far as motivation is concerned. He has just returned from a conference where Maslow's hierarchy of needs was discussed and some of his employees seem to fall in those categories. First there is Julie. She was just hired last week and her preoccupation at the moment seems to be finding a place to live, grocery stores, and the things like the fire and police department locations. Jericho wonders if she will ever start thinking about work. Then there is Jamie. When Jericho asked her to work late next month, she said it was no problem as long as there was a security person to walk her across the company campus to the underground parking lot. Jericho easily arranged for the security guard. Then there is Jason who just yesterday complained that his work was not challenging enough. He said he was not growing or using his full potential at what he was doing. Jessica also came to mind. What would he do with Jessica. She was their social butterfly, constantly flitting from one work station to another chatting with the employees and not only not getting her work done but also interrupting everyone else's work. And finally there was Lane who constantly needed attention and public recognition. If Lane accomplished a goal, he wanted everyone in the work area to realize he had made his goal. What a group of employees, thought Jericho.

85. Referring to Table 12-1, at which level is Julie currently functioning?
    A. Physiological needs
    B. Safety needs
    C. Social needs
    D. Esteem needs

    Answer: A Difficulty: 2

86. Referring to Table 12-1, at which level is Jamie when she is concerned about working late next month?
    A. Physiological needs
    B. Safety needs
    C. Social needs
    D. Esteem needs

    Answer: B Difficulty: 2

87. Referring to Table 12-1, Jason would like his work to take him to which level?
    A. Self-actualization
    B. Safety needs
    C. Social needs
    D. Esteem needs

    Answer: A Difficulty: 2

88. Referring to Table 12-1, Lane is at which level?
    A. Physiological needs
    B. Safety needs
    C. Social needs
    D. Esteem needs

    Answer: D Difficulty: 2

89. Referring to Table 12-1, Jessica is at which level?
    A. Physiological needs
    B. Safety needs
    C. Social needs
    D. Esteem needs

    Answer: C Difficulty: 2

Table 12-2
Weston has two very different first-line supervisors who report directly to him. Aaron really "cracks the whip" on his employees and firmly believes in strict controls and punishment for those employees who do not fulfill their job descriptions. Zach, on the other hand, has very few controls and believes that as long as people know what their objectives are, they will exercise self-control and self-direction. Aaron has been trying to use working conditions to increase the level of productivity in his department. Work conditions have not been very safe and employees have complained frequently that they felt unsafe at work. However, when conditions were improved, productivity was unaffected. Zach had chosen to use responsibility and the opportunity for growth to increase his productivity levels and he had been much more successful.

90. Referring to Table 12-2, Aaron is what type of manager?
    A. Theory X
    B. Theory Y
    C. Democratic
    D. Laissez-faire

    Answer: A Difficulty: 2

91. Referring to Table 12-2, Zach is what type of manager?
    A. Theory X
    B. Theory Y
    C. Dictatorial
    D. Autocratic

    Answer: B Difficulty: 2

Chapter 12:   *Motivating and Rewarding Employees*

92. Referring to Table 12-2, employees were at which level in the hierarchy of needs in Aaron's department?
    A. Physiological
    B. Social
    C. Safety
    D. Esteem

    Answer: C Difficulty: 2

93. Referring to Table 12-2, Aaron was trying to use what types of factors to increase productivity?
    A. Motivators
    B. Hygiene factors
    C. Social factors
    D. Esteem factors

    Answer: B Difficulty: 2

94. Referring to Table 12-2, Zach was using which types of factors to increase productivity levels?
    A. Motivators
    B. Hygiene factors
    C. Social factors
    D. Esteem factors

    Answer: A Difficulty: 2

Table 12-3
It seems Bill will never determine what motivates his group of 10 employees. He realizes everyone is different but that certainly complicates motivational issues. It seems like the only thing that motivates Jerri is the desire to have an impact and to be influential. She loves to be in charge. If she is not "in charge" she contributes very little to the project, whereas if she is in charge she will work beyond the level of anyone else. Nancy always wants to succeed. She seems to have a desire to excel at all she does. Then there is Tim. Bill gave Tim an assignment last month where he had to work by himself for the majority of the project with very little interaction from anyone else. Furthermore, it had taken him away from the workplace the majority of the month. Tim's productivity level fell dramatically and Bill wondered why.

95. Referring to Table 12-3, which need is highest for Jerri, according to McClelland?
    A. Need for achievement
    B. Need for power
    C. Need for affiliation
    D. Need for success

    Answer: B Difficulty: 2

96. Referring to Table 12-3, which need is highest for Nancy, according to McClelland?
    A. Need for achievement
    B. Need for power
    C. Need for affiliation
    D. Need for success

    Answer: A Difficulty: 2

97. Referring to Table 12-3, Nancy will probably avoid all but which of the following tasks?
    A. Very easy tasks
    B. Very difficult tasks
    C. Tasks that cause her to stretch personally
    D. Tasks where the success is due in large part to luck

    Answer: C Difficulty: 3

98. Referring to Table 12-3, which need is probably highest for Tim?
    A. Need for achievement
    B. Need for power
    C. Need for affiliation
    D. Need for success

    Answer: C Difficulty: 2

99. Referring to Table 12-3, which of the following people would demonstrate a high level of productivity if the project assigned to them provided them a very competitive situation where the status of being placed on that project was quite high, although a large part of the success of the project would be due to luck?
    A. Nancy
    B. Tim
    C. Jerri
    D. Bill

    Answer: C Difficulty: 3

Essay

100. Describe the motivational process.

    Answer:
    The process of willingly exerting high levels of effort toward organizational goals, conditioned by the individual's ability to satisfy some need
    Begins with an unsatisfied need, which creates tensions and the desire to alleviate that tension

Chapter 12: Motivating and Rewarding Employees

101. Compare and contrast Maslow's hierarchy of needs and McGregor's Theory X and Theory Y.

    Answer:
    Maslow's hierarchy of needs states that there are five needs that all individuals have - physiological, safety, social, esteem, and self-actualization
    Individuals progress up the pyramid to the next level after a need is substantially satisfied
    Theory X states that individuals do not like to work, do not like responsibility, have little ambition and must be coerced, controlled or threatened
    Theory Y states that work is as natural as play, individuals will seek out responsibility, and that individuals will exercise self-control and self-direction if they are committed to the organizational goals

102. Explain the three key variables in expectancy theory.

    Answer:
    Effort-performance - does the individual have the requisite skills and knowledge in order to accomplish the task
    Performance-reward - if the performance occurs will the reward also occur
    Attractiveness - how important is the reward to that individual

103. Describe three of the significant workplace issues that affect motivation in today's work force.

    Answer:
    Diverse work force
    Pay-for-performance
    Competency-based compensation
    Employee stock ownership programs
    Motivating minimum-wage employees

104. Explain the effects of two cultural differences and the effect of the cultural differences on motivation.

    Answer:
    Diverse work force - management must be flexible
    The opportunity to learn, convenient work hours and good interpersonal relationships are more important to women than to men
    The self-interest concept and high individualism is more important in the U.S., Great Britain, and Australia so group efforts will be more difficult to institute
    In collectivist nations, like Japan, Mexico, Singapore, employees will be more receptive to team-based job design, group goals, and group performance evaluations
    Need for achievement works only where there is a willingness to accept a moderate degree of risk and a concern for performance like the U.S.
    Humiliation of employees will work in China but prove very ineffective in the United States

Chapter 13: Leadership and Supervision

True/False

1. Not all leaders are managers, nor are all managers leaders.

   Answer: T Difficulty: 2 Page: 389

2. The terms leader and manager are synonymous.

   Answer: F Difficulty: 2 Page: 389

3. Charisma and enthusiasm are traits that have been found to consistently differentiate leaders from nonleaders.

   Answer: F Difficulty: 3 Page: 390

4. An autocratic leader would allow employees to participate in decision making.

   Answer: F Difficulty: 1 Page: 391

5. A democratic-participative leader only gathers information from employees and makes the final decision himself/herself.

   Answer: F Difficulty: 2 Page: 391

6. According to Lewin, quantity of work done was equal for managers using the laissez-faire and democratic leadership styles.

   Answer: F Difficulty: 3 Page: 391

7. Lewin found that using a democratic leadership style could contribute to both quantity and quality of work performed.

   Answer: T Difficulty: 2 Page: 391

8. Tannenbaum and Schmidt suggested that in the long run, managers should move toward an employee-centered leadership style.

   Answer: T Difficulty: 2 Page: 394

9. A production-oriented leader emphasizes interpersonal relations and takes a personal interest in the needs of employees.

   Answer: F Difficulty: 2 Page: 395

10. Fiedler assumed that an individual will change his or her leadership style to fit the situation.

    Answer: F Difficulty: 2 Page: 398

Chapter 13: Leadership and Supervision

11. Relationship-oriented leaders perform best in either very favorable or very unfavorable conditions.

    Answer: F Difficulty: 2 Page: 399

12. Susan tells employees exactly what is expected of them, schedules work to be done and gives specific guidance on how the tasks should be completed. She is a supportive leader.

    Answer: F Difficulty: 2 Page: 401

13. Vroom and Yetton believed that leader behavior must be adjusted to reflect the task structure.

    Answer: T Difficulty: 2 Page: 402

14. Situational leadership focuses on the readiness of the follower.

    Answer: T Difficulty: 2 Page: 403

15. A person with high task-high relationship would use a selling leadership style, according to Hersey and Blanchard.

    Answer: T Difficulty: 2 Page: 403

16. At stage R4, according to Hersey and Blanchard, the leader's role is often reduced to dealing with exceptions.

    Answer: T Difficulty: 2 Page: 404

17. Self-confidence, vision, and behavior that is out of the ordinary are all key characteristics of charismatic leaders.

    Answer: T Difficulty: 2 Page: 406

18. Charismatic leaders may be ideal for an organization facing stability but a liability during times of crisis.

    Answer: F Difficulty: 1 Page: 406

19. Transactional leadership is built on transformational leadership

    Answer: F Difficulty: 1 Page: 407

20. Transactional leadership is more strongly correlated with lower turnover rates, higher productivity, and higher employee satisfaction.

    Answer: F Difficulty: 2 Page: 408

21. Trust is attributed to a leader in terms of honesty, competence, and ability to inspire.

    Answer: F Difficulty: 2 Page: 408

22. The increasing use of empowerment is a result, at least in part, to the downsizing and restructuring of organizations today.

    Answer: T Difficulty: 3 Page: 410

23. Men tend to use a more democratic leadership style than women.

    Answer: F Difficulty: 1 Page: 411

24. Effective leaders do not use any one style of leadership.

    Answer: T Difficulty: 2 Page: 411

25. Leadership may not always be important in an organization.

    Answer: T Difficulty: 3 Page: 413

26. The lowest level on the management hierarchy are supervisors.

    Answer: T Difficulty: 1 Page: 414

27. Heavy reliance on technical skills, coping with role conflict, and coping with restrained authority are unique characteristics of supervisors.

    Answer: T Difficulty: 2 Page: 414

Multiple Choice

28. The profits of Wang Seng Liang came at the expense of
    A. The customer
    B. His employees
    C. His family
    D. The environment

    Answer: B Difficulty: 2 Page: 388

29. Wang Seng Liang realized that he was a major impediment to his company and turned it over to
    A. His brother
    B. A CEO hired from the United States
    C. The employees
    D. His son

    Answer: D Difficulty: 2 Page: 388

Chapter 13:   Leadership and Supervision

30. Patrick Wang Shui Chung created an environment in which _____ was/were used extensively.
    A. Technology
    B. Environmental scanning
    C. Teams
    D. Pay-for-performance programs

    Answer: C Difficulty: 2 Page: 388

31. All but which of the following statements is true?
    A. Managers are appointed
    B. Leaders may be appointed or may emerge
    C. All leaders have the capability of performing the other managerial functions
    D. Ideally all managers should be leaders

    Answer: C Difficulty: 3 Page: 389

32. Which of the following is generally not true about a manager?
    A. He or she is appointed
    B. He or she has legitimate power
    C. His or her influence is based on formal authority of position
    D. He or she emerges from a group

    Answer: D Difficulty: 2 Page: 389

33. All but which of the following are traits that differentiate leaders from nonleaders?
    A. Drive
    B. Honesty and integrity
    C. Charisma
    D. Intelligence

    Answer: C Difficulty: 3 Page: 390

34. All but which of the following are traits that differentiate leaders from nonleaders?
    A. Job-relevant knowledge
    B. Self-confidence
    C. Enthusiasm
    D. Intelligence

    Answer: C Difficulty: 3 Page: 390

35. Which of the following is needed in addition to traits to explain leadership?
    A. Enthusiasm
    B. Situations
    C. Charisma
    D. Networking

    Answer: B Difficulty: 2 Page: 390

36. A leader who typically tends to centralize authority, dictate work methods and make unilateral decisions is using which leadership style?
    A. Democratic
    B. Laissez-faire
    C. Autocratic
    D. Democratic-consultative

    Answer: C Difficulty: 1 Page: 391

37. A leader who tends to involve employees in decision making, delegates authority and gathers input from employees but makes the final decision himself/herself is using which leadership style?
    A. Democratic-participative
    B. Laissez-faire
    C. Autocratic
    D. Democratic-consultative

    Answer: D Difficulty: 2 Page: 391

38. A leader who tends to involve employees in decision making, delegates authority and allows the employees to have direct input into the final decision with the leader serving as only one input from the group is using which leadership style?
    A. Democratic-participative
    B. Laissez-faire
    C. Autocratic
    D. Democratic-consultative

    Answer: A Difficulty: 2 Page: 391

39. A leader that allows their employees complete freedom to make decisions and to complete work in whatever way they think is best is using which leadership style?
    A. Democratic-participative
    B. Laissez-faire
    C. Autocratic
    D. Democratic-consultative

    Answer: B Difficulty: 2 Page: 391

40. Which leadership style was ineffective on every performance criterion, according to Lewin?
    A. Democratic-participative
    B. Laissez-faire
    C. Autocratic
    D. Democratic-consultative

    Answer: B Difficulty: 2 Page: 391

Chapter 13:   Leadership and Supervision

41. Work quality and group satisfaction were highest using which leadership style, according to Lewin?
    A. Dictatorial
    B. Laissez-faire
    C. Autocratic
    D. Democratic

    Answer: D Difficulty: 2 Page: 391

42. Quantity of work accomplished was equal using which two types of leadership styles, according to Lewin?
    A. Dictatorial and autocratic
    B. Laissez-fair and autocratic
    C. Democratic and autocratic
    D. Laissez-faire and democratic

    Answer: C Difficulty: 3 Page: 391

43. All but which of the following are forces which Tannenbaum and Schmidt determined were important for managers in deciding which leadership style to use?
    A. Forces within the themselves
    B. Forces within the situation
    C. Forces within top management
    D. Forces within employees

    Answer: C Difficulty: 2 Page: 393

44. In the long-run, which leadership style should mangers move toward, according to Tannenbaum and Schmidt?
    A. Autocratic
    B. Laissez-faire
    C. Democratic-participative
    D. Democratic-consultative

    Answer: C Difficulty: 3 Page: 394

45. A leader who is characterized as high in _____ , according to the Ohio State Studies, assigns group members to particular tasks, expects workers to maintain definite performance standards and emphasizes deadlines.
    A. Employee-oriented
    B. Initiating structure
    C. Consideration
    D. Participation

    Answer: B Difficulty: 2 Page: 395

46. A leader who is high in _____, according to the Ohio State Studies, is characterized by mutual trust and respect for employees' ideas and feelings. He or she also shows concern for employees' comfort, well-being and satisfaction.
    A. Autocratic structure
    B. Initiating structure
    C. Consideration
    D. Production-oriented

    Answer: C Difficulty: 2 Page: 395

47. A leader who is _____ in both initiating structure and consideration achieved high employee performance and satisfaction more frequently than one who rated _____ on initiating structure and/or consideration
    A. Low, low
    B. High, high
    C. High, low
    D. Low, high

    Answer: C Difficulty: 3 Page: 395

48. A leader who emphasizes the technical aspects of the job, is concerned with accomplishing the group's tasks is said to be _____, according to the Michigan studies.
    A. Employee oriented
    B. Initiating
    C. Considerate
    D. Production-oriented

    Answer: D Difficulty: 2 Page: 395

49. According to the Michigan studies, leaders who were _____ were associated with higher group productivity and higher job satisfaction.
    A. Employee oriented
    B. Initiating
    C. Considerate
    D. Production-oriented

    Answer: A Difficulty: 3 Page: 396

50. The managerial grid developed by Blake and Mouton says that the best leadership style is which style?
    A. 9,1
    B. 1,9
    C. 5,5
    D. 9,9

    Answer: D Difficulty: 2 Page: 396

Chapter 13: Leadership and Supervision

51. The managerial grid developed by Blake and Mouton emphasizes which two variables?
    A. Employee-oriented, production oriented
    B. Concern for people, concern for production
    C. Initiating structure, consideration
    D. Concern for people, consideration

    Answer: B Difficulty: 2 Page: 396

52. All but which of the following are theories that isolate key situational variables in order to understand leadership success?
    A. Fiedler model
    B. Path-goal theory
    C. Hersey and Blanchard's model
    D. The Ohio studies

    Answer: D Difficulty: 1 Page: 397

53. The theory that effective group performance depends on the proper match between the leader's style of interacting with employees and the degree to which the situation gives control and influence to the leader is which of the following?
    A. Fiedler model
    B. Path-goal theory
    C. Hersey and Blanchard's model
    D. The Ohio studies

    Answer: A Difficulty: 1 Page: 397

54. According to Fiedler, which of the following measures whether a person is task- or relationship-oriented?
    A. Least-preferred coworker question
    B. Most-preferred coworker question
    C. Employee orientation
    D. Production orientation

    Answer: A Difficulty: 1 Page: 397

55. Fiedler has identified three contingency dimensions that define the key situational factors for determining leadership effectiveness. They are all but which of the following?
    A. Leader-member relations
    B. Task structure
    C. Consideration
    D. Position power

    Answer: C Difficulty: 2 Page: 398

56. Fiedler assumes that a person's leadership style is
    A. Constantly changing
    B. Fixed
    C. Changeable upon demand
    D. A progressing, developing skill

    Answer: B Difficulty: 2 Page: 398

57. The theory that it is a leader's job to assist followers in attaining their goals and to provide the necessary direction and support is which of the following?
    A. Fiedler model
    B. Path-goal theory
    C. Hersey and Blanchard's model
    D. The Ohio studies

    Answer: B Difficulty: 1 Page: 400

58. Which theory of leadership states that the leader's job is to clarify the objectives they wish their employees to reach and to remove roadblocks that employees find as they work toward their objectives?
    A. Fiedler model
    B. Path-goal theory
    C. Hersey and Blanchard's model
    D. The Ohio studies

    Answer: B Difficulty: 2 Page: 400

59. According to House, the _____ leader lets employees know what is expected of them, schedules work and gives specific guidelines.
    A. Directive
    B. Achievement-oriented
    C. Participative
    D. Supportive

    Answer: A Difficulty: 1 Page: 401

60. Janice is a friendly and outgoing manager who constantly shows concerns for the needs of her employees. She is demonstrating which type of leadership style according to House?
    A. Directive
    B. Achievement-oriented
    C. Participative
    D. Supportive

    Answer: D Difficulty: 2 Page: 401

Chapter 13: Leadership and Supervision

61. A leader that sets challenging goals and expects employees to perform at their highest level is which of the following leadership styles, according to House?
    A. Directive
    B. Achievement-oriented
    C. Participative
    D. Supportive

    Answer: B   Difficulty: 1   Page: 401

62. Jake always consults with his employees and uses their suggestions before making a decision. He is demonstrating which type of leadership style, according to House?
    A. Directive
    B. Achievement-oriented
    C. Participative
    D. Supportive

    Answer: C   Difficulty: 2   Page: 401

63. Which of the following models argued that leadership behavior must adjust to reflect the task structure?
    A. Path-goal
    B. Leader-participation
    C. Fiedler's model
    D. Blake and Mouton's model

    Answer: B   Difficulty: 2   Page: 402

64. According to the leader-participation model,
    A. Increased participation results in lower productivity
    B. Leaders should adjust their style to the situation
    C. Leaders should use group decision-making whenever possible
    D. Employees should participate in management

    Answer: B   Difficulty: 2   Page: 402

65. A model of leadership behavior that reflects how a leader should adjust his or her leadership style in accordance with the readiness of followers is which of the following?
    A. Path-goal
    B. Leader-participation
    C. Fiedler's model
    D. Situational leadership

    Answer: D   Difficulty: 1   Page: 403

66. All but which of the following are stages in follower readiness, according to Hersey and Blanchard?
    A. A follower is both unable and unwilling to do a job
    B. A follower is unable to do the job but willing to perform the task
    C. A follower is unable to do a job
    D. A follower is both able and willing to do the job

    Answer: C Difficulty: 2 Page: 403

67. A high task-low relationship would require which leadership style, according to Hersey and Blanchard?
    A. Delegating
    B. Telling
    C. Participating
    D. Selling

    Answer: B Difficulty: 2 Page: 403

68. A low task-high relationship would require which leadership style, according to Hersey and Blanchard?
    A. Delegating
    B. Telling
    C. Participating
    D. Selling

    Answer: C Difficulty: 2 Page: 403

69. According to Hersey and Blanchard, at R4 the leader primarily deals with
    A. The environment
    B. Forecasting
    C. The exceptions
    D. The routine tasks

    Answer: C Difficulty: 3 Page: 403

70. The theory that followers make attributions of heroic or extraordinary leadership abilities when they observe certain behaviors is known as which of the following?
    A. Charismatic leadership
    B. Transformational leadership
    C. Transactional leadership
    D. Autocratic leadership

    Answer: A Difficulty: 1 Page: 405

Chapter 13: Leadership and Supervision

71. All but which of the following differentiate charismatic leaders from noncharismatic leaders?
    A. A vision
    B. Ability to articulate the vision
    C. Environmental sensitivity
    D. Behavior that is ordinary

    Answer: D Difficulty: 2 Page: 406

72. When may a charismatic leader be most appropriate?
    A. All the time
    B. None of the time
    C. When there is an ideological component involved
    D. When there is no need for dramatic change

    Answer: C Difficulty: 2 Page: 406

73. Leaders who guide or motivate their followers toward established goals by clarifying role and task requirements are which of the following?
    A. Charismatic leadership
    B. Transformational leadership
    C. Transactional leadership
    D. Autocratic leadership

    Answer: C Difficulty: 2 Page: 407

74. Leaders who inspire followers to transcend their own self-interests for the good of the organization and are capable of having a profound and extraordinary effect on followers is which of the following?
    A. Charismatic leadership
    B. Transformational leadership
    C. Transactional leadership
    D. Autocratic leadership

    Answer: B Difficulty: 2 Page: 407

75. Leaders who pay attention to the concerns and developmental needs of individual followers, help followers to look at old problems in new ways, and are able to inspire followers to put extra effort into the group goals are which of the following?
    A. Charismatic leadership
    B. Transformational leadership
    C. Transactional leadership
    D. Autocratic leadership

    Answer: B Difficulty: 2 Page: 407

76. _____ is more strongly correlated with lower turnover rates, higher productivity, and higher employee satisfaction.
    A. Charismatic leadership
    B. Transformational leadership
    C. Transactional leadership
    D. Autocratic leadership

    Answer: B Difficulty: 3 Page: 408

77. The dominant component of credibility is
    A. Intelligence
    B. Charisma
    C. Honesty
    D. Trust

    Answer: C Difficulty: 2 Page: 408

78. A leader's _____ is judged in terms of his or her honesty, competence, and ability to inspire.
    A. Trust
    B. Credibility
    C. Intelligence
    D. Charisma

    Answer: B Difficulty: 2 Page: 408

79. The belief in the integrity, character and ability of a leader is defined as
    A. Trust
    B. Credibility
    C. Intelligence
    D. Charisma

    Answer: A Difficulty: 2 Page: 408

80. The most critical characteristics in determining another's trustworthiness are
    A. Integrity and openness
    B. Loyalty and consistency
    C. Integrity and competence
    D. Competence and consistency

    Answer: C Difficulty: 3 Page: 408

81. All but which of the following are reasons why the use of empowerment is increasing?
    A. The need for quick decisions
    B. The dynamic global village
    C. Mangers with larger spans of control
    D. Managers with smaller spans of control

    Answer: D Difficulty: 2 Page: 409

Chapter 13: Leadership and Supervision

82. Women tend to use a more _____ style of leadership.
    A. Autocratic
    B. Laissez-faire
    C. Democratic
    D. Dictatorial

    Answer: C Difficulty: 2 Page: 411

83. Men tend to use a more _____ leadership style.
    A. Employee-centered
    B. Task-centered
    C. Interpersonal-centered
    D. Charisma-centered

    Answer: B Difficulty: 2 Page: 411

84. The most effective leaders use _____ style.
    A. Autocratic
    B. Laissez-faire
    C. Democratic
    D. No single style is preferable

    Answer: D Difficulty: 2 Page: 411

85. Linda Wachner is recognized as the first woman to
    A. Become a world leader
    B. Become a Fortune 500 CEO
    C. Manage a company that has $1,000,000 in sales
    D. Manage a company that has $1,000,000 in profits

    Answer: B Difficulty: 2 Page: 412

86. All but which of the following can replace the need for a leader?
    A. Employee experience and professionalism
    B. Unambiguous and routine jobs
    C. Jobs that are intrinsically satisfying
    D. Ambiguous and nonroutine jobs

    Answer: D Difficulty: 2 Page: 413

87. The first or lowest level in the management hierarchy is which of the following?
    A. Top management
    B. Middle management
    C. Boundaryless managers
    D. Supervisors

    Answer: D Difficulty: 1 Page: 413

88. All but which of the following are characteristics of being a supervisor?
   A. Heavy reliance on technical expertise
   B. Heavy reliance on technological expertise
   C. Coping with constrained authority
   D. Coping with role conflict

   Answer: B Difficulty: 2 Page: 414

Scenario

Table 13-1
Patrick has just been hired in a management/leadership position for Trion's Inc. It should prove a challenging position due to the fact the Board of Directors wants to see the profit margin back to 5% in 18 months or less. Things have not been going well at Trion's Inc. Patrick wonders which leadership style will be more effective in order to accomplish the tasks that need to be done? He does not have much time so maybe he should centralize authority, dictate work methods and make the decisions, at least for awhile. However, that really is not the method Patrick prefers. He would rather involve employees in decision making, delegate authority and encourage participation in decision making to the point where his input simply becomes one vote in the group vote. From what he has observed, the last leadership style that was used with the group of employees was to allow employees to do whatever they wanted, giving them complete freedom to make decisions. The only input from the leader was to supply necessary materials and answer questions.

89. Referring to Table 13-1, if Patrick chooses the first option where he centralizes authority and dictates work methods, which leadership style will he be using?
   A. Democratic-participative
   B. Laissez-faire
   C. Autocratic
   D. Democratic-consultative

   Answer: C Difficulty: 2

90. Referring to Table 13-1, if Patrick uses his preferred style, which leadership style will be chosen?
   A. Democratic-participative
   B. Laissez-faire
   C. Autocratic
   D. Democratic-consultative

   Answer: A Difficulty: 3

Chapter 13: Leadership and Supervision

91. Referring to Table 13-1, which leadership style are the employees used to?
    A. Democratic-participative
    B. Laissez-faire
    C. Autocratic
    D. Democratic-consultative

    Answer: B Difficulty: 3

92. Referring to Table 13-1, according to Tannenbaum and Schmidt, which leadership style will be most effective in the long run?
    A. Democratic-participative
    B. Laissez-faire
    C. Autocratic
    D. Democratic-consultative

    Answer: A Difficulty: 3

93. Referring to Table 13-1, based on the information given, which leadership style should Patrick choose?
    A. Democratic-participative
    B. Laissez-faire
    C. Autocratic
    D. Democratic-consultative

    Answer: A Difficulty: 3

Table 13-2
Harry knows that there are a variety of differing ways to effectively lead; however, he would like to be more effective at his job as well as helping his first-line managers also be effective leaders. As he thinks about his first-line mangers, he realizes that they all demonstrate a wide variety of leadership styles. Jennie lets her employees know exactly what is expected of them and gives specific guidelines on how tasks are to be accomplished. Jace, on the other hand, always solicits employee information and suggestions before making a decision. Kate expects so much from her employees. She continuously sets challenging goals and expects her employees to reach those goals. Then there is Frank who is always outgoing and friendly, endlessly concerned with his employees and their welfare. Harry wonders what he could do to help the first-line mangers achieve their goals.

94. Referring to Table 13-2, Jennie uses which type of leadership style?
    A. Achievement-oriented
    B. Supportive
    C. Participative
    D. Directive

    Answer: D Difficulty: 2

95. Referring to Table 13-2, Jace uses which of the following leadership styles?
    A. Achievement-oriented
    B. Supportive
    C. Participative
    D. Directive

    Answer: C Difficulty: 2

96. Referring to Table 13-2, Kate demonstrates which leadership style?
    A. Achievement-oriented
    B. Supportive
    C. Participative
    D. Directive

    Answer: A Difficulty: 2

97. Referring to Table 13-2, Frank uses which leadership style?
    A. Achievement-oriented
    B. Supportive
    C. Participative
    D. Directive

    Answer: B Difficulty: 2

98. Referring to Table 13-2, which of the following could Harry do to help his first-line supervisors?
    A. Explain the task even if he thinks the supervisors understand
    B. Compensate for shortcomings in the supervisors
    C. Compensate for shortcomings in the work setting
    D. Compensate for shortcomings in the supervisors and the work setting

    Answer: D Difficulty: 3

Chapter 13:   Leadership and Supervision

Table 13-3
Eric has a wide variety of employees he is trying to lead. Everything from age, to experience, to enthusiasm varies. Some employees need so much direction and just the other day he upset one of the older, experienced workers, Hazel, by trying to help too much. After all she probably did know the job better than he and she was a very willing and capable worker. She had worked her job for 20 years. Yet he was only trying to be helpful. And he was trying to compensate for the day before when he had not told Joe enough. Joe was a new employee, very enthusiastic, but very little experience. Joe needed the roles defined and specific information on how to do some tasks. Hank, on the other hand, likes to share in decision making and Eric's main role is that of communication and facilitation.

99. Referring to Table 13-3, according to Hersey and Blanchard, Eric probably needs to focus more on which variable?
    A. Motivation
    B. Employee readiness
    C. The situation
    D. Eric's leadership preference

    Answer: B Difficulty: 2

100. Referring to Table 13-3, according to Hersey and Blanchard, which leadership style would probably work best with Hazel?
    A. Telling
    B. Selling
    C. Participating
    D. Delegating

    Answer: D Difficulty: 2

101. Referring to Table 13-3, where Hazel is concerned, Eric will probably only deal with
    A. Motivational issues
    B. Performance issues
    C. The exceptions
    D. Quality issues

    Answer: C Difficulty: 3

102. Referring to Table 13-3, according to Hersey and Blanchard, which leadership style would probably work best with Joe?
    A. Telling
    B. Selling
    C. Participating
    D. Delegating

    Answer: A Difficulty: 2

103. Referring to Table 13-3, according to Hersey and Blanchard, which leadership style would probably work best with Hank?
   A. Telling
   B. Selling
   C. Participating
   D. Delegating

   Answer: C Difficulty: 2

Essay

104. Compare and contrast managers and leaders.

   Answer:
   Leader has influence over others beyond what is dictated by any formal authority they may hold
   Leaders may be appointed or may emerge from a group
   Managers are appointed and have legitimate power that allows them to reward and punish

105. Describe three traits that differentiate leaders from nonleaders.

   Answer:
   Drive
   Desire to lead
   Honesty and integrity
   Self-confidence
   Intelligence
   Job-relevant knowledge

106. Compare and contrast Fiedler's contingency model and the situational leadership.

   Answer:
   Fiedler's contingency model identifies three variables: leader-member relations, task structure, and position power
   He believed that leadership styles were fixed thus it was necessary to match the leader with the situation
   Situational leadership states that a leader should adjust his/her style based upon follower readiness
   There are four choices based upon task and relationship behaviors: telling, selling, participating, and delegating

Chapter 13: Leadership and Supervision

107. Compare and contrast charismatic, transactional and transformation leaders.

    Answer:
    Charismatic leaders - their followers will make attributions of heroic or extraordinary leadership abilities when they observe certain behaviors
    Key characteristics include self-confidence, vision, ability to articulate the vision, strong conviction about the conviction, behavior that is out of the ordinary, and environmental sensitivity
    Transactional leaders - guide or motivate their followers toward established goals by clarifying role and task requirements
    Transformational leaders - inspire followers to transcend their own self-interests for the good of the organization and are capable of having a profound and extraordinary effect on followers

108. Describe the three important contemporary issues that are affecting leadership roles today.

    Answer:
    Credibility - a characteristic attributed to a leader in terms of honesty, competence, and ability to inspire
    Trust - the belief in the integrity, character, and ability of the leader
    Empowerment - allowing employees to make more decisions about areas they are affected by
    Increased use today due to downsizing/restructuring and the need for quick decision making in today's global village

Chapter 14: Communication and Interpersonal Skills

True/False

1. Effective communication is essential to successful employee performance.

    Answer: T Difficulty: 1 Page: 423

2. Everything a manager does involves communication.

    Answer: T Difficulty: 2 Page: 424

3. Communication involves only the transfer of meaning.

    Answer: F Difficulty: 2 Page: 424

4. Telephone static, constant interruptions, and loud voices are examples of the encoding process of communication.

    Answer: F Difficulty: 1 Page: 425

5. Beliefs and values act to influence communication

    Answer: T Difficulty: 1 Page: 425

6. A person's level of knowledge influences his or her ability to receive a message.

    Answer: T Difficulty: 1 Page: 426

7. Managers should stop the grapevine from occurring.

    Answer: F Difficulty: 2 Page: 427

8. Only 7% of the message that is sent is derived from the words used.

    Answer: T Difficulty: 3 Page: 428

9. E-mail is one of the most widely used methods today for organizational communication.

    Answer: T Difficulty: 2 Page: 428

10. The process of deliberately manipulating information to make it more favorable to the receiver is called selective perception.

    Answer: F Difficulty: 2 Page: 430

11. Feedback does not have to be conveyed in words.

    Answer: T Difficulty: 3 Page: 431

Chapter 14: Communication and Interpersonal Skills

12. Jargon can facilitate understanding when it is used within a group of those who know what it means, but it can cause innumerable problems when used outside that group.

    Answer: T Difficulty: 3 Page: 432

13. The average person speaks at a rate of 1,000 words per minute, but people have the capacity to hear and process at the rate of 150 words per minute.

    Answer: F Difficulty: 3 Page: 432

14. When men talk they emphasize connections and intimacy. When women talk they emphasize status and independence.

    Answer: F Difficulty: 2 Page: 433

15. Open communication is an inherent part of the Japanese work setting.

    Answer: T Difficulty: 2 Page: 433

16. Listening for feeling as well as content is an example of taking responsibility for the completeness of the message.

    Answer: T Difficulty: 2 Page: 435

17. Making eye contact is an important component in actively listening.

    Answer: T Difficulty: 2 Page: 436

18. Negative feedback is more readily and accurately perceived than positive feedback.

    Answer: F Difficulty: 2 Page: 436

19. Negative feedback should be descriptive rather than judgmental or evaluative.

    Answer: T Difficulty: 3 Page: 437

20. Feedback is most meaningful when there is a very short interval between the behavior and the receipt of the feedback.

    Answer: T Difficulty: 2 Page: 438

21. Managers abdicate their responsibility when they delegate.

    Answer: F Difficulty: 3 Page: 438

22. Managers need to learn to delegate if they are going to be effective.

    Answer: T Difficulty: 2 Page: 439

23. To delegate without instituting feedback controls is inviting problems.

    Answer: T Difficulty: 2 Page: 441

Multiple Choice

24. According to Tom Colesberry, information from whom provides him the best and most accurate feedback?
    A. Top management
    B. Middle management
    C. Customers
    D. Employees

    Answer: D Difficulty: 2 Page: 423

25. Many of the employees of Tom Colesberry's company speak only
    A. English
    B. French
    C. Spanish
    D. Italian

    Answer: C Difficulty: 2 Page: 423

26. _____ a manager does involves communication.
    A. A few things
    B. Some things
    C. Most things
    D. Everything

    Answer: D Difficulty: 2 Page: 424

27. For communication to be successful, meaning must be _____ and _____.
    A. Transferred, understood
    B. Transferred, imparted
    C. Understood, accepted
    D. Imparted, encoded

    Answer: A Difficulty: 2 Page: 424

28. The conversion of a message into some symbolic form is known as which of the following?
    A. Message
    B. Encoding
    C. Channel
    D. Decoding

    Answer: B Difficulty: 1 Page: 424

Chapter 14: Communication and Interpersonal Skills

29. A receiver's translation of a sender's message is known as which of the following?
    A. Message
    B. Encoding
    C. Channel
    D. Decoding

    Answer: D Difficulty: 1 Page: 424

30. Illegible print, telephone static, fans, and loud voices are all examples of which of the following?
    A. Noise
    B. Encoding
    C. Channel
    D. Decoding

    Answer: A Difficulty: 2 Page: 425

31. All but which of the following affect the encoding of a message?
    A. Skills
    B. Attitudes
    C. Socio-cultural system
    D. Technology

    Answer: D Difficulty: 2 Page: 425

32. The spoken word, paper, e-mail, and a memo are examples of which of the following?
    A. Noise
    B. Encoding
    C. Channel
    D. Decoding

    Answer: C Difficulty: 2 Page: 426

33. Which part of the communication process provides a check to the sender on whether understanding has been achieved?
    A. Noise
    B. Encoding
    C. Feedback
    D. Decoding

    Answer: C Difficulty: 2 Page: 426

34. The unofficial way that communication takes place in an organization that is neither authorized or supported by an organization is which of the following?
    A. Noise
    B. Grapevine
    C. Channel
    D. Decoding

    Answer: B Difficulty: 2 Page: 427

35. Which of the following statements is true concerning the grapevine?
    A. It is always accurate
    B. It is never accurate
    C. Management can stop the grapevine completely
    D. It contains some elements of truth

    Answer: D Difficulty: 2 Page: 427

36. All but which of the following are advantages of written communication?
    A. Provides a record of the communication
    B. Requires more time to prepare
    C. It can be stored for an indefinite time period
    D. More care is taken in the thought process about what is to be conveyed

    Answer: B Difficulty: 2 Page: 427

37. Body language, verbal intonation, the size of an office or the clothes that are worn are all examples of which of the following?
    A. Feedback
    B. Noise
    C. Body language
    D. Nonverbal communication

    Answer: D Difficulty: 2 Page: 428

38. Gestures, facial expressions, and leaning toward or away from a person are all examples of which of the following?
    A. Feedback
    B. Verbal intonation
    C. Body language
    D. Nonverbal communication

    Answer: C Difficulty: 2 Page: 428

Chapter 14: Communication and Interpersonal Skills

39. The emphasis that is given to words, the softness or loudness in speaking and the pitch used in speaking are all examples of which of the following?
    A. Feedback
    B. Verbal intonation
    C. Body language
    D. Nonverbal communication

    Answer: B Difficulty: 2 Page: 428

40. Which percentage of the oral message is derived from the facial expression and physical posture?
    A. 7%
    B. 25%
    C. 38%
    D. 55%

    Answer: D Difficulty: 3 Page: 428

41. Which percentage of the oral message is derived from the actual words used?
    A. 7%
    B. 25%
    C. 38%
    D. 55%

    Answer: A Difficulty: 3 Page: 428

42. One of the most widely used methods used today for organizational communication is which of the following?
    A. Closed-circuit television
    B. Telephone
    C. E-mail
    D. Cellular phones

    Answer: C Difficulty: 2 Page: 428

43. All but which of the following are barriers to effective communication?
    A. Filtering
    B. Feedback
    C. Emotions
    D. Selective perception

    Answer: B Difficulty: 2 Page: 430

44. The fact that individuals see and hear depending upon their needs, motivation, experience, background and other personal characteristics is which of the following?
    A. Filtering
    B. Feedback
    C. Emotions
    D. Selective perception

    Answer: D Difficulty: 1 Page: 430

45. Jacob just received the news that he has received the promotion for which he has waited two years. He is ecstatic. Every communication for the rest of the day and maybe tomorrow will be affected by which of the following?
    A. Filtering
    B. Emotions
    C. Language
    D. Nonverbal cues

    Answer: B Difficulty: 2 Page: 430

46. Age, education, culture and technological background are four variables that influence which of the following?
    A. Filtering
    B. Emotions
    C. Language
    D. Nonverbal cues

    Answer: C Difficulty: 3 Page: 430

47. Which of the following can reduce misunderstandings and inaccuracies in the communication process?
    A. Filtering
    B. Emotions
    C. Feedback
    D. Nonverbal cues

    Answer: C Difficulty: 1 Page: 431

48. All but which of the following are ways to overcome barriers in effective communication?
    A. Use feedback
    B. Actively listen
    C. Watch nonverbal clues
    D. Emphasize emotions

    Answer: D Difficulty: 2 Page: 431

Chapter 14: Communication and Interpersonal Skills

49. Individuals can listen at a rate of _____ words per minute where speaking occurs at _____ words per minute.
    A. 500, 100
    B. 750, 100
    C. 1000, 150
    D. 150, 1000

    Answer: C Difficulty: 3 Page: 432

50. All but which of the following are true statements?
    A. Hearing is passive, listening is active
    B. Many of us are poor listeners
    C. The difference between our hearing/processing rate and our speaking rate leave time for minds to wander
    D. Talking is more tiring than listening

    Answer: D Difficulty: 2 Page: 432

51. All but which of the following statements is correct?
    A. Men emphasize status and independence when they talk
    B. Women emphasize creating connections and intimacy
    C. Men assert their desire for independence and control by providing solutions
    D. Women present problems to gain advice

    Answer: D Difficulty: 3 Page: 433

52. All but which of the following is true?
    A. In the United States, managers rely heavily on formal communication
    B. In the United States, managers rely heavily on informal communication
    C. In Japan, communication is more informal
    D. Open communication is an inherent part of the Japanese work setting

    Answer: B Difficulty: 3 Page: 433

53. The biggest reason managers fail is due to
    A. Poor technological skills
    B. Poor human resource management skills
    C. Poor interpersonal skills
    D. Poor managerial skills

    Answer: C Difficulty: 1 Page: 434

54. All but which of the following are essential requirements for listening?
    A. Intensity
    B. Sympathy
    C. Acceptance
    D. Willingness to take responsibility for completeness

    Answer: B Difficulty: 2 Page: 435

55. All but which of the following are true statements concerning listening?
    A. Idle brain time should be used to summarize and integrate what has been said
    B. Put yourself in the speaker's shoes
    C. Judge content
    D. Listen for feeling as well as content

    Answer: C Difficulty: 2 Page: 435

56. All but which of the following are steps involved in learning to listen actively?
    A. Make eye contact
    B. Avoid interrupting the speaker
    C. Interrupt the speaker as often as necessary in order to clarify meaning
    D. Ask questions

    Answer: C Difficulty: 2 Page: 436

57. All but which of the following statements are true concerning feedback?
    A. Managers treat positive and negative feedback differently
    B. Positive feedback is less readily accepted
    C. Negative feedback often meets resistance
    D. Negative feedback is most likely to be accepted when it comes from a credible source

    Answer: B Difficulty: 2 Page: 436

58. "Coming into work late two out of three mornings this week is unacceptable", is an example of which of the following methods by which feedback can be improved?
    A. Focus on specific behaviors
    B. Keep feedback impersonal
    C. Keep feedback goal-oriented
    D. Ensure understanding

    Answer: A Difficulty: 2 Page: 437

59. Correcting an employee immediately after an incorrect behavior as opposed to waiting until their bi-annual performance review is an example of which of the following?
    A. Make feedback well-timed
    B. Keep feedback impersonal
    C. Keep feedback goal-oriented
    D. Ensure understanding

    Answer: A Difficulty: 2 Page: 438

Chapter 14:   Communication and Interpersonal Skills

60. Constantly criticizing someone for being late for work for a month when the entire city knows traffic is being rerouted daily due to major construction work is an example that falls under which of the following?
    A. Direct negative feedback toward behaviors that the receiver cannot control
    B. Keep feedback impersonal
    C. Keep feedback goal-oriented
    D. Ensure understanding

    Answer: A Difficulty: 2 Page: 438

61. The assignment of authority to another person to carry out specific activities is known as which of the following?
    A. Nonverbal language
    B. Feedback
    C. Delegation
    D. Participatory democracy

    Answer: C Difficulty: 1 Page: 438

62. All but which of the following are true statements concerning delegation?
    A. Proper delegation is not abdication
    B. Managers must delegate in order to be effective
    C. Mistakes are never a part of delegation
    D. Feedback controls should always be a part of delegation

    Answer: C Difficulty: 2 Page: 438

63. All but which of the following are actions that should be taken in order to effectively delegate?
    A. Clarify the assignment
    B. Allow employees to participate
    C. Delegation should take place only between the two people involved
    D. Establish feedback channels

    Answer: C Difficulty: 2 Page: 439

64. Which of the following should be delegated?
    A. The process to be used
    B. The exact steps to be taken
    C. The results to be achieved
    D. Exactly how the project is to be done

    Answer: C Difficulty: 2 Page: 440

65. All but which of the following are contingency factors in delegation?
    A. The size of the organization
    B. The importance of the duty or decision
    C. Task simplicity
    D. Employee qualities

    Answer: C Difficulty: 3 Page: 440

66. The manager specifically has established the parameters of the project he is delegating to Joe. This is an example of which of the following?
    A. Clarify the assignment
    B. Allow employees to participate
    C. Specify the range of the employees' discretion
    D. Establish feedback channels

    Answer: C Difficulty: 2 Page: 440

67. Determining due dates and dates for progress reports as well as periodically checking on how the employee is progressing is an example of which of the following?
    A. Clarify the assignment
    B. Allow employees to participate
    C. Specify the range of the employees' discretion
    D. Establish feedback channels

    Answer: D Difficulty: 2 Page: 441

68. The average manager spends _____ of his or her time dealing with conflict.
    A. 5%
    B. 10%
    C. 20%
    D. 40%

    Answer: C Difficulty: 2 Page: 441

69. The view that conflict is negative and must be avoided and that it indicates a malfunctioning within the organization is which of the following?
    A. Interactionist view
    B. Human relations view
    C. Traditional view
    D. Organizational view

    Answer: C Difficulty: 1 Page: 442

Chapter 14:   Communication and Interpersonal Skills

70. The view that conflict cannot only be a positive force in an organization but also that some conflict is absolutely necessary for an organization to perform effectively is known as which of the following?
    A. Interactionist view
    B. Human relations view
    C. Traditional view
    D. Organizational view

    Answer: A Difficulty: 2 Page: 442

71. Conflicts that support the goals of the organization are
    A. Dysfunctional conflicts
    B. Functional conflicts
    C. Variable conflict
    D. Unproductive conflict

    Answer: B Difficulty: 2 Page: 443

72. Whether a conflict is functional or dysfunctional is a matter of
    A. Easy determination
    B. Judgement
    C. Determining the facts
    D. The environment

    Answer: B Difficulty: 3 Page: 443

73. All but which of the following are the three causes of conflict?
    A. Communication differences
    B. Structural differences
    C. Management differences
    D. Personal differences

    Answer: C Difficulty: 2 Page: 444

74. Disagreements over goals, decision alternatives, performance criteria and resource allocation is an example of which of the following?
    A. Communication differences
    B. Structural differences
    C. Management differences
    D. Personal differences

    Answer: B Difficulty: 2 Page: 446

75. Which of the following options is ideal for resolving conflict?
    A. Avoidance
    B. Compromise
    C. Collaboration
    D. There is no one best method for every situation

    Answer: D Difficulty: 3 Page: 446

76. When the issue under dispute is not that important to you or when you want to build up credits for later issues, which of the following strategies would work best?
    A. Avoidance
    B. Accommodation
    C. Compromise
    D. Collaboration

Answer: B Difficulty: 2 Page: 446

77. When time pressures are minimal and when all parties seriously want a win-win situation, and when the issue is too important to be compromised, which of the following strategies would work best?
    A. Avoidance
    B. Accommodation
    C. Forcing
    D. Collaboration

Answer: D Difficulty: 2 Page: 446

78. A yes answer to all but which of the following questions may indicate a need for conflict stimulation?
    A. Do employees show unusually high resistance to change?
    B. Is there an abundance of new ideas?
    C. Are you surrounded by "yes" people?
    D. Regardless of the price, do managers maintain peace and cooperation?

Answer: B Difficulty: 3 Page: 448

79. All but which of the following are true statements?
    A. Managers must convey the message that conflict plays a legitimate role in the organization
    B. Ambiguous or threatening messages encourage conflict
    C. Only negative outcomes result from conflict
    D. Bringing in outsiders with divergent interests may add a fresh perspective to an organization

Answer: C Difficulty: 2 Page: 448

80. All but which of the following statements are true concerning devil's advocates?
    A. They play the role of the critic
    B. They act as a check against groupthink
    C. They can improve the decision making process for groups
    D. They will speed up the decision making process

Answer: D Difficulty: 2 Page: 449

Chapter 14: Communication and Interpersonal Skills

81. The bargaining strategy in which the identifying feature is that it operates under zero-sum conditions, which means any gain is at the expense of the other person is which of the following?
    A. Negotiation
    B. Distributive bargaining
    C. Integrative bargaining
    D. Win-win bargaining

    Answer: B Difficulty: 2 Page: 449

82. Which bargaining strategy involves at least one settlement where there is no loss to either party?
    A. Negotiation
    B. Distributive bargaining
    C. Integrative bargaining
    D. Win-win bargaining

    Answer: C Difficulty: 2 Page: 450

83. Which bargaining strategy tends to build animosities and deepen divisions between people?
    A. Negotiation
    B. Distributive bargaining
    C. Integrative bargaining
    D. Win-win bargaining

    Answer: B Difficulty: 3 Page: 451

Scenario

Table 14-1
The message received yesterday was certainly not the message Jon had intended to send. This morning after speaking to the fifth angry employee, he realized he had failed in communicating. He had worked so diligently to properly word the decrease in profits and the resulting lack of a bonus for the coming year. It was due, in large part, to foreign currency risk factors. When all foreign currency had been changed back to dollars, profits were gone and with it, the bonus. The employees had been so upset as soon as he said the words no bonus that he was not sure they had heard anything else. Now he had to try and communicate again.

84. Referring to Table 14-1, which of the following barriers occurred when the employees became upset?
    A. Emotion
    B. Selective perception
    C. Filtering
    D. Language

    Answer: A Difficulty: 2

85. Referring to Table 14-1, it seemed the employees heard only the parts of what he had to say that they wanted to hear. This is an example of which of the following?
    A. Filtering
    B. Emotions
    C. Language
    D. Selective perception

    Answer: D Difficulty: 3

86. Referring to Table 14-1, Jon had used the technical terms for the currency exchange problem, like exchange rate risk, hedging, forward contracts and differing exchange rates. He had tried to explain the difficult concepts using all the proper finance terminology. He had tried to be thorough in his explanation. Words evidently have differing meanings to differing people. This is an example of which communication barrier?
    A. Filtering
    B. Emotions
    C. Language
    D. Nonverbal cues

    Answer: C Difficulty: 3

87. Referring to Table 14-1, which of the following could Jon have used yesterday to determine the message sent was not the message received?
    A. Filtering
    B. Emotions
    C. Feedback
    D. Nonverbal cues

    Answer: C Difficulty: 2

88. Referring to Table 14-1, which of the following did the employees probably not do yesterday as they heard Jon's message?
    A. Constrain emotions
    B. Listen actively
    C. Overcome selective perception
    D. Overcome the language barriers

    Answer: B Difficulty: 3

Chapter 14: Communication and Interpersonal Skills

Table 14-2
Elaine knew that in order to be an effective manager she needed to delegate, yet it was extremely difficult for her. She was new to the organization and unsure yet exactly what the delegation process was and how it was to be used. There were seven layers in the organizational hierarchy and she alone had fifteen managers she was responsible for so she knew delegation had to occur. Looking in the company handbook, she noticed that for all decisions over $140,000 she needed her supervisor's approval. For everything over $250,000, Vice-Presidential approval was needed. Many of the tasks her managers were working on were very technical. Elaine was not sure if she had the expertise to make some decisions. She had a very competent group of people working for her, though. Their skill level, education, experience and motivation were superior. The final question in her mind though still focused on what was acceptable in the organization. Management seemed to trust the employees and place confidence in their decision making. It was a point Elaine still needed to check out.

89. Referring to Table 14-2, which of the following contingency factors of delegation is affected by the seven layers of organizational hierarchy?
    A. Task complexity
    B. Organizational culture
    C. The size of the organization
    D. The importance of the duty or decision

    Answer: C Difficulty: 1

90. Referring to Table 14-2, the dollar amounts for decision making are an example of which of the following?
    A. Task complexity
    B. Organizational culture
    C. The size of the organization
    D. The importance of the duty or decision

    Answer: D Difficulty: 2

91. Referring to Table 14-2, the expertise that Elaine is referring to would fall under which contingency factor?
    A. Task complexity
    B. Organizational culture
    C. The size of the organization
    D. The importance of the duty or decision

    Answer: A Difficulty: 2

92. Referring to Table 14-2, the skill level, education and experience of the employees would fall under which contingency factor of delegation?
    A. Qualities of the employees
    B. Organizational culture
    C. The size of the organization
    D. The importance of the duty or decision

    Answer: A Difficulty: 2

93. Referring to Table 14-2, the point that Elaine is pondering concerning the organization falls under which contingency factor?
   A. Task complexity
   B. Organizational culture
   C. The size of the organization
   D. The importance of the duty or decision

   Answer: B Difficulty: 2

Table 14-3
Stacie had just returned from a seminar on conflict management. Although it seemed she spent a lot of time dealing with conflict, it certainly was not her favorite aspect of being a manager. She thought back to some of the conflicts that she had encountered lately. There had been the conflict last week between two office staff members over the location of the department coffee pot. They could not agree on where it should be placed. Stacie had smiled, shook her head and walked away from that one. Then there had been the dispute among the middle managers over where to hold the company picnic. The argument had gotten rather heated but it made no difference to Stacie and she was not about to use some of her credits for something that unimportant to her. Then there was the ongoing debate over the restructuring of the company. Top management had said there was a time period of two years in which to complete a restructuring and they had wanted employee input from the bottom up so that it could be a win-win situation for everyone. All involved in this debate realized the importance of a positive resolution.

94. Referring to Table 14-3, what percentage of time does Stacie probably spend in conflict management?
   A. 5%
   B. 10%
   C. 20%
   D. 40%

   Answer: C Difficulty: 2

95. Referring to Table 14-3, what strategy did Stacie use in dealing with the coffee pot issue?
   A. Avoidance
   B. Forcing
   C. Collaboration
   D. Compromising

   Answer: A Difficulty: 2

96. Referring to Table 14-3, what strategy did Stacie use in dealing with the company picnic?
   A. Accommodation
   B. Forcing
   C. Collaboration
   D. Compromising

   Answer: A Difficulty: 2

Chapter 14: Communication and Interpersonal Skills

97. Referring to Table 14-3, which strategy was being used in the restructuring issue?
    A. Accommodation
    B. Forcing
    C. Collaboration
    D. Compromising

    Answer: C   Difficulty: 2

98. Referring to Table 14-3, which of the following is the ideal strategy for dealing with conflict?
    A. Avoidance
    B. Forcing
    C. Collaboration
    D. There is no one ideal strategy

    Answer: D   Difficulty: 3

Essay

99. Describe the communication process.

    Answer:
    A message is encoded by the sender and passed through a channel to a receiver who then decodes the message, feedback occurs
    When the message is transferred and understood, communication has taken place

100. Explain three techniques for overcoming communication barriers.

    Answer:
    Use feedback
    Simplify language
    Actively listen
    Constrain emotions
    Watch for nonverbal clues

101. Describe three steps for learning to actively listen.

    Answer:
    Make eye contact
    Exhibit affirmative nods and appropriate facial expressions
    Avoid distracting actions or gestures that suggest boredom
    Ask questions
    Paraphrase using your own words
    Avoid interrupting the speaker
    Do no overtalk
    Make smooth transitions between the roles of speaker and listener

102. Compare and contrast the five conflict management strategies, stating which one works best.

    Answer:
    There is no one best strategy. The strategy used must depend on the situation
    Avoidance - used when the issue is trivial
    Accommodation - used when the issue is unimportant
    Forcing - used when a quick, unpopular decision is required
    Compromise - used when time is short and the conflicting parties are equal in power
    Collaboration - used when a win-win solution is desired on an issue too important to compromise

103. List three steps involved in effectively developing negotiation skills.

    Answer:
    Research your opponent
    Begin with a positive overture
    Address problems, not personalities
    Pay little attention to initial offers
    Emphasize win-win solutions
    Be open to accepting third-party assistance

Chapter 15: Foundations of Control

True/False

1. Control is the final link in the functional chain of management

    Answer: T   Difficulty: 2   Page: 463

2. Control must precede planning.

    Answer: F   Difficulty: 2   Page: 463

3. Personal observation as a form of control measurement requires little time.

    Answer: F   Difficulty: 1   Page: 464

4. Statistics reports often ignore important facts as they focus on key areas only.

    Answer: T   Difficulty: 3   Page: 464

5. What is measured is often more critical than how it is measured.

    Answer: T   Difficulty: 3   Page: 465

6. Subjective measures are better than having no measures at all.

    Answer: T   Difficulty: 2   Page: 466

7. Deviations outside the range of variation are significant and receive management attention.

    Answer: T   Difficulty: 2   Page: 466

8. Basic corrective action corrects problems at once and gets performance back to where it should be.

    Answer: F   Difficulty: 1   Page: 467

9. A course of managerial action that can be taken when deviations are found is to simply do nothing.

    Answer: T   Difficulty: 2   Page: 467

10. If employees do not meet a standard, the first thing they attack is the standard.

    Answer: T   Difficulty: 3   Page: 468

Testbank

11. Concurrent control implements controls before an activity begins.

    Answer: F Difficulty: 1 Page: 468

12. The key to feedforward control is to take action before a problem occurs.

    Answer: T Difficulty: 2 Page: 469

13. The best known form of concurrent control is direct supervision.

    Answer: T Difficulty: 2 Page: 470

14. The major disadvantage of feedback control is that by the time the manager has the information, the problem has already occurred.

    Answer: T Difficulty: 2 Page: 470

15. In order to be effective, control systems should be stable and unchanging.

    Answer: F Difficulty: 2 Page: 471

16. The benefits of controlling for everything would not justify the cost.

    Answer: T Difficulty: 3 Page: 471

17. In well-designed control systems, attention should be called only to the exceptions.

    Answer: T Difficulty: 3 Page: 471

18. Control systems should vary to reflect the size of the organization.

    Answer: T Difficulty: 2 Page: 472

19. Concurrent control through direct supervision is probably most cost effective for small businesses.

    Answer: T Difficulty: 3 Page: 472

20. When providing employees with performance feedback, the manager should focus on specific rather than general work behaviors.

    Answer: T Difficulty: 2 Page: 473

21. Methods of controlling employee behavior and operations can be quite different in foreign countries.

    Answer: T Difficulty: 2 Page: 474

Chapter 15: Foundations of Control

22. In less-advanced countries, direct supervision and highly centralized decision making are the basic means of control.

    Answer: T Difficulty: 2 Page: 475

23. Employers have the right to monitor employees' e-mail, telephone conversations and computer.

    Answer: T Difficulty: 1 Page: 478

24. Employers do not have the right to keep employees from skydiving, smoking or drinking off the job.

    Answer: F Difficulty: 3 Page: 478

Multiple Choice

25. Which of the following does S.A.B. produce?
    A. Robes for the monarchy
    B. Leather goods
    C. Fine china
    D. Tailor-made clothing

    Answer: B Difficulty: 2 Page: 460

26. All but which of the following statements is true?
    A. S.A.B. expanded their facilities at a rent of nearly 100 times their previous rent
    B. S.A.B. opened a store in Japan
    C. The British pound weakened against the dollar
    D. Luxury items were in less demand

    Answer: B Difficulty: 2 Page: 460

27. The approach to control that emphasizes the use of external market mechanisms such as price competition and market share is which of the following?
    A. Market control
    B. Bureaucratic control
    C. Clan control
    D. Price control

    Answer: A Difficulty: 1 Page: 461

28. Organizations that have clearly specified and distinct products and services and considerable competition typically use which of the following?
   A. Market control
   B. Bureaucratic control
   C. Clan control
   D. Price control

   Answer: A Difficulty: 2 Page: 461

29. A control approach that emphasizes authority and relies heavily on administrative rules, policies and procedures is known as which of the following?
   A. Market control
   B. Bureaucratic control
   C. Clan control
   D. Price control

   Answer: B Difficulty: 1 Page: 461

30. A type of control that depends on standardization of activities, well-defined job descriptions and budgets would be an example of which of the following?
   A. Market control
   B. Bureaucratic control
   C. Clan control
   D. Price control

   Answer: B Difficulty: 2 Page: 462

31. A control approach where employee behaviors are regulated by shared values, norms, traditions, rituals, and other aspects of the organization's culture is known as which of the following?
   A. Market control
   B. Bureaucratic control
   C. Clan control
   D. Price control

   Answer: C Difficulty: 1 Page: 462

32. A company in which teams are widely used, like Microsoft, will frequently use which type of control?
   A. Market control
   B. Bureaucratic control
   C. Clan control
   D. Price control

   Answer: C Difficulty: 2 Page: 462

Chapter 15: Foundations of Control

33. The key to an effective control system is to design one that
    A. Monitors everything happening in the organization
    B. Monitors only the important activities in the organization
    C. Helps the organization to effectively and efficiently reach its goals
    D. Requires a minimum of management involvement

    Answer: C Difficulty: 2 Page: 462

34. Planning must _____ control.
    A. Follow
    B. Occur at the same time
    C. Precede
    D. Planning has no relationship to control

    Answer: C Difficulty: 2 Page: 463

35. All but which of the following are the steps involved in the control process?
    A. Measure actual performance
    B. Compare actual performance against the standard
    C. Develop the standard
    D. Take appropriate action to correct any deviations

    Answer: C Difficulty: 3 Page: 463

36. Objectives must be all but which of the following?
    A. Tangible
    B. Verifiable
    C. Ambiguous
    D. Measurable

    Answer: C Difficulty: 1 Page: 463

37. All but which of the following are common sources of information used by managers to measure actual performance?
    A. Personal observation
    B. Statistical reports
    C. Oral reports
    D. Jury of opinion

    Answer: D Difficulty: 3 Page: 463

38. Which of the following methods of measuring provides information that is not filtered by others and permits intensive coverage although it is quite time consuming?
    A. Personal observation
    B. Statistical reports
    C. Oral reports
    D. Written reports

    Answer: A Difficulty: 2 Page: 463

39. Which of the following methods of measurement reports only on key areas and may ignore important facts?
    A. Personal observation
    B. Statistical reports
    C. Oral reports
    D. Written reports

    Answer: B Difficulty: 2 Page: 464

40. Which of the following methods allows for faster feedback, though it is filtered, and with today's technology can be taped for future reference?
    A. Personal observation
    B. Statistical reports
    C. Oral reports
    D. Written reports

    Answer: C Difficulty: 2 Page: 465

41. Controls are needed primarily for all but which of the following areas?
    A. Information
    B. Finances
    C. Technology usage
    D. People

    Answer: C Difficulty: 2 Page: 465

42. The acceptable parameters of variance between actual performance and the standard is which of the following?
    A. Clan control
    B. Statistical reports
    C. Range of variation
    D. Written reports

    Answer: C Difficulty: 1 Page: 466

43. Managers can do all but which of the following when taking managerial action?
    A. They can do nothing
    B. Correct the performance
    C. Revise the standard
    D. Change the measurement

    Answer: D Difficulty: 2 Page: 467

44. When problems are corrected at once to get performance back on track, _____ has been used.
    A. Mechanistic control
    B. Immediate corrective action
    C. Basic corrective action
    D. Remedial corrective action

    Answer: B Difficulty: 1 Page: 467

Chapter 15:   Foundations of Control

45. When questions of why are asked and what caused the deviations in performance is investigated, and then corrective action is taken, a manager is using which of the following?
    A. Mechanistic control
    B. Immediate corrective action
    C. Basic corrective action
    D. Remedial corrective action

    Answer: C Difficulty: 2 Page: 467

46. When measured performance does not meet the set standard, the first thing employees are apt to attack is
    A. Management
    B. Processes used
    C. The standard
    D. Technology

    Answer: C Difficulty: 3 Page: 468

47. Control that prevents anticipated problems is which of the following?
    A. Feedforward control
    B. Concurrent control
    C. Feedback control
    D. Management control

    Answer: A Difficulty: 1 Page: 469

48. An organization that hires additional personnel as soon as a major contract has been awarded is using which control system?
    A. Feedforward control
    B. Concurrent control
    C. Feedback control
    D. Management control

    Answer: A Difficulty: 2 Page: 469

49. Control that takes place while an activity is in progress is known as which of the following?
    A. Feedforward control
    B. Concurrent control
    C. Feedback control
    D. Management control

    Answer: B Difficulty: 1 Page: 470

50. Direct supervision is the best-known form of this type of control.
    A. Feedforward control
    B. Concurrent control
    C. Feedback control
    D. Management control

    Answer: B Difficulty: 2 Page: 470

51. Control action that is taken to correct a problem that has already occurred is which of the following?
    A. Feedforward control
    B. Concurrent control
    C. Feedback control
    D. Management control

    Answer: C Difficulty: 1 Page: 470

52. Financial statements are an example of which type of control?
    A. Feedforward control
    B. Concurrent control
    C. Feedback control
    D. Management control

    Answer: C Difficulty: 3 Page: 470

53. All but which of the following are qualities of an effective control system?
    A. Accuracy
    B. Timeliness
    C. Emphasis on the exception
    D. Singular criteria

    Answer: D Difficulty: 3 Page: 471

54. All but which of the following are qualities of an effective control system?
    A. Strategic placement
    B. Complexity
    C. Economy
    D. Corrective action needed

    Answer: B Difficulty: 3 Page: 471

55. Which is probably most cost effective for a small business?
    A. Feedforward control
    B. Concurrent control
    C. Feedback control
    D. Empirical control

    Answer: B Difficulty: 3 Page: 472

Chapter 15: Foundations of Control

56. All but which of the following statements are true?
    A. Very large organizations will typically have highly formalized and impersonal feedforward and feedback controls
    B. The higher one moves in the organization's hierarchy, the greater the need for a multiple set of criteria
    C. The type and extent of controls should be consistent with the organization's culture
    D. If control is costly, and the repercussions from the error are small, the control system must be elaborate

    Answer: D Difficulty: 2 Page: 472

57. All but which of the following should occur when providing performance feedback to an employee?
    A. Put the employee at ease
    B. Focus on general behaviors
    C. Support feedback with hard data
    D. Let the employee speak

    Answer: B Difficulty: 2 Page: 473

58. All but which of the following should occur when providing performance feedback to an employee?
    A. Detail a future plan of action
    B. Keep comments impersonal and job-related
    C. Do not let the employee speak
    D. Make sure the employee knows the purpose of the feedback session

    Answer: C Difficulty: 2 Page: 473

59. In a large organization, which control recommendations should be made?
    A. Elaborate, comprehensive controls covering every area
    B. Decreased number and breadth of controls
    C. Few, easy to measure criteria
    D. Formal, impersonal, extensive rules and regulations

    Answer: D Difficulty: 2 Page: 474

60. In a small organization, which control recommendation should be made?
    A. Many criteria
    B. Increased number and breadth of controls
    C. Elaborate, comprehensive controls
    D. Informal, personal, management by walking around

    Answer: D Difficulty: 2 Page: 474

61. All but which of the following statements are true?
    A. Methods of controlling employee behavior can be quite different in foreign countries
    B. Collecting data that is comparable between countries is an easy task for multinationals
    C. Distance creates a tendency to formalize controls
    D. In less-advanced countries, direct supervision and highly centralized decision making are the basic means of control

    Answer: B Difficulty: 3 Page: 475

62. All but which of the following statements is true?
    A. Sometimes the controls can run the organization
    B. Manipulation of control data is random
    C. Controls must be both flexible and reasonable
    D. When rewards are at stake, individuals tends to manipulate data to appear in a favorable light

    Answer: B Difficulty: 3 Page: 476

63. Employers have the right to monitor all but which of the following?
    A. Employees' e-mail
    B. Tap an employee's work telephone
    C. Bug an employee office
    D. Monitor the employee restroom

    Answer: C Difficulty: 2 Page: 478

64. Employers have the right to dictate whether or not employees engage in all but which of the following off-the-job activities?
    A. Skydiving
    B. Drinking alcoholic beverages - off-the-job
    C. Smoking
    D. Religious practices

    Answer: D Difficulty: 2 Page: 478

Chapter 15: Foundations of Control

Scenario

Table 15-1
Jina realizes her unit needs to make some changes in its control system. However, she is uncertain which will work best for her organization. They are just one unit among five. She could base her unit's performance on their distinct product and turn her unit into a profit center and evaluate against the company total. She could also use more heavily the rules, policies, regulations, and procedures already in place. She has not enforced very strictly many of the regulations established by the home office. Part of the reason for this is that her unit is fairly self-regulating. The work groups set their goals and insure those goals are attained. Little latitude is allowed for a worker who does not meet the group norms.

65. Referring to Table 15-1, if Jina looks at her unit as a profit center which form of control will she be using?
    A. Bureaucratic control
    B. Market control
    C. Clan control
    D. Regulated control

    Answer: B Difficulty: 2

66. Referring to Table 15-1, what form of control would the home office prefer Jina use?
    A. Bureaucratic control
    B. Market control
    C. Clan control
    D. Regulated control

    Answer: A Difficulty: 3

67. Referring to Table 15-1, what form of control is her unit currently using?
    A. Bureaucratic control
    B. Market control
    C. Clan control
    D. Regulated control

    Answer: C Difficulty: 2

68. Referring to Table 15-1, what should any form of control that Jina chooses ultimately help her to do?
    A. Monitor everything that happens in the unit
    B. Monitor only the important activities in the unit
    C. Helps her effectively and efficiently reach its goals
    D. Involve a minimum of management involvement

    Answer: C Difficulty: 3

69. Referring to Table 15-1, which of the following statements are correct?
   A. Control must precede planning
   B. Planning must precede control
   C. No control mechanisms are necessary
   D. Everything within Jina's unit must be monitored

   Answer: B Difficulty: 2

Table 15-2
Sam has not been receiving the information that he needs from his current control system. By the time Sam receives the information, the activity has occurred and there is nothing that can be done. Direct supervision is used extensively on the floor now. So some activities have been changed before they became costly mistakes but Sam would like to do better. He would like to fix things before they broke and anticipate more of the problems that occurred.

70. Referring to Table 15-2, Sam is currently using which form of control?
   A. Feedforward control
   B. Concurrent control
   C. Feedback control
   D. Management control

   Answer: C Difficulty: 2

71. Referring to Table 15-2, the control that is occurring on the floor is an example of which of the following?
   A. Feedforward control
   B. Concurrent control
   C. Feedback control
   D. Management control

   Answer: B Difficulty: 2

72. Referring to Table 15-2, supervision is the best-known form of which type of control?
   A. Feedforward control
   B. Concurrent control
   C. Feedback control
   D. Management control

   Answer: B Difficulty: 3

73. Referring to Table 15-2, which form of control would Sam like to use?
   A. Feedforward control
   B. Concurrent control
   C. Feedback control
   D. Management control

   Answer: A Difficulty: 2

Chapter 15: Foundations of Control

74. Referring to Table 15-2, which of the types of control requires Sam to gather timely and accurate information that may be hard to develop?
   A. Feedforward control
   B. Concurrent control
   C. Feedback control
   D. Management control

   Answer: A Difficulty: 3

Table 15-3
Jared has been hired to establish a control system for SRP Inc. Jared knows several decisions must be made before the control system can be implemented. Several contingencies must also be considered. One of the first decisions that must be made is where to place the controls and what needs to be controlled. Jared also knows the organization is relatively small and will be for some time and that management intends to decentralize extensively. Furthermore, management has indicated that if-then guidelines are to be implemented. Jared looks forward to designing a system that will work well for the company for years to come.

75. Referring to Table 15-3, the first step deals with which of the following qualities of control?
   A. Accuracy
   B. Understandability
   C. Strategic placement
   D. Multiple criteria

   Answer: C Difficulty: 2

76. Referring to Table 15-3, controls should be implemented for
   A. Everything that goes on in the organization
   B. Areas where variations are unlikely to occur
   C. Areas where variations will cost little
   D. All critical activities, operations, and events

   Answer: D Difficulty: 3

77. Referring to Table 15-3, the need for the standards to be challenging yet attainable is which of the following qualities?
   A. Reasonable criteria
   B. Understandability
   C. Strategic placement
   D. Multiple criteria

   Answer: A Difficulty: 2

78. Referring to Table 15-3, since the organization is small, what control recommendations should Jared make?
    A. Informal, personal, management by walking around
    B. Formal, impersonal, extensive rules and regulations
    C. Increased number of controls to monitor everything
    D. Reduced number of controls

    Answer: A Difficulty: 2

79. Referring to Table 15-3, the if-then guidelines refers to which of the following?
    A. Economy
    B. Understandability
    C. Strategic placement
    D. Corrective action

    Answer: D Difficulty: 2

Essay

80. Compare and contrast the three differing approaches to designing a control system.

    Answer:
    Market control - emphasizes the use of external market mechanisms such as price competition or market share
    Bureaucratic control - emphasizes strict compliance to the administrative rules and regulations established
    Clan control - emphasizes the control of employee behaviors through the culture of the organization and such things as traditions, values and norms

81. Compare and contrast the three types of control.

    Answer:
    Feedforward control - anticipates problems
    Concurrent control - corrects problems as they happen
    Feedback control - corrects problems after they occur

82. Explain three qualities of an effective control system.

    Answer:
    Accuracy
    Timeliness
    Economy
    Flexibility
    Understandability
    Reasonable criteria
    Strategic placement
    Emphasis on the exception
    Multiple criteria
    Corrective action

Chapter 15:   Foundations of Control

83. Explain three contingency factors that will influence control systems.

    Answer:
    Size of the organization
    One's position in the organization
    Degree of centralization
    Organizational culture
    Importance of the activity

84. Discuss the ethical dilemmas involved in monitoring employees on- and off-the-job.

    Answer:
    On-the-job - employers can read employee e-mail, tap employee telephones, and even monitor employee restrooms
    Off-the-job - employers can prohibit certain risky activities like skydiving and riding motorcycles as well as prohibit things like smoking and drinking

    The ethical dilemma revolves around the rights of employees versus the rights of employers

Chapter 16: Control Tools and Techniques

True/False

1. MIS focuses specifically on providing management with information, not data.

   Answer: T Difficulty: 2 Page: 488

2. MIS organizes information in some meaningful way and can access the data in a reasonable amount of time.

   Answer: F Difficulty: 3 Page: 488

3. Since information is so central to managers today, without the use of computer they would have a difficult time performing their managerial functions.

   Answer: T Difficulty: 2 Page: 489

4. When a manager becomes an end-user, he or she takes responsibility for information control.

   Answer: T Difficulty: 1 Page: 490

5. MIS is not a source of competitive advantage for an organization.

   Answer: F Difficulty: 2 Page: 490

6. MIS increases a manager's decision making ability.

   Answer: T Difficulty: 1 Page: 492

7. MIS is making organizations taller and more mechanistic.

   Answer: F Difficulty: 2 Page: 492

8. MIS is changing the status hierarchy in organizations.

   Answer: T Difficulty: 2 Page: 493

9. MIS makes it possible to obtain more complete and accurate information.

   Answer: T Difficulty: 1 Page: 494

10. Effective control systems allow organizations to produce higher-quality products and services but at a higher price.

    Answer: F Difficulty: 2 Page: 494

Chapter 16: Control Tools and Techniques

11. The transformational process is as relevant to service organizations as it is to manufacturing organizations.

    Answer: T Difficulty: 2 Page: 495

12. Labor and materials are examples of indirect costs.

    Answer: F Difficulty: 2 Page: 495

13. Labor and materials are examples of indirect costs.

    Answer: F Difficulty: 2 Page: 495

14. Purchasing control seeks to ensure availability, acceptable quality, continued reliable sources, and at the same time reduced costs.

    Answer: T Difficulty: 2 Page: 495

15. A rapidly growing trend in business is to turn suppliers into partners.

    Answer: T Difficulty: 2 Page: 496

16. If demand and lead times are not known and/or not constant, then EOQ can be used.

    Answer: F Difficulty: 2 Page: 501

17. A system that flags the fact inventory needs to be replenished when it reaches a certain level is known as fixed-interval reordering systems.

    Answer: F Difficulty: 2 Page: 502

18. The ultimate goal of JIT is to reduce a company's inventory and its associated costs to zero.

    Answer: T Difficulty: 3 Page: 502

19. Fixing a tire on a bus, after it has blown due to the miles driven on it, would be an example of conditional maintenance.

    Answer: F Difficulty: 2 Page: 503

20. Continuous improvement programs emphasize actions to identify mistakes after they have occurred, while quality control programs emphasize the prevention of mistakes.

    Answer: F Difficulty: 2 Page: 503

21. The entire batch of light bulbs is deemed acceptable based upon the calculation of sample risk error. This is an example of process control.

    Answer: F   Difficulty: 2   Page: 504

22. Deming believed ultimately it was the responsibility of employees to increase the quality of goods/services produced.

    Answer: F   Difficulty: 2   Page: 504

23. Leverage ratios refer to the use of borrowed funds to finance a business.

    Answer: T   Difficulty: 2   Page: 506

24. Profit ratios describe how efficiently management is using an organization's resources.

    Answer: F   Difficulty: 2   Page: 506

25. Internal audits go beyond verifying the financial statements.

    Answer: T   Difficulty: 2   Page: 507

26. Cost-benefit analysis is useful when costs are known and the standards against which the costs are measured are also clearly known.

    Answer: F   Difficulty: 3   Page: 507

27. The purpose of ABC is to reflect production costs accurately.

    Answer: T   Difficulty: 2   Page: 508

28. The concept of ABC is the allocation of costs solely on the basis of usage.

    Answer: T   Difficulty: 2   Page: 508

Multiple Choice

29. To address the supply problem at Mount Sinai Hospital in Toronto, Robert Cullen introduced which of the following?
    A. Restructuring plan
    B. New management
    C. A better control system
    D. Pay-for-performance compensation

    Answer: C   Difficulty: 2   Page: 487

Chapter 16: Control Tools and Techniques

30. To address the supply problem at Mount Sinai Hospital in Toronto, Robert Cullen changed which of the following?
    A. From several layers of management to a few layers
    B. Reduced the number of middle management
    C. From several suppliers to one supplier
    D. From manual labor to machines

    Answer: D Difficulty: 2 Page: 487

31. All but which of the following are the three primary areas that require effective controls?
    A. Information
    B. Operations
    C. Finance
    D. Planning

    Answer: D Difficulty: 2 Page: 488

32. A system used to provide management with needed information on a regular basis is which of the following?
    A. Operation management
    B. Maintenance control
    C. Management information system
    D. Data processing system

    Answer: C Difficulty: 1 Page: 488

33. An MIS system focuses specifically on providing management with _____ not merely _____.
    A. Cost controls, measurements
    B. Data, information
    C. Information, data
    D. Productivity, increased motivation

    Answer: C Difficulty: 2 Page: 488

34. Since information is so important to managers today, they would have a difficult time performing their managerial functions without
    A. Employees
    B. Computers
    C. Budgets
    D. Using motivational techniques

    Answer: B Difficulty: 2 Page: 489

35. All but which of the following are steps in designing a management information system?
    A. Analyze information requirements
    B. Aggregate the decisions
    C. Implement the system
    D. Analyze only the information needed by top management

    Answer: D Difficulty: 1 Page: 489

36. All but which of the following can be sources of an organization's competitive advantage?
    A. Cost leadership
    B. Product differentiation
    C. Information technology
    D. Management skills

    Answer: D Difficulty: 1 Page: 490

37. All but which of the following are the words that Mark Kats, chief MIS architect for Levi Strauss and Co., lives by?
    A. Rethink
    B. Retry
    C. Redesign
    D. Retool

    Answer: B Difficulty: 2 Page: 491

38. The goal of MIS for Levi Strauss and Company is to have information available to
    A. All employees
    B. Top management
    C. All managers
    D. The employees who need the information

    Answer: C Difficulty: 2 Page: 491

39. Since MIS significantly alters the quantity and quality of information as well as the speed with which it can be obtained, MIS will improve
    A. Customer service
    B. Motivation
    C. Managerial decision making
    D. Profits

    Answer: C Difficulty: 2 Page: 492

40. MISs are making organizations _____ and more _____.
    A. Taller, mechanistic
    B. Flatter, organic
    C. Taller, organic
    D. Flatter, mechanistic

    Answer: B Difficulty: 3 Page: 492

Chapter 16: Control Tools and Techniques

41. The most important effect that computer-based control systems have had on the power structure is to _____ the control of top management.
    A. Increase
    B. Decrease
    C. Not change
    D. There is no relationship between MISs and power

    Answer: A Difficulty: 3 Page: 493

42. All but which of the following statements are true concerning MIS?
    A. MIS can be a source of an organization's competitive advantage
    B. MIS improves management's decision making ability
    C. With MIS, the span of control for a manager has become less wide
    D. MIS has allowed organizations to become more organic without giving up control

    Answer: C Difficulty: 2 Page: 492

43. All but which of the following statements are true concerning MIS?
    A. MIS changes the status hierarchy in an organization
    B. MIS permits more lateral and diagonal communication
    C. MIS entirely eliminates the need for face-to-face communication
    D. MIS decreases the problem of distortion and filtering of information

    Answer: C Difficulty: 2 Page: 493

44. All but which of the following statements are true concerning MIS?
    A. MIS can be a source of an organization's competitive advantage
    B. MIS improves management's decision making ability
    C. With MIS, the span of control for a manager has become less wide
    D. MIS has allowed organizations to become more organic without giving up control

    Answer: C Difficulty: 2 Page: 492

45. All but which of the following statements are true concerning MIS?
    A. MIS eliminates the need for face-to-face communication
    B. MIS permits more lateral and diagonal communication
    C. MIS make it possible to obtain more complete and accurate measuring control
    D. MIS permits more accurate, timely information

    Answer: A Difficulty: 2 Page: 494

46. Every organization has an operations system that transforms _____ into _____.
    A. Inputs, outputs
    B. Outputs, inputs
    C. Information, data
    D. Profits, costs

    Answer: A Difficulty: 1 Page: 494

47. An organization that produces nonphysical outputs that are intangible, cannot be stored in inventory and incorporate the customer in the actual process is known as
    A. Operations management
    B. The transformation process
    C. A service organization
    D. A manufacturing organization

    Answer: C Difficulty: 1 Page: 495

48. The study and application of the transformation process to organizations is known as which of the following?
    A. Operations management
    B. The transformation process
    C. A service organization
    D. A manufacturing organization

    Answer: A Difficulty: 1 Page: 495

49. All but which of the following are the primary subsystems in operations management?
    A. Cost controls
    B. Inventories
    C. Maintenance
    D. Quantity controls

    Answer: D Difficulty: 1 Page: 494

50. All but which of the following are examples of direct costs?
    A. Materials
    B. Rent
    C. Labor
    D. Wages

    Answer: B Difficulty: 2 Page: 495

51. All but which of the following are examples of indirect costs?
    A. Insurance
    B. Materials
    C. Rent
    D. Management salaries

    Answer: B Difficulty: 2 Page: 496

Chapter 16: Control Tools and Techniques

52. Cost-centers are held responsible for which of the following?
    A. Indirect costs
    B. Direct costs
    C. All costs
    D. Their share of costs

    Answer: B Difficulty: 3 Page: 496

53. Purchasing control seeks to ensure all but which of the following?
    A. Availability
    B. Acceptable quality
    C. Increased costs
    D. Reliable sources

    Answer: C Difficulty: 1 Page: 496

54. A rapidly growing trend in business is to turn suppliers into
    A. Partners
    B. Customers
    C. Competitors
    D. Stockholders

    Answer: A Difficulty: 2 Page: 496

55. All but which of the following can be achieved when suppliers are partners?
    A. Reduced costs
    B. Increased costs
    C. Higher quality inputs
    D. Fewer defects

    Answer: B Difficulty: 2 Page: 497

56. A system that flags the fact inventory needs to be replenished when it reaches a certain level is known as which of the following?
    A. Just-in-time inventory
    B. Fixed-interval reordering system
    C. Fixed-point reordering system
    D. Economic order quantity model

    Answer: C Difficulty: 2 Page: 497

57. A technique for balancing purchase, ordering, carrying, and stockout costs to derive the optimum quantity for a purchase order is which of the following?
    A. Just-in-time inventory
    B. Fixed-interval reordering system
    C. Fixed-point reordering system
    D. Economic order quantity model

    Answer: D Difficulty: 2 Page: 497

58. The EOQ model seeks to balance all but which of the following costs?
    A. Purchase costs
    B. Indirect costs
    C. Ordering costs
    D. Stockout costs

    Answer: B Difficulty: 3 Page: 497

59. Costs such as paperwork, follow-up, inspection upon arrival, and processing costs are which of the following types of costs?
    A. Purchase costs
    B. Ordering costs
    C. Stockout costs
    D. Carrying costs

    Answer: B Difficulty: 2 Page: 497

60. Costs such as profits foregone from orders lost, the cost of establishing goodwill and additional expenses incurred to expedite late shipments are which of the following types of costs?
    A. Purchase costs
    B. Ordering costs
    C. Stockout costs
    D. Carrying costs

    Answer: C Difficulty: 2 Page: 497

61. The point where ordering costs equal carrying costs is which of the following?
    A. Indirect costs
    B. Direct costs
    C. Economic order quantity
    D. Least cost order quantity

    Answer: C Difficulty: 2 Page: 500

62. The relationship between holding costs and ordering costs is
    A. Direct
    B. Inverse
    C. Constant
    D. There is no relationship between holding costs and ordering costs

    Answer: B Difficulty: 3 Page: 500

63. If which two conditions cannot be met, then EOQ should not be used?
    A. Production periods and quantities needed
    B. Demand and lead times
    C. Lead times and production periods
    D. Demand and quantities needed

    Answer: B Difficulty: 3 Page: 501

Chapter 16:   Control Tools and Techniques

64. A system that uses time as the determining factor for reviewing and reordering inventory items is which of the following?
    A. Just-in-time inventory
    B. Fixed-interval reordering system
    C. Fixed-point reordering system
    D. Economic order quantity model

    Answer: B Difficulty: 1 Page: 502

65. With which of the following systems, inventory items arrive when they are needed in the production process instead of being stored in stock?
    A. Just-in-time inventory
    B. Fixed-interval reordering system
    C. Fixed-point reordering system
    D. Economic order quantity model

    Answer: A Difficulty: 2 Page: 502

66. Which of the following systems reduces a company's inventory and its associated costs to zero?
    A. Just-in-time inventory
    B. Fixed-interval reordering system
    C. Fixed-point reordering system
    D. Economic order quantity model

    Answer: A Difficulty: 2 Page: 502

67. All but which of the following are approaches to maintenance control?
    A. Preventative
    B. Preparatory
    C. Conditional
    D. Remedial

    Answer: B Difficulty: 1 Page: 503

68. The greater the cost of money, time, liability, or increased loss of goodwill, the greater the benefits from
    A. Preventative maintenance
    B. Preparatory maintenance
    C. Conditional maintenance
    D. Remedial maintenance

    Answer: A Difficulty: 2 Page: 503

69. Jon's Taxi Service sends all of its cars into the shop for a complete tune-up every 3,500 miles. This is an example of which of the following?
    A. Preventative maintenance
    B. Preparatory maintenance
    C. Conditional maintenance
    D. Remedial maintenance

    Answer: A Difficulty: 2 Page: 503

70. Jon's Taxi Service checks the oil and tire pressure of all cars every time they fill up with gasoline. Any necessary air or oil is added at this time. This an example of which of the following?
    A. Preventative maintenance
    B. Preparatory maintenance
    C. Conditional maintenance
    D. Remedial maintenance

    Answer: C Difficulty: 2 Page: 503

71. Jon's Taxi Service changes all lights, headlights, taillights, overhead lights, after they burn out. This is an example of which of the following?
    A. Preventative maintenance
    B. Preparatory maintenance
    C. Conditional maintenance
    D. Remedial maintenance

    Answer: D Difficulty: 2 Page: 503

72. Continuous improvement programs emphasize actions to _____ mistakes, while quality control programs emphasize identifying mistakes _____ they have occurred.
    A. Fix, before
    B. Prevent, after
    C. Fix, after
    D. Prevent, before

    Answer: B Difficulty: 3 Page: 503

73. A quality control procedure in which an evaluation of purchased or manufactured material or products that already exists is taken and a decision is made to accept or reject the whole lot based upon the product evaluation is which of the following?
    A. Process sampling
    B. Acceptance sampling
    C. Attribute sampling
    D. Variable sampling

    Answer: B Difficulty: 2 Page: 504

74. A quality control procedure in which items are sampled during the transformation process in order to determine if the process is under control is known as which of the following?
    A. Process sampling
    B. Acceptance sampling
    C. Attribute sampling
    D. Variable sampling

    Answer: A Difficulty: 1 Page: 504

Chapter 16: Control Tools and Techniques

75. A quality control technique where after inspecting the item and comparing it to the standard, the item is either accepted or not accepted is known as which of the following?
    A. Process sampling
    B. Acceptance sampling
    C. Attribute sampling
    D. Variable sampling

    Answer: C Difficulty: 2 Page: 504

76. According to Deming, who is responsible for quality control?
    A. Employees
    B. Top management
    C. Suppliers
    D. All management

    Answer: D Difficulty: 2 Page: 504

77. All but which of the following are points proposed by Deming for improving quality in an organization?
    A. Plan for the long-term
    B. Plan for the short-term
    C. Establish statistical controls over production processes
    D. Require employees to do quality work

    Answer: B Difficulty: 2 Page: 505

78. All but which of the following are points proposed by Deming for improving quality in an organization?
    A. Deal with the fewest number of suppliers
    B. Drive out fear
    C. Deal with a larger number of suppliers
    D. Do not be sucked into adopting strictly numerical goals, like zero defects

    Answer: C Difficulty: 2 Page: 505

79. Managers use ratios to compare to all but which of the following?
    A. Past years
    B. Other companies in different industries
    C. Other companies in the same industry
    D. Leading companies in the same industry

    Answer: B Difficulty: 2 Page: 505

80. An organization's current assets divided by its current liabilities is which of the following?
    A. Current ratio
    B. Acid test ratio
    C. Debt-to-assets ratio
    D. Inventory turnover ratio

    Answer: A Difficulty: 1 Page: 505

81. Which of the following ratios can help a manager control debt levels?
    A. Current ratio
    B. Acid test ratio
    C. Times-interest-earned ratio
    D. Inventory turnover ratio

    Answer: C Difficulty: 2 Page: 506

82. One of the most widely used measures of a business firm's profitability is
    A. The current ratio
    B. The profit-margin-on-revenues ratio
    C. The return-on-investment ratio
    D. The total assets turnover ratio

    Answer: C Difficulty: 2 Page: 507

83. Which of the following is designed to check an organization's control mechanisms?
    A. The current ratio
    B. The return-on-investment ratio
    C. Audits
    D. Cost-benefit analysis

    Answer: C Difficulty: 2 Page: 507

84. Managers can use _____ to identify problems and to ensure that organizational activities are progressing as planned.
    A. External audits
    B. Internal audits
    C. Cost-benefit analysis
    D. Profit-margin-on-revenues ratio

    Answer: B Difficulty: 3 Page: 507

Chapter 16:   Control Tools and Techniques

85. _____ is useful when the amount of costs is known, but the standard against which those costs must be compared is ambiguous or difficult to measure.
    A. Activity-based accounting
    B. Cost-benefit analysis
    C. Operations management
    D. Ratio analysis

    Answer: B Difficulty: 2 Page: 507

86. A procedure whereby costs for producing a good or service are allocated on the basis of the activities performed and the resources employed is which of the following?
    A. Activity-based accounting
    B. Cost-benefit analysis
    C. Operations management
    D. Ratio analysis

    Answer: A Difficulty: 2 Page: 508

87. The concept of ABC is to allocate costs based upon
    A. Profit percentage
    B. Sales percentage
    C. Market share
    D. Usage

    Answer: D Difficulty: 2 Page: 508

88. When specific costs that are incurred in the production of a good/service are charged directly to the task, it is called
    A. Activity-based accounting
    B. Cost-benefit analysis
    C. Operations management
    D. Ratio analysis

    Answer: A Difficulty: 2 Page: 508

Scenario

Table 16-1
Tim's Tune-ups is having a major inventory control problem. It seems he never has the parts on hand that he needs when he needs them and furthermore a large amount of current assets are tied up in inventory causing cash flow problems. His current system is to every Saturday go through the parts he carries and see if he is low in any areas. If he is he places an order and usually by Monday afternoon he has parts again. However, it seems like he is always running out of some items and has plenty of other items. Since very few customers schedule their appointments ahead of time, Tim never knows exactly what demand will be or what parts will be needed at what times. This also makes his inventory problems more difficult. His banker wants Tim to carry little in inventory and reduce his cost of inventory but Tim is concerned then he will not have the parts on hand he needs. He is considering ordering parts by flagging differing items when they only have so many left and then ordering that part immediately. Then he could better keep track of those parts he uses more and less often.

89. Referring to Table 16-1, what inventory system is Tim currently using?
    A. EOQ
    B. JIT
    C. Fixed-interval reordering system
    D. Fixed-point reordering system

    Answer: C Difficulty: 2

90. Referring to Table 16-1, which of the following systems will not work very well due to the unknown demand and lead time for ordering?
    A. EOQ
    B. JIT
    C. Fixed-interval reordering system
    D. Fixed-point reordering system

    Answer: A Difficulty: 3

91. Referring to Table 16-1, if Tim wanted to reduce his inventory to zero and thus reduce his cost of inventory, what inventory system would he use?
    A. EOQ
    B. JIT
    C. Fixed-interval reordering system
    D. Fixed-point reordering system

    Answer: B Difficulty: 2

Chapter 16: Control Tools and Techniques

92. Referring to Table 16-1, which system is Tim considering using?
    A. EOQ
    B. JIT
    C. Fixed-interval reordering system
    D. Fixed-point reordering system

    Answer: D Difficulty: 2

93. Referring to Table 16-1, since Tim cannot depend upon his suppliers to consistently and quickly deliver the parts he needs, which of the following systems would not work for inventory control?
    A. EOQ
    B. JIT
    C. Fixed-interval reordering system
    D. Fixed-point reordering system

    Answer: B Difficulty: 3

Table 16-2
Bill has been sent to determine where the problems are in the production line of his company. There has been a lot of "down time" lately which has resulted in lost sales. Something needs to be done quickly. Arriving at the factory he finds all the line workers outside taking a break. Evidently an important piece of equipment has broken down and shut down not only that section of the line but the whole line since that part must be completed before the rest of the product can be finished. Bill goes inside to find the foreman and the maintenance personnel completely overhauling the machine. The foreman tells Bill the only time he is authorized to fix the machine is when it completely breaks down. Then it takes a complete overhaul to get it up and running again. Bill asks if it is ever checked on a regular basis, like after every 200 hours of use. The foreman reminds him he can only call maintenance in the event of a major breakdown. When Bill asks the foreman if it is ever maintained before a problem arises, the foreman just laughs. Bill decides a different type of maintenance system needs to be implemented.

94. Referring to Table 16-2, what kind of maintenance is being used for the key piece of equipment?
    A. Conditional maintenance
    B. Remedial maintenance
    C. Preventative maintenance
    D. Quality control

    Answer: B Difficulty: 2

95. Referring to Table 16-2, Bill's question to the foreman about the check after every 200 hours is reference to what type of maintenance.
    A. Conditional maintenance
    B. Remedial maintenance
    C. Preventative maintenance
    D. Quality control

    Answer: A Difficulty: 2

96. Referring to Table 16-2, maintenance before a problem arises is which of the following types of maintenance control?
    A. Conditional maintenance
    B. Remedial maintenance
    C. Preventative maintenance
    D. Quality control

    Answer: C Difficulty: 2

97. Referring to Table 16-2, all but which of the following statements would increase the working time of the downed piece of equipment?
    A. Design redundancy into the equipment
    B. Facilitate fast repair
    C. Keep the equipment back out of the way so it is not in the road when it does go down
    D. Use a modular piece of equipment so it can be easily removed and replaced

    Answer: C Difficulty: 3

98. Referring to Table 16-2, all but which of the following may be occurring due to that piece of equipment being down so frequently?
    A. Lost sales
    B. Delayed product deliveries
    C. Higher costs
    D. Lower costs

    Answer: D Difficulty: 2

Table 16-3
Jennica is analyzing the financial reports of the company. She is to present the key numbers to the Board of Directors tomorrow and she wants to make sure all the numbers are correct and she fully understands what is going on with finances in the company. She glances down through the following figures and quickly checks the calculations.

Current assets	150,000
Inventories	25,000
Current liabilities	125,000
Total debt	300,000
Total assets	500,000
Profits	100,000
Sales	1,000,000

99. Referring to Table 16-3, what is the correct current ratio for Jennica's company?
    A. 150,000
    B. 1.2
    C. .83
    D. .30

    Answer: B Difficulty: 2

Chapter 16: Control Tools and Techniques

100. Referring to Table 16-3, what is the correct acid test ratio for the company?
    A. .5
    B. 1
    C. 125,000
    D. 1.5

    Answer: B Difficulty: 2

101. Referring to Table 16-3, the debt-to-assets ratio is which of the following?
    A. .60
    B. 1.60
    C. .416
    D. 125,000

    Answer: B Difficulty: 2

102. Referring to Table 16-3, the profit margin-on-revenues is which of the following?
    A. 5%
    B. 10%
    C. 20%
    D. 30%

    Answer: B Difficulty: 2

103. Referring to Table 16-3, the return on investment is which of the following?
    A. 5%
    B. 10%
    C. 20%
    D. 66%

    Answer: C Difficulty: 2

Essay

104. Explain the importance of an MIS-management information system.

    Answer:
    Provides managers with accurate and current information
    Allows access to more information to more managers
    Prevents some of the filtering and distortion that occurs when information has to work its way up the hierarchy

105. Compare and contrast data and information, giving an example of each.

   Answer:
   Data - raw, unanalyzed facts
   Example - current assets are $500,000 and current liabilities are $300,000
   Information - data that has been organized into a usable form
   Current ratio is current assets divided by current liabilities which is 1.66 which means that for every $1 of current liabilities there is $1.66 of current assets

106. Describe cost centers and direct and indirect costs and their relationship to cost centers.

   Answer:
   Cost centers - units for which managers are held responsible for the costs incurred in that center, specifically the direct costs
   Direct costs - incurred in proportion to the output produced, e.g., labor
   Indirect costs - costs that are unaffected by the amount of output, e.g., rent

107. Explain two types of maintenance control systems that an organization can use.

   Answer:
   Preventative - maintenance before a breakdown occurs
   Remedial - maintenance performed when a breakdown occurs
   Conditional - maintenance performed in response to an inspection

108. Compare and contrast external audit and internal audit.

   Answer:
   External audit - verification of the accounting/financial records of an organization by an outside, independent firm
   Internal audit - a verification of an organization's own accounting/financial record by its own staff